Wanganella

and the Australian Trans-Tasman Liners

HUDDART PARKER LINE

T.S.M.V. WANGANELLA

HUDDART PARKER LINE

T.S.M.V. "WANGANELLA" 10,000 Tons

This Twin Screw Luxury Motor Liner maintains a fast, regular service between

AUSTRALIA AND NEW ZEALAND

Suites, Single Rooms, Deck Cabins, Two and Three Berth Cabins. Service and Cuisine Unsurpassed.

Particulars and Bookings at all Offices and Agencies

Wanganella

and the Australian Trans-Tasman Liners

Peter Plowman

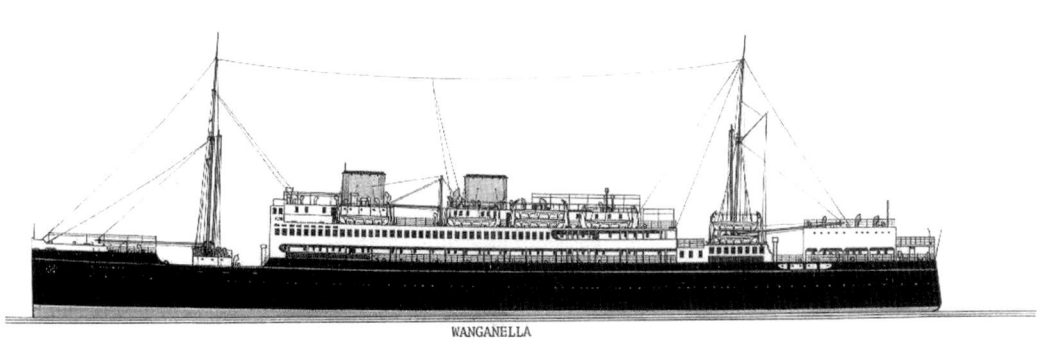
WANGANELLA

ROSENBERG
in association with
transpress NZ

First published in Australia in 2009
by Rosenberg Publishing Pty Ltd
PO Box 6125, Dural Delivery Centre NSW 2158
Phone: 61 2 9654 1502 Fax: 61 2 9654 1338
Email: rosenbergpub@smartchat.net.au
Web: www.rosenbergpub.com.au

Published in New Zealand in 2009
by *transpress* NZ, P.O. Box 10-215
Wellington, NZ

© Copyright Chiswick Publications Pty Ltd 2009

All rights reserved. No part of this publication may be
reproduced, stored in a retrieval system,
or transmitted, in any form or by any means, electronic,
mechanical, photocopying,
recording or otherwise, without the prior permission of the
publisher in writing.

The National Library of Australia Cataloguing-in-Publication

Plowman, Peter.
Wanganella and the Australian Trans-Tasman Liners.

1st ed.
Includes index.
ISBN 9781877058806. (Australian edition)
ISBN 9781877418099. (New Zealand edition)
Wanganella (Ship)–History.
Passenger ships–Australia–New Zealand–History.
Hospital ships–Australia–New Zealand–History.
Cruise ships–Australia–New Zealand–History.

387.5420994

Printed in Thailand by Kyodo Nation Printing Services

Contents

Introduction		6
Acknowledgments		8
1	Early Days	13
2	First Blood	22
3	The First Huddart Parker Ships	31
4	Into a New Century	44
5	*Ulimaroa*	55
6	World War I	64
7	The 1920s	74
8	*Wanganella*	80
9	The 1930s	95
10	World War II	108
11	Post-War Problems	118
12	On the Rocks	122
13	A Slow Decline	143
14	Cruising	151
15	The Final Years	171
16	Under Foreign Owners	176
17	Workers' Hostel	184
Index		188

Introduction

A couple of years ago I had the idea of writing a book about the six motor liners that entered service for Australian owners between 1936 and 1939, the *Manunda*, *Westralia*, *Wanganella*, *Manoora*, *Duntroon* and *Kanimbla*. After working on this for a while I realised that the concept was not viable. While five of the ships operated around the coast of Australia, the sixth, *Wanganella*, was on a totally different service, across the Tasman Sea to New Zealand. As a result I split the concept into two books, one about the coastal liners, the other covering the services across the Tasman Sea. The first of these books, *Coast to Coast*, was published in November 2007.

I have always thought that *Wanganella* was a liner with a most interesting story, and deserving of special attention, which I have been able to give it in this book. In the past very little has been written about *Wanganella* and the earlier ships that maintained the Australian presence on the Tasman trade, and I hope this book will redress that. In contrast, a great many books have been published over the years about the passenger ships operated by the Union Steam Ship Company of New Zealand, but in each one the Australian ships have received scant mention.

The only Australian company to maintain a service across the Tasman Sea was Huddart Parker Limited, who survived numerous attempts by the Union Line to drive them off the route in the early days, and eventually the two agreed to share the route in several cooperative agreements. As a result both companies enjoyed many years of success until travellers turned to the airplane in the 1950s.

There was a time when the only way to travel between Australia and New Zealand was by ship. Up to the late 1870s these ships were mostly owned by Australian companies and primarily intended to transport cargo, with minimal attention being paid to the requirements and comfort of passengers making such voyages. This changed in 1879 when the Union Line introduced *Rotomahana*, which immediately rendered all existing tonnage obsolete, and all the Australian companies left the trade.

Towards the end of 1892, the Union Line suddenly found itself faced with major competition when an Australian-owned company rejoined the trade. James Huddart, one of the founders of Huddart, Parker & Company Limited, established a separate company, the New Zealand & Australasian Steamship Company, to operate a service between Australia and New Zealand. The Union Line retaliated by placing their best ships in direct competition with the newcomers, and also started a rate war that drove fares down to totally uneconomic levels. In March 1893 the Australian company withdrew, leaving the Tasman trade to the Union Line once again.

Despite the failure of James Huddart's venture, Huddart Parker Limited decided to expand their sphere of operation from the Australian coastal trade to include New Zealand, entering the service across the Tasman Sea in November 1893. The first trans-Tasman departure for Huddart Parker Limited was taken by *Tasmania*, on 29 November 1893.

The Union Line tried the same tactics as before in an attempt to stifle the competition, but this time they were up against a much stronger opponent who was able to ride out the fare wars, and instead of buckling under the pressure Huddart Parker Limited added two more vessels, *Elingamite* and *Anglian*, to the trade during 1894.

In 1897 a brand-new vessel, *Westralia*, was placed on the Tasman trade, but almost immediately Huddart Parker suffered the loss of *Tasmania*, which was wrecked on the New Zealand coast. As a result of this disaster, Huddart Parker ordered another new ship for the trade, which entered service in 1899 as *Zealandia*.

The first decade of the twentieth century would see both Huddart Parker Limited and the Union Steam Ship Company of New Zealand regularly introducing a succession of new liners of increasing size on the Tasman trade. Although the two companies were not engaged in fare wars any more, and operated their ships on a joint schedule, there was still considerable competition to attract passengers.

At the end of 1902 Huddart Parker took delivery of *Victoria*, which was followed in 1904 by the very similar *Wimmera*. These two vessels and *Zealandia* maintained the Tasman trade for the next few years, though they were soon eclipsed by new vessels built for the Union Line, in particular the *Maheno*, built in 1905.

In January 1908 the brand-new *Ulimaroa* was placed on the Tasman trade by Huddart Parker, and would remain the mainstay of their Tasman operation for the next twenty years. The new ship, along with *Wimmera* and *Victoria*, maintained the

Huddart Parker presence on the Tasman up to 1913, when *Riverina* replaced *Wimmera*. These three ships remained on the trade until January 1916, when *Ulimaroa* was taken over for war service. In January 1918 *Victoria* was sold, so the sinking of *Wimmera* in July 1918 was a major blow to the company, as it left only *Riverina* to maintain the service.

The post-war years were very difficult, with long waits for ships to be returned from military duty, and numerous maritime strikes. In November 1921 *Riverina* was transferred to the route between Sydney and Hobart, leaving *Ulimaroa* as the sole Huddart Parker representative crossing the Tasman. This situation lasted until April 1932, when *Ulimaroa* was replaced by *Zealandia*, but at the same time Huddart Parker was actively seeking a new ship for the Tasman route.

Just at that time a brand-new ship was offered for sale in Britain, and it was purchased by Huddart Parker. Originally named *Achimota*, the liner was renamed *Wanganella*, and it arrived in Sydney from Britain on the last day of 1932. On 12 January 1933, *Wanganella* departed on its first voyage to New Zealand, and the start of an amazing career.

For three years *Wanganella* operated in conjunction with *Monowai* of the Union Line, which was a comparable vessel, but in 1936 the New Zealand company introduced their brand-new *Awatea*, which totally outclassed both *Wanganella* and *Monowai* in every way. *Awatea* was one of the most outstanding liners of the 1930s, but *Wanganella* was able to maintain her place on the Tasman trade for the next three years.

The outbreak of World War II soon affected the Tasman trade. *Wanganella* was taken over for duty as a hospital ship, a role she fulfilled in the most admirable way. *Awatea* became a troopship, and was sunk in 1942, while *Monowai* served in a variety of roles.

The end of the war in 1945 did not herald an immediate return to normal coastal services, however, as *Wanganella* and *Monowai* were retained under military control for some time. Late in 1945, *Wanganella* was handed back to Huddart Parker Limited, but it would take almost a year to refit the liner for commercial service again. Instead of returning to the Tasman trade, *Wanganella* was first sent on a voyage to Vancouver, so it was not until January 1947 that the liner left Sydney for New Zealand again.

The voyage almost ended in tragedy, when *Wanganella* ran aground on Barrett Reef at the entrance to Wellington Harbour, and remained there for seventeen days. After being salvaged, the work of repairing the damage lasted almost two years, and it was not until December 1948 that *Wanganella* returned to service.

Meanwhile *Monowai* had been released from military duty, but also required a major refit, finally returning to commercial service in January 1949. For the next ten years these two liners would maintain a regular service across the Tasman Sea, but in May 1960 *Monowai* was withdrawn.

Wanganella struggled on operating a lone ship service, but passenger numbers were rapidly dwindling as more people began travelling by aircraft than by sea. In 1961 Huddart Parker Limited ended their interest in the Tasman trade when the company was sold, but *Wanganella* continued to operate to New Zealand, now wearing the funnel colours of McIlwraith, McEacharn Limited.

On 25 July 1962, *Wanganella* arrived in Sydney for the last time under the Australian flag. By then the ship had been sold to Hang Fung Shipping of Hong Kong, and began a new career as a cruise ship, with an occasional Tasman voyage as well. Unfortunately the new venture was not a success, and in July 1963 there came another sale, this time to an American company involved in the construction of a hydro-electric power scheme in the South Island of New Zealand.

On 29 August 1963 *Wanganella* arrived in Doubtful Sound, and a few days later moved to Deep Cove, which would be home for the next six years, serving as a hostel for workers employed on the hydro-electric construction.

When the massive project was completed there was no further need for the old liner, and *Wanganella* was sold again, at the end of 1969, to a Hong Kong company. Plans to return the ship to active service proved impossible to implement, and on 5 June 1970 *Wanganella* arrived at a ship-breaking yard in Taiwan.

So ended the career of one of the most notable liners ever to fly the Australian flag.

Over the years Huddart Parker changed the style of their title on several occasions, sometimes involving the inclusion of a comma between the two names. To make things as simple as possible for the reader, I decided to settle on a standard form by referring to the company simply as either Huddart Parker, or Huddart Parker Limited. The company originally gave its ships a plain black funnel, which was changed to yellow very early in the twentieth century. Unfortunately, despite extensive searching, I have not been able to ascertain exactly when this change occurred.

While I have made every endeavour for accuracy, any errors, omissions or misinterpretations included in this book are entirely my own responsibility.

Acknowledgments

For many years I have been keeping records on passenger ships that have been owned by Australian companies with a view to eventually using the information in books. The material contained in this volume has come from many sources, including newspapers, maritime magazines and various published works, and also from various contacts.

The inspiration for this book came some years ago, when I received a received a large number of pictures of *Wanganella* on Barrett Reef from a former crew member, Robert W. 'Bobby' Brookes, who lived in Launceston.

I was first contacted by Bobby Brookes in the early 1990s, when I was editor of the magazine *Australian Sea Heritage*. Over the next few years we maintained a regular correspondence, especially during the period I was writing a book on Australian paddle boats, to which Bobby contributed some excellent pictures and much useful information on the paddlers that once graced Port Phillip Bay. I had mentioned my interest in *Wanganella* to him, and was extremely pleased when the package of photographs arrived. This caused me to begin serious research on the *Wanganella*, and the other Australian ships that traded across the Tasman Sea to New Zealand. I had asked Bobby if he could provide me with his memories of being a crew member on *Wanganella* at the time of the grounding, but sadly he passed away before he could do so.

Other useful information and photographs came from various friends, who were most generous in loaning me items from their collections.

One of the most important finds was the December 1932 issue of the magazine *The Motor Ship*, containing a detailed description of *Wanganella* when it was brand new, which was kindly loaned to me by Stephen Card. I am also very grateful to Paul Joyce for the loan of a 1950s-era *Wanganella* brochure, complete with deck plan and interior pictures, as well as several menus and photographs.

Other valuable photographs and information for the book have been provided by Dallas Hogan, John Jeremy, Nick Tolerton and Bob McDougall, to whom I express my warmest appreciation.

Thanks are also expressed to Warwick Abadee for providing me with a copy of the story Norman Lapin wrote of his 1936 *Wanganella* cruise, and to Norman Lapin for permission to publish it.

A particular stroke of luck occurred when I met David Parker, great-great-grandson of T.J. Parker, one of the founders of Huddart Parker Limited. David's grandfather and father had both worked for the company, and among the material David had was an almost complete collection of the Huddart Parker in-house magazine, *The Beacon*, published from 1955 to 1961. David very kindly allowed me to borrow these magazines, which provided a wealth of information and illustrations of the career of *Wanganella* through these years, making up a large part of the liner's post-war history.

Illustrations included in this book were taken by a number of photographers, while others have been in my collection for many years. However, there were a few gaps that needed filling with previously unpublished photographic and brochure material. This included pictures from the collection of the late Fred Roderick which are now held by the New South Wales Branch of the World Ship Society.

The Whitehead Collection is held by the Victoria Branch of the World Ship Society, and I am extremely grateful to John Bone, the Branch President, for granting me permission to use a number of photographs from that collection. I am sure they will be greatly appreciated by readers. Fortunately, the entire Whitehead Collection has been scanned by John Asome, and I particularly thank Glen Stuart for taking the time to locate the photographs and email them to me.

I was also greatly assisted with photographs by John Mathieson, David Cooper, Ian Edwards and Tim Ryan, to each of whom I express my thanks.

I had always hoped to include some colour photographs, and have been able to obtain copies of a selection of very interesting paintings. The superb paintings of *Wanganella* and *Monowai*, *Riverina* and *Ulimaroa* in the first colour insert were done for me by my good friend Stan Stefaniak. Stan is a superb maritime artist, and I am pleased to have the opportunity to bring his work to a wider audience through this book.

The paintings of *Wanganella* and *Wimmera* owned by John Hannan are part of his amazing maritime art collection, and I am extremely grateful to him for permission to use them in this book.

I have been most fortunate in obtaining a variety of colour slides from the 1960s of *Wanganella*, *Westralia* and *Monowai*. These were taken by John Bennett, Lindsay Rex, the late Dennis Brook, the late Fred Roderick, the late Ron Knight and the late Richard McKenna, the latter slides being supplied by Don Finlayson from the McKenna Collection held by the Western Australian Maritime Museum.

To all those people who so generously helped me with this book I extend my sincere thanks.

Painting of *Wimmera* (John Hannan collection).

Postcard of Dickson Gregory painting of *Wimmera* (Dallas Hogan collection).

Painting of *Riverina* by Stan Stefaniak.

Painting of *Ulimaroa* by Stan Stefaniak.

Hand-coloured postcard of *Wanganella* in the 1930s.

Painting of *Wanganella* in the early 1950s by David Hogan (John Hannan collection).

Cover of Christmas Day 1953 menu depicting the main lounge on *Wanganella* (Paul Joyce collection).

1

Early Days

Australia and New Zealand are separated by 2000 kilometres of the Tasman Sea. The two islands that make up the majority of New Zealand were discovered by Europeans at much the same time as Australia, but the first attempts at settling the new lands were made in Australia in 1788. It was probably inevitable that the first Europeans to try settling in New Zealand would arrive there from Australia, in 1792.

The first European settlement in Australia was a penal colony on the shores of Port Jackson, better known as Sydney Harbour. The first few years were difficult for the early arrivals, a major problem being a shortage of food. From time to time store ships would be sent to the new colony, along with other vessels carrying more convicts.

One of these ships, the *Britannia*, under the command of Captain William Raven, arrived in Port Jackson on 26 July 1792. This vessel had been granted a three-year fishing licence, primarily for whales, from the East India Company, the first contract for private enterprise in the new colony.

In early October 1792, eleven officers of the New South Wales Corps formed a syndicate and chartered the *Britannia* to bring cattle and other goods to the colony to 'tend to the comforts of themselves and the soldiers of the Corps'. It was planned that the ship would make a voyage to another recently settled colony at the Cape of Good Hope on this speculative venture, where it was thought the necessary goods could be obtained.

As the *Britannia* would have to sail in an easterly direction to take advantage of the prevailing winds, it was decided to have the ship take a party of seal hunters to New Zealand, who would be picked up on the return voyage. This was because, during his voyage of discovery in 1770, Captain Cook had reported an abundance of fur seals were to be found on the south-west coast of the South Island of New Zealand.

Britannia departed Port Jackson on 24 October, and sailed across the Tasman Sea, arriving in early November at Dusky Sound. Here the sealing party disembarked, and began the first European settlement in New Zealand. This voyage marks the beginning of sea communications between the two countries. The sealing party built the first European style houses in New Zealand, but living conditions were extremely harsh. After several months, the sealers feared they had been abandoned, and began constructing a vessel so they could sail back to Sydney.

Britannia had voyaged on to the Cape of Good Hope, and returned as planned to Dusky Sound, picking up the sealing party, along with 4500 sealskins. The half-finished boat was left behind, and *Britannia* returned to Port Jackson on 20 June 1793.

In 1795 a vessel named *Endeavour*—not the *Endeavour* used by Captain Cook in his voyages of discovery—left Sydney for Dusky Sound. The captain planned to complete the half-finished boat at Dusky Sound, and use it to catch seals. As *Endeavour* closed on the coastline it ran aground in Facile Harbour, a cove in Dusky Sound, and became the first known shipwreck in New Zealand. There were 244 persons on board, including 46 convicts who had stowed away, and at least two women.

The survivors were left in desperate circumstances, being forced to live off what they could catch on the land and in the sea. During 1796 the half-finished boat left at Dusky Sound by the sealers was completed, and many of the marooned people made their way back to Sydney in it and a rescued longboat from the wrecked *Endeavour*. The 35 people who were left behind in Dusky Sound were not rescued until May 1797, by which time they were starving.

For the next fifty years there was no regular service between Australia and New Zealand, but sailing ships continued to make occasional voyages between the two countries, mainly to carry supplies to the European settlements that began developing in various parts of both islands of New Zealand, to conduct trade with the Maoris, or for sealing and whaling expeditions. During this period quite a few ships were lost, as the coastline of New Zealand was extremely dangerous, and poorly mapped.

The first steamships appeared in Australian waters in 1831. They were paddle boats, and their activities were usually confined to coastal trading. However, in 1847 the paddle steamer *Juno* made a voyage to New Zealand and back, becoming the first steamship to complete the journey.

Built by Caird & Co. at Greenock in 1836 to the order of the St George Steam Packet Co., the 621 gross ton *Juno* was purchased in 1841 by Benjamin Boyd, who at that time was about to become a major business figure in New South Wales as the founder of the Royal Bank of Australasia, and in attempting to establish his own settlement, Boydtown, on Twofold Bay near Eden. *Juno* made the voyage to Australia under sail, as was common in those times even for steamships, departing London on 26 June 1841. After arriving in Sydney on 25 March 1842, the vessel lay at anchor in Sydney Harbour for the next five years.

In May 1847 the *Shipping Gazette* in Sydney carried an item regarding the *Juno* which noted that 'the result of the trial of this steamer to Twofold Bay to test her boilers (which having been put in previous to her departure from England, had not been previously tried) has, we understand, proved most satisfactory'. The vessel was then chartered by the Commissariat in New South Wales for a voyage to New Zealand, to carry supplies to British forces stationed there. It is possible that Benjamin Boyd saw this as an opportunity to establish a regular service across the Tasman.

On 13 June 1847, *Juno* left its berth in Sydney, but did not pass through Sydney Heads until the following morning. On board were nine passengers—eight males, including Benjamin Boyd, and one lady who was accompanying her husband—while the cargo included live sheep, cattle and horses. The voyage was beset by difficulties. For the first week the vessel battled through a strong north-easterly gale, which finally eased on the evening of 23 June. However, the wind then veered to the west, causing a nasty cross-sea, which put such a strain on the pintles of the rudder that it eventually fell off and was lost.

For three days the *Juno* wallowed helplessly in seas that were too rough for repairs to be attempted, but on 26 June a temporary rudder was put in place. When *Juno* reached the Bay of Islands it anchored for further repairs to the temporary rudder, which was made larger. On 4 July *Juno* left for Auckland, but again ran into heavy seas, which destroyed the temporary rudder. *Juno* was forced to turn around and return to the Bay of Islands, where another rudder was constructed and fitted in place. Leaving again on 6 July, *Juno* steamed to Auckland in just fifteen hours, despite battling a strong headwind.

The voyage from Sydney to Auckland had taken 23 days. Of the 1000 sheep on board when the voyage began, only 670 survived, while 49 of the 79 head of cattle were still alive to go ashore in Auckland. However, all the horses made the voyage safely.

Juno remained in Auckland for just over six weeks, then left for Sydney on 22 August. A series of problems soon arose that forced the vessel to return to Auckland for repairs, and it was not until 11 September that *Juno* was able to leave again for Sydney. Nothing was recorded of the return voyage, which must have been better than the trip over.

By then Benjamin Boyd's interests in Australia were in a state of total collapse, and the *Juno* was sold in 1848 to W. Sprott Boyd, no relation to Benjamin Boyd, who planned to use the vessel on a service between Sydney and Adelaide. When a subsidy was not forthcoming from the South Australian Government, this service was quickly terminated. *Juno* was sold to the Spanish Government in 1851, and sent to the Philippines. It made a voyage back to Australia in 1853, but on the return voyage from Sydney to Manila was wrecked on the north coast of New South Wales on 22 October 1853.

The first regular steamship service across the Tasman Sea did not commence until 1854, as a New Zealand venture. The Auckland Provincial Council offered the Auckland Steam Navigation Company an annual subsidy of £5,000 to operate a regular monthly service between Auckland and Sydney. This company had recently taken delivery of a new ship, the *William Denny*, built by Denny Bros at Dumbarton in 1853. It had an iron hull, measured 595 gross tons, and was powered by steam engines of 200 hp driving a single propeller.

The *William Denny* maintained a regular schedule over the next three years, being the only steamer on the Tasman trade. The service came to a sudden end when, on 3 March 1857, the *William Denny* ran aground near North Cape, at the top of North Island. At first it was thought the steamer could be salvaged, but two weeks after it went ashore, a heavy gale struck the area and the *William Denny* broke up. The Auckland Steam Navigation Company did not acquire a replacement vessel, and the steamer service across the Tasman Sea came to a halt.

It was reported in 1858 that the Otago Provincial Council offered to provide an annual subsidy of £4,000 for two years to the owners of a steamer named the

Queen to operate a regular service between Otago and Melbourne with a call at Invercargill, but there is no record of this ship ever making a voyage across the Tasman.

It was not until 1859 that a regular steamship service across the Tasman Sea was resumed. The newly formed Intercolonial Royal Mail Steam Packet Company was provided with an annual subsidy of £24,000 by the British Government to operate regular services between Sydney and New Zealand for a period of ten years. Departures from Sydney would be monthly, with two vessels leaving after the P&O liner arrived from Britain with the mails. One of the steamers would go directly to Auckland, while the other would call at Nelson, New Plymouth, Wellington, Port Cooper and Otago.

The new company took delivery of three new ships. Two, *Lord Ashley* and *Lord Worsley*, were 435 gross ton sister ships, built at Hull in England in 1857, having iron hulls 188 feet/57.3 m long with a beam of just under 25 feet/7.6 m and a single propeller, with engines of 80 nhp. They provided accommodation for 30 first class and 11 second class passengers. In April 1858, Shaw, Savill & Co. placed advertisements in London newspapers that the *Lord Ashley* was due to leave shortly for Auckland and Port Chalmers, carrying passengers and cargo. On its delivery voyage *Lord Ashley* became the first commercial steamship to make a direct passage from Britain to New Zealand, being followed by *Lord Worsley* a few months later.

The third ship was the 363 gross ton *Airedale*, built at South Stockton in England in 1857, with an iron hull and single propeller, which was used for a connecting service from Nelson, Picton and Wellington to Lyttelton and Dunedin.

A fourth vessel to be operated by the company was the 1122 gross ton *Prince Alfred*, built in 1854 by Wm Denny at Dumbarton for Pearson & Coleman, of Hull, and sold to the Intercolonial company in 1858.

The first Tasman sailing was taken by *Lord Ashley* in November 1858, being joined during 1859 by *Lord Worsley* and *Prince Alfred*. While passengers and cargo were carried along with the mails, the service only survived through the large subsidy. During 1860, *Lord Ashley* made only seven return trips between Sydney and Auckland, which increased to fifteen in 1861, but was down to nine in 1862. It was during that year that ownership of the Intercolonial company was changed to the Panama & Australian Royal Mail Steam Packet Company, following which *Lord Ashley* was used primarily on coastal trades in New Zealand, with only one or two trips to Sydney each year.

In 1872, *Lord Ashley* was sold to John Manning of Sydney, and spent some years operating from Sydney to Rockhampton. Converted into a collier in June 1877, operating from Newcastle to Sydney, *Lord Ashley* was wrecked on a reef off Terrigal on 8 September 1877.

In 1859 a well-established Australian coastal trading firm, McMeckan, Blackwood & Company, of Melbourne, decided to enter the New Zealand trade. This company had been operating a fleet of sailing ships on the Australian coastal trades for many years, and was generally known as the 'Blue Emu Line' because their house flag featured an emu in blue on a white background.

McMeckan, Blackwood formed the Adelaide, Melbourne & Otago Steamship Company, to operate a regular service between those ports. As this was not in direct competition with the services being operated by the Intercolonial Royal Mail Steam Packet Company, it was able to operate successfully, even without a subsidy.

Among the ships placed in the fleet of the Adelaide, Melbourne & Otago Steamship Company were the *Omeo* and *Alhambra*. Built in 1858, *Omeo* was a barque-rigged, iron-hulled single-screw steamer, which was placed on the Tasman trade as soon as it arrived in Australia. *Alhambra* had been built in 1855 for the P&O Steam Navigation Company, being purchased by McMeckan, Blackwood in 1859 and also going straight onto the New Zealand trade.

The whole Tasman trade changed dramatically when, on 8 June 1861, gold was discovered in the Otago region. The possibility of quick wealth lured thousands of miners, and soon the demand for passages from Australia to Otago far outstripped the available vessels.

Just about anything that could float was advertised as offering passages to Otago, from vintage sailing ships to paddle steamers and cargo ships. Unfortunately some of these vessels were not up to the voyage, and disappeared without trace in the midst of the Tasman Sea. Despite this, the gold rush continued, and on some days as many as 3000 hopeful miners would rush ashore at Dunedin and immediately head off to the goldfields.

The gold rush was a bonanza for McMeckan, Blackwood & Company, whose ships sailed fully loaded on every voyage out of Melbourne. A number of new companies sprang up almost overnight to cash in on the trade, most of them surviving only a short time, though usually making exceptional profits for the owners. In addition to passengers, a trade soon developed in providing food and general supplies to the goldfields, since the miners were interested only in digging, not farming. Some old clipper ships were used also to carry sheep to New Zealand at this time, forming the basis of what would became a major industry.

One of the steamers to carry passengers between Australia and New Zealand during this period was the *South Australian*, owned by Samuel White, who had a flour mill at Aldinga, 45 kilometres south of Adelaide. White migrated from Britain, arriving in Aldinga in 1850. Over the next decade and a half he became one of the leading citizens in the district, which by the mid-1860s was populated by about 500 people. White was also heavily involved in the development of Port Willunga, about 2 kilometres from Aldinga. His activities as a flour merchant brought him into contact with several shipowners, and he obtained a part share in several vessels then operating on the local coastal trade to Port Adelaide.

In 1863, Samuel White ordered a new vessel to be built for him by the John Key shipyard in Scotland, which was launched in April 1864, and completed three months later. Named *South Australian*, it was 633 gross tons, had an iron hull 222 feet/67.7 m long, and was powered by two geared oscillating steam engines of 180 hp driving a single propeller, for a service speed of 10 knots. Accommodation was installed for 40 saloon class and 140 second class passengers, and the cargo capacity was 560 tons.

South Australian reached Port Adelaide in September 1864, and shortly afterward began operating a regular service to Melbourne. At the time, *South Australian* was one of the largest and fastest vessels operating on the coastal trades but, faced with serious competition from McMeckan, Blackwood, the service was soon in trouble.

In October 1864, after only one return trip to Melbourne, *South Australian* was chartered by the South Australian Government for £1,000 to carry a group of settlers to Escape Cliffs on Adam Bay, in the Northern Territory. This voyage departed Adelaide on 29 October, going up the east coast of Australia. The ship returned to Adelaide on 1 January 1865 via the west coast, having completed one of the first circumnavigations of Australia. *South Australian* then resumed its service between Adelaide and Melbourne, again in competition with the steamers operated by McMeckan, Blackwood.

With *South Australian* struggling to survive, in September 1865 White concluded an arrangement with the Otago Steam Ship Company, of Dunedin, to operate *South Australian* on a regular service across the Tasman Sea from Melbourne to ports in South Island, and to Wellington in the North Island. The Otago Company held the mail contract between Melbourne and the Otago region, which was originally operated by their own vessels, the 872 gross ton *Scotia*, and *Albion* of 806 gross tons, both built in 1863 by Denny Bros.

The barque-rigged *Scotia* was the first completed, but had a very short career. On 3 June 1864 *Scotia* was on a voyage from Melbourne to Otago when it went aground on a reef off Stirling Point, at Bluff, while entering that port, and became a total loss.

The Otago Company then chartered a vessel named *Hero*, which had been built in 1861 for service across the North Sea, and in 1863 was briefly owned by the famous Black Ball Line. Later the same year the vessel was bought by Bright Bros & Co. of Melbourne, and on arrival in Australia was immediately chartered to the Otago Company until *South Australian* was brought in to partner *Albion*.

South Australian departed Melbourne on 7 October 1865 on its first voyage to New Zealand. On board were 238 passengers, mostly miners heading for the goldfields. The first port of call was Hokitika, on the west coast of South Island, then the vessel went on to call at Nelson, Wellington, Lyttelton and Port Chalmers, the port for Dunedin. On the return trip the ship went around the southern tip of South Island, with a call at Bluff, then directly back to Melbourne.

In all, *South Australian* made eleven voyages from Melbourne to New Zealand, sometimes following the same route as the first trip, but on occasion going to Bluff and Port Chalmers first, then back via Cook Strait. On 21 August 1866, *South Australian* departed Port Chalmers on its final voyage under the arrangement with the Otago Steam Ship Company. When the ship had disembarked its passengers and unloaded cargo in Melbourne, it was laid up.

By then Samuel White was in serious financial trouble, mostly caused by the poor returns obtained by *South Australian* since it entered service. The ship was seized by the bank that held the mortgage, and offered for sale by auction in January 1867, but the reserve price was not reached. A short time later, *South Australian* was sold to McMeckan, Blackwood for £11,500. The new owners spent an additional £3,000 giving the vessel an extensive refit, prior to returning it to the Tasman trade under the banner of the Adelaide, Melbourne & Otago Steamship Company, but operating only between Melbourne and Port Chalmers, with a call at Bluff.

Still named *South Australian*, the vessel departed Melbourne on 21 March 1867, under the command of Captain Hugh Mackie, a very experienced master, who was formerly on the *Gothenburg*. On the morning of 28 March, *South Australian* arrived in Port Chalmers, remaining in port for five days.

On the afternoon of 2 April, *South Australian* left

its berth to commence the return trip to Melbourne, clearing the port at 4.20 pm. As it was only a short run to Bluff, and the ship was due to arrive there the next morning after dawn, speed was reduced to slow as it proceeded down the east coast of South Island in a very calm sea.

About six hours into the trip, *South Australian* ran aground on rocks about half a kilometre off the shore and 6 kilometres south of Coal Point in South Otago. Despite the grounding occurring when the ship was travelling at slow speed, it remained stuck firmly on the rocks. During the next day the passengers and crew were evacuated safely, and work began on salvaging the cargo. This included gold valued at £13,000, which was saved, but only a small portion of the rest of the cargo had been removed when, a week after the ship went aground, it broke in two and began to break up.

At a subsequent inquiry into the accident, the master and ship's officers were all exonerated. It was found that the compass deviation card supplied to the ship by authorities in Melbourne had been wrongly formulated, which had caused the ship to follow an incorrect course.

Although the ship was insured for £20,000, the owners encountered unexpected difficulties in making their claim. When Samuel White had sold the ship in 1867, he had not cancelled the insurance policy he held on the ship, and he died the following year. The matter of the insurance payment for the *South Australian* was not resolved for quite a few years. Eventually the wreck was sold at auction to scrap dealers for just £165.

The Intercolonial Royal Mail Steam Packet Company did not benefit as much from the gold rush and even with its generous subsidy was having trouble surviving economically. Their operation was not helped when both *Prince Alfred* and *Lord Worsley* were lost. *Lord Worsley* left Nelson on 31 August 1862, but early the following morning ran aground in Namu Bay, becoming a total loss.

It was also in 1862 that a new vessel, *Claud Hamilton*, was added to the Intercolonial fleet. An iron-hulled, single-screw steamer of 668 gross tons, and 200 feet/61 m long, *Claud Hamilton* was a particularly attractive ship, with a clipper bow, three lofty masts and single funnel. By the time this vessel reached Sydney, however, the Intercolonial Royal Mail Steam Packet Company was no longer in business.

In 1863 the Panama, Australia & New Zealand Royal Mail Steam Packet Company was formed, which had capital of £375,000, and in addition was subsidised by both the British and New Zealand governments. The new company was intended to operate a through service from London to New Zealand and Australia in two sea sections, with passengers travelling overland across Panama. It was also planned that the ships then owned by the Intercolonial Royal Mail Steam Packet Company would be transferred to the new company when it commenced operation. However, this took some time to occur, and it was not until 15 June 1866 that the *Kaikoura* left Sydney on the first voyage to New Zealand and Panama.

Other ships to be used on this trade included *Otago* and *Tararua*, both built in 1863. The 977 gross ton *Otago*, which was 236 feet/72 m long, was a two-funnelled, iron-hulled single-screw steamer, which completed its delivery voyage from Glasgow to Melbourne in the fast time of 52 days. On arrival in Australia, *Otago* was immediately placed on a service to New Zealand until the longer service began. *Tararua*, which was a three-masted iron-hulled single-screw steamer, also operated on the Tasman trade when it first arrived in Australia.

For a short time this service prospered, but with the completion of a railway line between San Francisco and New York, a trip across the United States became more attractive to travellers than the much harder trek across Panama. The Panama, Australia & New Zealand Royal Mail Steam Packet Company struggled on for a further two years, but on 22 December 1868 the *Rakaia* made the final departure from Sydney for Panama; the company folded in early 1869, and its vessels were sold. *Otago*, *Tararua* and *Claud Hamilton* were purchased by McMeckan, Blackwood, and without any change of name remained on the Tasman trade in the fleet of the Adelaide, Melbourne & Otago Steam Ship Company, which now enjoyed a virtual monopoly on the steamship services between Australia and New Zealand, and was operating weekly departures.

The only competition of any substance was provided by the Australasian Steam Navigation Company (ASN), which in 1868 had begun a service from Melbourne to Sydney and then Auckland. However, departures were never on a regular basis, and the ships used were normally employed on services along the east coast of Australia. Departures became more regular in 1875, when ASN began operating a mail service from Sydney and Auckland to Honolulu and San Francisco using two vessels, *City of Melbourne* and *Wonga Wonga*.

The first departure was taken by the *City of Melbourne*, which departed Sydney on 16 January 1875. On 11 September 1876 the *City of Melbourne* came close to foundering in the huge storm off the New South Wales south coast that sank the Howard Smith Limited steamer *Dandenong* off Jervis Bay, with the loss of 40 lives, and has always been known as the 'Dandenong gale'.

It is worth mentioning here that on 20 February 1876 a submarine telegraphic cable came into operation between Australia and New Zealand. The 2000 kilometre long cable was laid by two ships sent specially from England for the task.

By the mid-1870s, McMeckan, Blackwood & Company owned the largest fleet of steamers in Australia, engaged on both coastal services and the Tasman trade. During 1875, two new steamers, the identical sisters *Arawata* and *Ringarooma*, were added to the fleet of the Adelaide, Melbourne & Otago Steam Ship Company. Built at Whiteinch in England, they were 1096 gross tons, and proved to be quite fast, becoming the largest vessels to be owned by McMeckan, Blackwood. The two new vessels joined *Tararua* and *Albion* in maintaining the regular service to New Zealand.

The same year a new competitor appeared on the Tasman trade, when the Union Steam Ship Company of New Zealand was incorporated on 12 July 1875. Initially the new company concentrated on New Zealand coastal services, but expanded very rapidly. In June 1876 the New Zealand Steam Navigation Co. Ltd, of Wellington, was bought up, along with the four small vessels it owned, and the following month the Albion Shipping Co. which owned only one vessel, was purchased.

On 4 October 1876, the *Wakatipu*, owned by Captain Angus Cameron, but operating on behalf of the Union Line, departed Port Chalmers for Wellington and then Sydney, inaugurating the trans-Tasman service of the Union Line. In January 1877 the company took delivery of their first new vessel, the *Rotorua*, which left Port Chalmers on 10 January 1877 for Sydney, with a call at Onehunga on the way.

In 1878 the Union Line advised McMeckan, Blackwood & Company that they intended to enter the trade from Otago to Melbourne, which would have provided stiff competition for the Australian company. By that time McMeckan, Blackwood had pulled out of the Australian coastal trades, and appeared to be losing interest in being shipowners, preferring to trade as agents instead. On 19 November 1878, the Union Line purchased the Adelaide, Melbourne & Otago Steam Ship Company from McMeckan, Blackwood & Co., along with the four vessels it owned, *Albion*, *Arawata*, *Ringarooma* and *Tararua*.

Rotorua, the first vessel built for the Union Line.

This sale brought to a close the shipowning activities of McMeckan, Blackwood, and their distinctive house flag with its blue emu disappeared from the seas forever. The Union Line kept the four ships they had purchased on the same trade, without change of name. For the next fourteen years the Tasman trade was totally dominated by the Union Line, with virtually no serious competition.

Among the ships the Union Line placed on the trans-Tasman trade was *Te Anau*, built in 1879 by the Denny shipyard at Dumbarton. The vessel was 1652 gross tons, and fitted with triple-expansion machinery driving a single propeller, giving a service speed of 13 knots. *Te Anau* was typical of the steamers then being operated on the Tasman trade.

An interesting description of *Te Anau* and its early career was published in the February 1959 issue of *Sea Breezes* magazine, in a letter written by E. B. Jackson, of Nelson in New Zealand. He wrote:

> The *Te Anau* was flush-decked and carried 132 first-class passengers in the 'tweendecks. Steerage passengers numbering 72 were carried in the forward compartment.
>
> The vessel possessed a raised fo'c'sle head, bridge deck amidships surmounted by a flying bridge, while right aft was a handsome teak deckhouse containing the smoking room, 'social hall' and first-class saloon companionway. Two holds were available for cargo, one forward and one aft. Five lifeboats were carried, besides rafts.
>
> Her appearance was enhanced by two well-raked masts fitted with top-masts (an indication that sail was at one time carried). The tall single funnel was stepped amidships, abaft the navigating bridge. The cutwater was straight and bore some ornamentation while the stern was of the counter variety. The plating of the hull was extended to form a continuous bulwark around the main deck.
>
> The *Te Anau* visited my home port of Nelson many times during her career as a coastal passenger vessel. She was also in the Intercolonial trade between this country and Australia, and on March 7, 1880, when 400 miles [640 km] out from Bluff (southernmost port of New Zealand) en route to Melbourne, she had the misfortune to strip her propeller and arrived back in Bluff under sail. She was commanded by Capt. McQuoy for many years, a true old-time seafarer.
>
> I can only add that the saloon, quite a handsome apartment, and lit overhead by a large teak skylight, was situated right aft, sailing ship style. All cabins were very small, lighting by oil lamps and washing facilities somewhat primitive, according to modern standards. However, she was the typical passenger cargo carrier of her day and served her owners faithfully and well over a long period.

In 1916 the craft was converted to a cargo carrier and in 1924 was sold to shipbreakers who stripped the hull after which it was used in connection with the Wanganui Harbour works. The skipper's cabin was purchased by a Wanganui resident and used by him as a garden house.

Also in 1879, the Union Line placed another vessel on the Tasman trade, the *Rotomahana*, which would become one their most famous ships. Built in Scotland, *Rotomahana* made history in being the first vessel constructed of mild steel, and also the first to be fitted with bilge keels. In design she was totally unlike any other vessel ever owned by the Union Line, but this is said to have been because the vessel was originally ordered as the private yacht of a wealthy prince, who died before it was completed. Subsequently the vessel was sold while still on the stocks to the Union Line. Launched on 6 June 1879, fitting out took only six weeks, and the vessel was completed on 14 July.

Rotomahana was quite small by today's standards, just 1727 gross tons and 298 feet/90.8 m long. Her stately appearance was enhanced by a clipper bow and jib-boom, complete with figurehead and decorative scroll work. The single compound engine installed was quite large for a ship of that size, comprising a high-pressure cylinder with a diameter of 42 inches/1.2 m, while the low-pressure cylinder had an 82-inch/2 m diameter. Steam was supplied by six boilers, each with a working pressure of 70 pounds per square inch/482.3 kPa. The single propeller was also quite large, with a diameter of 14 feet 6 inches/4.4 m. On trials *Rotomahana* reached a top speed of 15.5 knots, very fast for the times.

On her delivery voyage *Rotomahana* left London on 5 August 1879, boarded 100 passengers at Plymouth and, under the command of Captain T. Underwood, voyaged by way of South Africa to reach Melbourne on 22 September. After several days in port, she crossed the Tasman Sea in just 3 days 16 hours, arriving in Port Chalmers on 1 October 1879.

Rotomahana was placed on the trans-Tasman trade, and caused enormous interest at every port visited due to her yacht-like lines and internal fittings, with accommodation for 140 first class, 80 second class and 80 steerage class passengers. The first and second class staterooms and public rooms were panelled in fine woods, such as mahogany, polished bird's-eye maple, rosewood, satinwood and teak, while the lounges featured elaborate carvings, beautiful mirrors and quality furnishings.

In November 1879, *Rotomahana* began operating across the Tasman Sea, her first crossing being to Sydney. Her return trip to Auckland tested the sea-keeping qualities of the vessel to the full, as reported in the *New Zealand Herald* on 26 November:

> By all accounts the storm was in the form of a cyclone ... and under such circumstances the escape of the steamer from a greater disaster than what occurred is due in great measure to the skill and coolness displayed by Captain Underwood and his officers during the trying time ... The damage done to the steamer by the huge seas which occasionally broke on board is very small; £200 will cover the cost while the same amount will cover the loss of the cargo that was swept away from the deck.
>
> The steamer left Sydney at 9 am on Thursday 20th with strong westerly winds and for the first five hours was kept on her course, the wind gradually increasing to a gale. At 2 pm it had increased to hurricane force with mountainous seas running and the vessel was then obliged to run before the storm more than four points off her course until 2 am on the 21st, the steam in the meantime being throttled off and yet she made 17 knots running clean away from her screw action.
>
> The sea during the major portion of this time was really frightful to witness, standing up in the wake of the vessel as high as the crosstrees, and the steamer appearing as a mere straw upon the crest of the huge waves. In such weather as this, one of the hands named A. McLellan was swept overboard, on the night of the 20th, by a huge sea breaking on board which lifted the man clean off the bridge, beside smashing the boat and doing other damage.
>
> The arrival of the steamer at Russell on Monday was a time of great rejoicing to the passengers and it was determined to celebrate their arrival by a convivial gathering in the saloon of the vessel that evening.

On her next trans-Tasman voyage from New Zealand, *Rotomahana* arrived in Hobart for the first time on the morning of 9 December 1879, berthing alongside the Argyle Street Pier. An article in the *Mercury* newspaper the next day stated '*Rotomahana* far eclipses any steamer that has before visited Hobart Town'. The vessel's stay in Hobart was very short, as she departed at 12.30 pm for Melbourne. On her return trip to New Zealand, *Rotomahana* called back at Hobart on 19 December, and subsequently became a regular visitor to the port. Unfortunately, a limited cargo capacity combined with excessive coal consumption at high speed made *Rotomahana* a very expensive ship to operate, and she was often laid up during off-peak periods.

Despite their position of total domination on the Tasman, the Union Line was soon looking to have William Denny & Bros of Dumbarton build more new ships for the trade. The first to be delivered was *Manapouri*, of 1783 gross tons, which was launched

Rotomahana in Sydney (Dallas Hogan collection).

on 20 December 1881 and arrived in New Zealand in May 1882. This vessel was notable in being the first merchant vessel in the world to have incandescent lighting installed. A sister ship, *Wairarapa*, arrived in New Zealand in November 1882. This pair could carry about 200 passengers each, and were the fastest ships operating across the Tasman, with a service speed of 13 knots, though this claim was sometimes challenged.

On 9 January 1883, *Manapouri* departed Auckland bound for Sydney, being followed nearly three hours later by the larger *City of Sydney*, a 3020 gross ton liner operated by the Pacific Royal Mail Line between San Francisco and Sydney. It was generally thought the larger liner would beat the Union Line vessel, but *Manapouri* arrived in Sydney 3 hours and 10 minutes ahead of its rival, to record a narrow victory.

In 1885 the Union Line found themselves faced with a bit of competition on the Tasman trade, the 2749 gross ton *Triumph*. In September 1885 the owners of the *Triumph* began offering passages from Auckland to Sydney via Wellington for as little as £7. This rate was immediately matched by the Union Line, which was quickly able to drive out the potential rival. It was a tactic the Union Line would repeat whenever other companies entered the Tasman trades, with varying degrees of success.

In October 1885 the largest Union Line vessel to date, *Mararoa*, of 2465 gross tons, arrived in New Zealand from the Denny shipyard. Originally intended to operate across the Tasman, *Mararoa* was instead placed in service across the Pacific to San Francisco, but proved unsuitable for this trade. After only four trans-Pacific voyages, *Mararoa* was transferred to the Tasman routes.

To replace *Mararoa* on the Pacific trade, the 3433 gross ton *Monowai* was built by Denny & Bros, and left Sydney in March 1890 on its first voyage to San Francisco. *Monowai* proved to be so slow that official complaints were received by the Union Line from the New Zealand Government. After only one round trip, *Monowai* was transferred to the Tasman trades, but after only a few trips had to be returned to the Pacific trade, as the Union Line had no other vessel available for that trade.

Going into 1892, the Union Line was maintaining services between Australia and New Zealand using a variety of ships. The mainstays of the trade were the sisters *Manapouri* and *Wairarapa*, along with the larger *Mararoa*, while *Rotomahana* was also still operating for most of the year as well. By the end of that year, however, the Union Line would be facing serious competition.

Wairarapa

2

First Blood

Towards the end of 1892, the Union Line suddenly found itself faced with major competition on the Tasman, when after a 14-year absence an Australian-owned company joined the trade. In 1891, James Huddart, one of the founders of Huddart, Parker & Company Limited, established a separate company, the New Zealand & Australasian Steamship Company, to operate regular services across the Tasman between Australia and New Zealand.

James Huddart was the nephew of Captain Peter Huddart, who in 1852 had arrived in Port Phillip Bay from Britain as master of the sailing ship *Aberfoyle*, and came ashore to explore the possibilities offered by the colony. He settled in Geelong, establishing himself in Yarra Street North as a merchant and shipbroker. His major interest was importing coal to Melbourne from Newcastle, and the business soon flourished.

In the early 1860s, Captain Huddart brought out his nephew, James Huddart, from Britain to join him in the business. James was a man of vision and ambition, and soon opened a branch office in Ballarat. Shortly afterward, Captain Huddart left Australia, returning to his British home in Cumberland, leaving James Huddart in sole control of the business.

By 1875, James Huddart was operating two sailing ships of his own, *Medea*, of 453 gross tons, and *Queen Emma*, of 314 gross tons, on the coal trade between Newcastle and Melbourne.

Thomas J. Parker had arrived in Australia from Britain in 1853, and soon established a business representing the family firm based in London, J. and D. Parker & Company, as merchants and importers. Parker actually brought his office with him from Britain, in the form of a small prefabricated iron building, which was erected in Little Malop Street, Geelong.

In 1854, Parker also became the Geelong agent for Captain William Howard Smith, who was operating a regular daily return service from Melbourne to Geelong with the steamer *Express*, of which he was master and half owner, his partner being the vessel's engineer, J. B. Skinner, while the chief officer was Thomas Webb. In 1855, Parker established the Express Steamer Agency, and appointed John Traill as manager to look after this side of his business.

Of Scottish ancestry, John Traill was born 1826 on the Scottish east coast and educated at Edinburgh. At the age of 28, in 1854 he migrated to Australia and settled in Geelong, initially becoming manager of Smith Barker & Skinner, who operated in the coastal shipping trade between Melbourne and Geelong. In 1860 Traill married, and later had four children.

When Captain Howard Smith decided to enter the inter-state coal trade in 1862, he sold his half-share in the *Express* to Thomas Parker, who then moved to Melbourne and continued to operate it on the Melbourne–Geelong service. Howard Smith's place as master of the ship was taken by Thomas Webb.

When J. B. Skinner died in 1867, his half-share in the *Express* was bought by John Traill and Captain Webb, which brought them into a partnership with Parker. In 1869 Parker had a larger vessel built in Scotland for the trade, the *Despatch*, which he owned outright. The *Express* was relegated to a reserve steamer, and sold in 1874 to E. P. Houghton, of Dunedin, in New Zealand. *Express* ended its career in New Zealand waters, being wrecked at Riverton on 9 March 1877.

The *Despatch* was an enormous success on the trade between Melbourne and Geelong, being a great improvement on the *Express*. The venture proved so profitable that in 1875, Parker and his two partners, Traill and Webb, bought a wooden-hulled barque, the *Olivia Davies*, of 523 gross tons, built in America in 1864. This vessel was placed in the coal trade between Newcastle and Melbourne, bringing them into competition with James Huddart.

On 1 August 1876, the coal-importing business interests of Thomas J Parker and James Huddart, along with John Traill and Captain Tom Webb as equal partners, were merged to form Huddart, Parker & Company. The shipping service operated by Parker on Port Phillip Bay between Melbourne and Geelong was not included in the new company until 1886.

Over the next few years the new company added four more sailing vessels to their fleet, and in 1878 opened an office in Melbourne. Two years later their first steamer, *Nemesis*, was delivered for the coal trade, followed by two more ships in the next two years, *Lindus* and *Wendouree*, replacing the entire sailing-ship fleet.

In 1885 two more steam colliers were added to the fleet, *Burrumbeet* and *Corangamite*, and when the latter vessel was wrecked in December 1886, a replacement was built, entering service in 1887 as *Elingamite*.

In 1889 Huddart, Parker & Company was reformed into a limited liability company with a capital of £300,000. Each partner held one quarter of the shares and James Huddart was appointed chairman. By 1890, the headquarters of Huddart Parker had moved from offices on the wharves at Geelong to Collins Street in Melbourne. At the same time John Traill moved his family into a recently built house in St Kilda Road, which was named Ulimaroa. His descendants lived in the house, which is still standing, until 1960.

By 1891, Huddart Parker was operating a fleet of five steamers on the coal trade between Newcastle and Melbourne, offering a small amount of passenger accommodation. The company had also entered the Bass Strait passenger trade between Melbourne and northern Tasmania in April 1890, using the diminutive *Coogee*, which had been bought in 1888 and initially used on the service between Geelong and Melbourne.

Despite all these developments on the Australian coastal trades, by 1890 James Huddart found his attention diverted by the proposal to develop an 'All Red Route' for travel between Britain and Australia via the Pacific. With British possessions always shown in red on maps, the route was so called because it was planned that passengers could travel by Canadian Pacific Line ships from Liverpool to Canada, then join Canadian Pacific Railways for the journey overland to Vancouver. What was then required was a British company to operate a steamship service to Australia, and James Huddart decided he would provide this.

Huddart placed orders with the C. S. Swan & Hunter shipyard at Newcastle, in England, for the construction of two sister ships, to be completed in 1892. These ships would be owned outright by James Huddart, but managed for him by Huddart Parker. Unfortunately, when the two ships were completed the arrangements for the trans-Pacific service had not been finalised, and James Huddart was forced to find alternative employment for his vessels, or lay them up. As they were too large to join the Australian coastal trade, Huddart opted to enter the trans-Tasman trade, giving his new company the impressive title of the New Zealand & Australasian Steamship Company, to operate in direct competition with the Union Steam Ship Company.

It was something of a surprise when James Huddart decided to branch out on his own into the New Zealand trade, at the same time relinquishing his position as chairman of Huddart Parker, though retaining a financial interest in the company. Huddart was replaced as chairman of Huddart Parker by Thomas Webb, who was succeeded in 1895 by John Traill. Although the new company was a totally separate entity from Huddart, Parker & Company Limited, they were appointed to be managing agents of the two new ships when they entered service.

The first of the ships was launched on 28 May 1892 and named *Warrimoo*, reaching 17 knots on trials before being handed over to James Huddart on 23 July. Two days later, on 25 July 1892, the second vessel was launched and named *Miowera*, and work began on fitting it out to join *Warrimoo*.

Departing Newcastle in England on 31 August 1892, *Warrimoo* ran into a full gale while passing through the English Channel, reportedly coping well with the heavy seas, and arrived in Plymouth at 5.15 pm on 2 September to embark passengers, leaving there at 4 pm on 3 September.

The voyage to Sydney was made without any further stops, *Warrimoo* passing the Cape of Good Hope on 22 September, and Cape Leeuwin on 6 October. Rounding Wilson's Promontory at 4 am on 11 October, and Gabo Island at 8.30 that evening, *Warrimoo* steamed up the New South Wales coast to pass through Sydney Heads at 10.15 pm on 12 October.

The distance steamed from Plymouth to Sydney was 12 456 miles/19 930 km, and the voyage had been completed in a steaming time of 37 days 18 hours.

Prior to the arrival of the vessel in Sydney, advertisements began promoting the new service, such as this one appearing in the *Sydney Morning Herald* on 10 October:

NEW ZEALAND & AUSTRALASIAN
STEAMSHIP COMPANY

STEAM BETWEEN SYDNEY AND NEW
ZEALAND

FIRST CLASS PASSENGER STEAMSHIP
WARRIMOO, 5,000 TONS, SPEED 17 KNOTS
Commander, J.C. ARTHUR, R.N.R

The above company will initiate this service with this splendid steamer, built especially for this trade, dispatching her hence on or about the 14th inst.
THE BERTHING ACCOMMODATION is simple and luxurious. The Dining Saloon is a magnificent apartment 50ft in length, and the same width as the ship. There are 50 State Rooms, all well furnished, and fitted with patent spring mattresses, iron folding beds, and the most improved sanitary appliances. There is a complete installation of Electric Light, with a reserve engine in case of emergency. A complete system of Electric Bells. The Ladies Boudoir is handsomely furnished, and above the Dining Saloon is a spacious Music Hall.

SALOON CAPACITY, 180
SECOND CABIN, 100

The MIOWERA, sister ship,
JAMES STOTT, Commander,
will follow at an early date.

FARES

	Saloon		Steerage	
	Single	Return	Single	Return
AUCKLAND	£5 0 0	£8 0 0	£2 10 0	£4 0 0
NAPIER	£5 0 0	£8 0 0	£2 10 0	£4 0 0
WELLINGTON	£5 0 0	£8 0 0	£2 10 0	£4 0 0
LYTTELTON	£6 0 0	£9 10 0	£3 0 0	£5 0 0
DUNEDIN	£6 10 0	£10 10 0	£3 10 0	£5 10
BLUFF	£7 0 0	£11 10 0	£3 15 0	£6 0 0

For further particulars, apply to
HUDDART, PARKER, and CO., LIMITED
Managing Agents

Two days after *Warrimoo* arrived in Sydney, an extensive description of the vessel appeared in the *Sydney Morning Herald*, including the following excerpts:

What the public feel the most interest in is that which conduces best towards making first a safe voyage, and next a comfortable one. The matter of speed also accounts for a good deal, no doubt.

With regard to safety, the vessel is divided into numerous watertight compartments. In order to bring her within the scope of Admiralty requirements for a troopship and scout, she has to be as nearly unsinkable as it is possible to build a ship.

Built of steel, the *Warrimoo* is constructed on the three deck grade, with long poop extending over engines and boilers, long topgallant forecastle, and a complete water ballast arrangement on the double-bottom system. The decks are of specially selected teak wood of unusual thickness, and the strength of the vessel generally is considered in excess of Lloyd's and Board of Trade rules, the exceptional weight of the framing admitting of hold beams being dispensed with. Her fine lines, double bottom, numerous watertight compartments, and high rate of speed combine to render the vessel eminently fitted to fly the white ensign should the emergency ever arise.

Also with regard to safety from a passenger point of view is the provision made for saving life. In this respect she has eight lifeboats, two of which are constructed of steel, and under the pillow of every passenger on board a lifebelt is placed day and night.

She is fitted with rolling chocks, of steel plates of exceptional width, which will add very much to the comfort of the passengers by diminishing rolling and pitching motions, and the question of ventilation has not been overlooked. In these semi-tropical latitudes pure air and plenty of it are no less vital at sea than an abundance of shower-bath accommodation and unlimited supply of fresh water. 'There is not a stuffy place on board', was the declaration of one of the officers yesterday, and marble baths are provided, with fittings of electro-plated silver to match the mountings in the saloon and staterooms. Every berth and compartment, including the vessel's holds, are ventilated on the latest and most approved methods known to naval architects.

The whole of the passenger accommodation is on the main deck, with alleyways running after from the break of the three-quarter poop, thus affording a fine current of air right through on both sides of the ship.

The dining saloon is a magnificent apartment, immediately under the poop. It is 50 feet in length and its width extends over the whole breadth of the ship. The panelling is of chaste design, the polished framing and panels in walnut, maple and carved oak presenting a very fine effect. Upwards of 100 revolving chairs, upholstered in blue Utrecht velvet, are arranged round the tables, and along the port and starboard sides of the saloon there are sofas upholstered to match. The

Warrimoo in the 1890s (WSS Victoria).

antique sideboards and rich surroundings impart an air of grandeur to the saloon, the effect being heightened by the subdued light from the tinted glass in a large cupola skylight, which, in addition to the large sidelights admits air and light to the apartment.

There are about 50 staterooms, all richly furnished, and fitted with patent spring mattresses, iron folding beds, and patent folding lavatory. The upholstery, selected by Mrs. Huddart, wife of the managing owner, is the same as in the dining saloon. There is a complete electric light installation, with reserve engine to meet emergencies, and electric bells are connected with all the berths, fore and aft.

The smoking hall, which is on the forward deck, is a handsome apartment, the panelling of which is carried out in slabs of polished vein marble, ornamented with chaste gilded designs between pilasters of Parmarga marble, the whole being surmounted with a crimson ermine friese, with gilded lines. The seats are fitted with arms, the tables are of tinted bronze with marble tops, and the floor is laid with encaustic tiles of bright colours and rich design.

A richly furnished boudoir is reserved for the ladies, and there is a spacious music hall directly over the dining saloon, to which entrance is obtained by a descending corridor of exceptional width, the balustrades being richly carved.

There are an exceptional number of fresh water tanks, and machinery capable of condensing upwards of 10,000 gallons is fitted on board. The engines and boilers have been built by the Wallsend Slipway and Engineering Company, Limited. The diameter of shifting and strength of the engines generally are much in excess of Lloyd's rules. The guaranteed speed is 16 knots per hour, but as a matter of fact, the vessel made 16½ knots against the tide, and with her propeller only partly immersed, so that even better results may be anticipated when the ship is loaded.

All the latest improvements have been introduced in connection with the deck appliances, including patent silent winches, three steam whips, Muir and Caldwell's steering gear, stockless anchors, and patent cold air refrigerating machinery for the preservation of dead meat and fruit is also provided.

With passengers having boarded the previous evening, at 6.30 am on Saturday, 15 October, *Warrimoo* departed on the first voyage by the new company to New Zealand. There were reported to be a total of 58 passengers on board, 37 saloon class and 21 steerage. The route for the service would be from Sydney to Auckland, then Wellington, and down the east coast of the South Island, calling at Lyttelton, Dunedin and Bluff before crossing the Tasman Sea to Melbourne, then up the Australian east coast to Sydney.

Once two ships were in service, the route would be operated in both directions, and also include a call at Hobart. It was no doubt the hope of the owners that the two ships would attract the majority of Australians wishing to travel to and from New Zealand, but it would also be essential to secure a good number of New Zealand passengers.

On 17 October this advertisement was published in the *New Zealand Herald* of Auckland by L. D. Nathan & Co., the New Zealand agents for the New Zealand & Australasian Steamship Company:

> The splendid passenger steamer
> WARRIMOO
> (J. C. Arthur, Commander)
> is due at Auckland from Sydney
> on Tuesday, 18th inst.
> The first-class new steamship will be
> despatched for Southern Ports and
> Melbourne on or about
> Wednesday next, 19th inst and affords an
> unrivalled opportunity for passengers from
> New Zealand for Victoria.
> Speed, 17 knots.
> FREIGHT AND PASSAGE
> AT LOWEST CURRENT RATES
> Saloons and State Rooms are magnificent,
> and all appointments most perfect
> and elaborate. Electric light and bells
> are fitted throughout.
> The WARRIMOO has accommodation
> for 180 Saloon and 100 Second Cabin
> Passengers, and possesses all modern
> scientific improvements, ensuring safety
> and the utmost immunity from discomfort.
> The WARRIMOO left Sydney on Saturday
> last, and will arrive here today
> (Tuesday), leaving next day, en route for
> Melbourne which port she will reach in
> time to enable passengers to witness the
> Melbourne Cup.

Another advertisement inserted by the agents in the same newspaper on the same day read:

> MELBOURNE CUP
>
> The SS WARRIMOO
>
> It is arranged to reach Melbourne in time
> to enable passengers to witness the CUP,
> and the great speed at command enables
> her to carry out her timetable with the
> precision of an express train.
> In addition to the inducement of a
> pleasure trip in this really superb vessel,
> in which all the latest improvements are
> combined, passengers can avail them-
> selves of SUPERIOR ADVANTAGES at
> the VERY LOWEST RATES of passage
> that her arrival in Australasian waters
> has brought into force.
> Special rates and facilities offered for
> Return trip via Sydney

Warrimoo arrived in Auckland for the first time at 1.50 am on 18 October, having completed its first voyage across the Tasman in 3 days 19 hours. This was longer than had been anticipated, and the slower trip was attributed to the alleged inferior coal taken as bunkers in Sydney.

Warrimoo stayed in Auckland less than twelve hours, though attracting a lot of interest during that time. At noon the vessel departed for ports on the east coast of New Zealand.

The new service posed a major threat to the established services of the Union Line, and they responded by immediately reducing their fares to the same level as the Australian company. At the start of October 1892 the Union Line had been charging £6 saloon class and £4 steerage for a passage from Auckland to Melbourne, but by the end of the month these had been reduced to £5 and £2-10-0 respectively.

The Union Line began including extra information on their vessels in their advertisements, with *Mararoa* being described as 'so well and favourably known, especially built for the trade, fitted with cool chambers and electric light throughout. SALOON AMIDSHIPS FULL WIDTH OF SHIP'. The Union Line also pressed the captains of their vessels to make fast passages, to counter the publicity being accorded *Warrimoo*. At 5.40 pm on 20 October, *Mararoa* left Wellington for Sydney, passing through the Heads at 9 am on 24 October, thus completing the voyage in 88 hours. While this was not a new record, it was much faster than the regular schedule.

Warrimoo arrived back in Sydney on the afternoon of 2 November. It only had 13 saloon and 30 second class passengers on board, but apparently most of the passengers from New Zealand had disembarked in Melbourne. On 3 November the following item appeared in the shipping section of the *Sydney Morning Herald*:

> Her maiden trip round the east coast ports of New Zealand right down to Bluff and across to Melbourne, thence on back to Sydney, was completed by the new steamship *Warrimoo* last evening. At the New Zealand ports, also at Melbourne, this being her first visit, she proved an object of a good deal of interest, and though her rate of speed has perhaps been a little under what was predicted by some of her admirers, the vessel has made a most favourable impression at all ports, and has done well.

She carried a good many passengers to Melbourne from New Zealand for the Cup week, and just before the voyage across to Port Phillip terminated, Major-General Richardson, on behalf of *Warrimoo*'s passengers, presented Captain J. C. Arthur, R.N.R., with a testimonial and expressed the pleasure the passengers had felt at the appearance, attendance and general comfort of the new ship.

Of the trip from the Bluff, Captain Arthur reports leaving at 6 pm on the 26th October, and arriving at Port Phillip Heads at 1 am on the 30th ultimo, thus making the run in 79 hours, the fastest time on record. She left Melbourne on the 31st ultimo, clearing the Heads at 9 pm, and entering Sydney Heads at 3 pm on the 2nd instant, having experienced moderate variable winds and fine weather throughout the passage. The *Warrimoo* sails again for New Zealand ports, via Melbourne and the Bluff, on Saturday next, at 1 pm.

As mentioned above, *Warrimoo* departed Sydney on 5 November on its second trip to New Zealand, following the reverse route to the first voyage. The Union Line had scheduled two of their ships to depart two days previously, *Waihora* going to Auckland and east coast ports, while *Mararoa* went to Wellington and Lyttelton.

For its third trip, which departed Sydney on 24 November, *Warrimoo* again went to Auckland first; on its next departure, Saturday, 10 December, following the reverse route, going first to Melbourne and then Hobart for the first time. The vessel was advertised to carry passengers to both these ports, the saloon fare to Melbourne being £2, and ten shillings in steerage, while Hobart was £4-10-0 in saloon accommodation, and £1-15-0 steerage, which was the same as the regular fares on these routes. However, the fare to Bluff was only £5-10-0 in saloon class and £2-10-0 steerage, with further ports being only slightly more expensive.

A week after *Warrimoo* departed on this voyage, the second vessel to be built for the New Zealand & Australasian Steamship Company, *Miowera*, departed Sydney on its first voyage to New Zealand, going first to Auckland. On its delivery voyage, *Miowera* had first loaded cargo and embarked passengers in London, leaving there on 26 October. The vessel arrived in Sydney on 12 December, and next day the *Sydney Morning Herald* reported:

The *Miowera* arrived yesterday – 38 hours from Port Phillip to Sydney Heads. This is equal to a mean speed of 13½ knots per hour. Perhaps this is not the speed *Miowera* is equal to under best conditions; but it is worth noticing as the performance of a vessel on her first voyage, and following a straight out run of 13,000 miles as the *Miowera* has to Melbourne. The weather conditions were also very unfavourable, and a mean steaming speed of 13.7 knots against heavy head seas, strong head current, and fresh contrary winds is not often logged by an intercolonial steamer over a distance of 522 miles.

The new ship, like her sister vessel the *Warrimoo*, is under the flag of the New Zealand and Australasian Steam Ship Company. She was built under the immediate personal supervision of the managing director, Mr. James Huddart, who also voyaged out by her to Melbourne. She has on board for here and New Zealand a good many passengers in saloon and second cabin, and a few minutes conversation held with some of them was sufficient to satisfy any curiosity there might be as to the liberal treatment they had received on board, the great steadiness of the *Miowera* in a rough seaway, and the jolly time they had generally.

Though she is built on the same lines as the *Warrimoo*, there are minor improvements made in the passenger spaces of the ship, the saloon fittings, lavatory accommodation, and the staterooms, all tending to render shipboard life more comfortable to the traveller. The thorough ventilation of the vessel from end to end, and in and through each cabin and compartment, is compassed by a special system, and in warm weather or in tropical latitudes, this abundance of fresh air will be appreciated.

The saloons and state cabins are fitted up and furnished in luxurious style. The dining saloon and staterooms are on the main deck. The general effect is tasteful and elegant. Polished woods have been freely made use of in the fittings, and the rich hangings and expensive cut Utrecht velvet employed in the upholstery work add to the general sumptuousness of the apartment. The saloon is lit by a large stained-glass cupola or skylight of beautiful design, and the social hall or lounge over the saloon is luxuriously appointed.

There are marble baths and lavatories, and the appointments of the various cabins are those of a first class hotel. The electric light is installed throughout, and each cabin has its electric bell. The saloon can dine 120 passengers comfortably. For the ladies there is a handsome boudoir, and for the gentlemen there is a smoking room, the latter being very cosy and comfortable in its arrangements.

The vessel is rigged with three light spars stepped without yards, in accordance with the most modern practice, but capable of carrying sufficient canvas in the shape of three trysails to steady her in a heavy beam sea. On each side of the funnel is a large metal cross bearing a representation of the five stars which form the Southern Cross, the whole design giving a picturesque finish to the appearance of the steamer as seen from the land.

Miowera (WSS Victoria).

In the matter of safety, it may be mentioned that the *Miowera* belongs to the description of vessels termed unsinkable, from the numerous watertight compartments into which she is partitioned. There is quite an array of lifeboats at the davits, and two of these are of steel. A lifebelt is also provided for each passenger.

Captain Stott, who is, by the way, well known in the New Zealand trade, reports of the maiden voyage that she left Gravesend on 26th October, and was in the Bay of Biscay during the gale that overtook the ill-fated *Roumania* off the Portugal coast. The *Miowera* proved herself an excellent sea boat, and in the opinion of Captain Stott and his officers, as well as of the passengers, she could not have been more sea-kindly or comfortable. The breakwater at the forecastle is slightly higher than that of the *Warrimoo*, and the steamer faced a heavy ahead sea without taking anything more than spray on board.

On 1st November at 11am, the *Miowera* passed Santa Cruz, the passengers obtaining a fine view of the town, as also a clear sight until dark of the far-famed Peak of Teneriffe. Owing to the coal supply being limited, the steamer was not afforded an opportunity of taking full advantage of the N.E. trades, but her log shows daily records of 308, 311, 330, 310, 319 and 312 knots during their continuance. The equator was passed on November 7, where also the S.E. trades were met. These proved very fresh, and culminated in a strong S.E. gale, with a heavy sea, which reduced the speed of the steamer at times to eight knots.

This adverse weather was carried to Cape Town, the light on Robbin Island being made at exactly the time and position foreshadowed by Captain Stott, and although it was his first visit to the port no difficulty was found in anchoring off the breakwater in the darkness at 4 am on November 17. Here four passengers were landed and an equal number embarked.

A departure from Cape Town was taken at 4.40 pm on the same day, and in order to be on the safe side of coal consumption the revolutions were limited to about 57 per minute. After clearing the Aghulhas Banks, on the edge of which a well defined current reduced the speed of the ship, a course was shaped for St Paul's Island, the easting being run down between the 38th and 39th parallels. Fine weather was experienced to St Paul's. Ninepin Rock was passed at 6.20 pm, two miles off. The steam whistle was blown, and the island examined with telescopes, but there was no sign of living persons, nor could any animals be seen.

After passing St Paul's the revolutions were increased to about 62, and, the weather continuing favourable, with following breezes and seas, good progress was made, despite the fact that the *Miowera* was in deep-loaded trim aft. The last few days runs were about the average, viz 317 and 314 knots. Mr. Foreman, chief engineer, reports a daily consumption of 37 tons. Amusements of all kinds were carried out on the trip, and a happier voyage could not be desired.

The newspaper also included a list of the cargo carried on the voyage to Australia, which included such items as 34 cases horseshoes, 2 cases drapery, 28 cases wine, 15 cases stationery, 2 cases sewing machines, 13 cases furniture, 3 cases paper, 6 cases photo goods, 16 cases cheese, 13 cases nails, 11 bales twine, 4 casks ink and gum, 9 cases felt hats, 2 parcels canvas, 3 cases shirts, 2 iron tanks candlewick, 1 tank candlemoulds, 3 tanks sugar, 10 cases varnish, 10 cases claret, 25 cases gin, 200 cases whiskey, 10 cases hams, 234 cases cocoa and 203 cases sardines.

Warrimoo and *Miowera* were identical in size, being 3529 gross tons, 357 feet/108.7 m long, with a breadth of 42 feet 3 inches/13 m, and moulded depth of 28 feet/8.5 m. They were powered by triple-expansion machinery driving a single propeller, giving a service speed of 15 knots. Accommodation was provided on each ship for a maximum of 233 first class and 127 second class passengers. They had very distinctive funnel markings, white with a black top, and on the white a blue cross with the Southern Cross star pattern in gold.

Miowera departed Sydney on its first voyage to New Zealand on 17 December, carrying 400 passengers. The New Zealand & Australasian Steamship Company was now able to offer regular departures on the Tasman trade, and immediately proved to be major competition to the Union Line.

The Australian company had undercut the fares being charged by the New Zealand firm, who immediately responded by reducing their fares to match. This started a rate war, as each company began to undercut the other. In November the Union Line fares had gone down to £3 saloon class and £1-10-0 steerage for the journey across the Tasman, and this was immediately matched by the New Zealand & Australasian Steamship Company.

As fares tumbled, many people who had not previously been able to afford a trip across the Tasman Sea found it was now within their means. In an attempt to attract extra passengers, the New Zealand & Australasian Steamship Company announced that their ships would include an excursion into Milford Sound during voyages to and from Melbourne. This had been done before by ships of the Union Line, but not on a regular basis.

The ships of the New Zealand & Australasian Steamship Company and the Union Line were soon carrying full loads of passengers, but the fares being charged were so low that neither company was operating the service at a profit. With only two steamers at their disposal, the New Zealand & Australasian Steamship Company could not match the frequency of departures offered by the Union Line, nor was the Australian company able to secure any mail contracts or other subsidies.

In addition, the Union Line began arranging that, whenever possible, they would provide direct competition to the Australian company by having one of their fastest ships depart Sydney on the same day as a vessel of the New Zealand & Australasian Steamship Company, and follow the same schedule around the New Zealand coast and on to Melbourne, while another vessel would make a more direct voyage to the South Island ports.

The first time this occurred was on 14 January 1893, when *Miowera* departed Sydney on its second voyage to New Zealand at noon, being followed at 1 pm by *Talune*, bound for Wellington, Lyttelton, Dunedin and Bluff. At 2 pm *Rotomahana* left Sydney, following the same route as *Miowera*. The Union Line had hoped their vessel would be

Rotomahana berthed in Hobart (Maritime Museum of Tasmania).

able to beat *Miowera* to Auckland, but *Miowera* managed to create a new record for the crossing, 3 days 10 hours 52 minutes, one hour and eight minutes faster than the previous record passage by *Mararoa*. Although *Rotomahana* also made a fast passage, it arrived in Auckland almost four and a half hours after *Miowera*.

With their two ships in service, the New Zealand & Australasian Steamship Company could provide a departure from Sydney roughly every two weeks. *Miowera* always made the round trip in a clockwise direction, calling at Auckland first, while *Warrimoo* followed the reverse route, its next departure being on 21 January. The following advertisement appeared in the *Sydney Morning Herald* on Tuesday, 7 February 1893, with the owners using a shortened form of their name:

NEW ZEALAND LINE
NEW AND IMPROVED STEAM SERVICE
BETWEEN AUSTRALIA AND NEW
ZEALAND
EVERY TEN DAYS

WARRIMOO
5,000 tons, 4,500 I.H.P.
SATURDAY, 11th FEBRUARY at 12 noon
CALLING AT MELBOURNE, MILFORD AND
GEORGE'S SOUND, BLUFF,
PORT CHALMERS, LYTTELTON,
WELLINGTON, AUCKLAND.
WITHOUT TRANSHIPMENT

Followed by her sister ship,
MIOWERA
(via Auckland) on February 25

Passengers have an opportunity (weather, etc, permitting) of viewing the magnificent scenery of MILFORD AND GEORGE'S SOUNDS.
All staterooms are of exceptionally large size and superbly fitted, whilst the Dining, Music, Smoking, and Social Saloons are furnished on a scale hitherto unknown on the coast.
Stewardesses carried in the second cabin as well as in the saloon.
Passengers are granted SPECIAL TICKETS for the round voyage at LOW RATES, from Sydney back to Sydney, by the same steamer, and have the option of breaking their journey at any port.
Fare £10 10s
HUDDART, PARKER, and CO., LTD.,
Agents.

As fares and freight charges continued to tumble, it soon became evident that one company or the other was going to be forced out of the Tasman passenger shipping business. By the middle of 1892 Australia was in the grip of a financial depression, with 23 banks going out of business in the first half of the year, and many companies being forced to close down. Going into 1893 the financial situation began to slowly improve, and by the middle of the year some of the banks were able to re-open, and the future began to look a bit brighter.

However, James Huddart had been finalising plans to establish his intended service from Australia to Canada. He was successful in obtaining the mail contract between Sydney and Vancouver, and annual subsidies of £10,000 from the New South Wales Government and £25,000 from the Canadian Government. The new service to Canada was ready to commence in May 1893, and James Huddart was to take *Miowera* and *Warrimoo* out of the unprofitable Tasman trade.

Miowera left Sydney on 18 March 1893 on what was destined to be its last voyage to New Zealand, going as usual via Auckland first. Prior to the vessel returning to Sydney, it was noted in the company advertisements that after *Miowera* arrived back in Sydney on 6 April it was due to have an overhaul, and no future departure date was provided. Meanwhile, *Warrimoo* had left Sydney on 4 March, and departed again on 27 March, on each occasion going to Melbourne and Hobart first, but the departure by *Warrimoo* on 15 April went to Auckland first.

Huddart named his new service the Canadian-Australian Royal Mail Line, and the funnel colour of the two ships was changed to buff with a black top, while the hulls were repainted white. On 18 May 1893, *Miowera* departed Sydney for Brisbane, Honolulu, Victoria and Vancouver, with *Warrimoo* following a few weeks later. The Brisbane call was included in the hope it would encourage the Queensland Government to offer a subsidy as well, and when this was not forthcoming Brisbane was omitted from the itinerary. However, the Fijian Government offered a subsidy, so a call at Suva was substituted.

When the New Zealand & Australasian Steamship Company withdrew its ships from the Tasman service, the Union Line once again had the trade to themselves, and immediately raised their fares and freight charges to the levels they had been prior to October 1892. No doubt they thought they would once again be the only company operating across the Tasman, but that situation was to change very quickly.

3

The First Huddart Parker Ships

Despite the failure of James Huddart's New Zealand & Australasian Steamship Company on the trans-Tasman service, Huddart Parker Limited decided to expand their sphere of operation from the Australian coast to include New Zealand, entering the service across the Tasman Sea in November 1893. By then the financial situation in Australia was showing continuing signs of improvement, and the future appeared much brighter.

The first trans-Tasman departure for Huddart Parker Limited was taken by *Tasmania*, the latest addition to their fleet, built in 1892 by C. S. Swan & Hunter at Newcastle-on-Tyne in England. The 2252 gross ton vessel had been launched by Mrs Huddart on 12 April 1892, and on sea trials in late May 1892 had achieved 14 knots from the triple-expansion engine connected to a single propeller.

Departing Newcastle-on-Tyne on 4 June 1892, *Tasmania* voyaged non-stop around South Africa to arrive in Melbourne on 23 July, and went to Newcastle for bunkers before berthing in Sydney for the first time. As the name implied, *Tasmania* had been built for the service from Sydney to Hobart, and was also registered at the Tasmanian port. Although primarily designed as a cargo carrier, *Tasmania* provided comfortable cabin accommodation.

The *Sydney Morning Herald* on 1 August 1892 carried a full description of the ship, which included the following:

> Lying alongside her owners' wharf at the foot of Margaret Street is the new express steamer *Tasmania*, the finest, fastest and largest steamer under the house flag of Messrs Huddart, Parker, and Co.
>
> The saloon accommodation is extensive, providing as it does sleeping berths for 100 saloon passengers and 80 fore-cabin passengers, all on the upper deck, thus securing excellent ventilation throughout. The saloon and all the cabins have handsome encaustic tiled floors, covered with pretty rugs and carpets to suit either warm or cold weather. The berths are of the patent fold-up system, with spring mattresses. There

Tasmania, the first Huddart Parker trans-Tasman liner (WSS Victoria).

are marble baths fitted with cold sea water, and having the additional luxury of hot sea water in lieu of steam for heating the baths. There is a handsome marble smokeroom amidships, with tiled floor, and there is a richly decorated music saloon and social hall, in addition to the handsome dining saloon, all of which are fitted luxuriously.

The electric light installation of the *Tasmania* is exceptionally good, and to ensure a constant supply of light the owners have provided two dynamos with two engines. There are also electric bells throughout the saloon. The vessel is divided into several watertight compartments, and has a cellular double bottom the whole length, securing additional safety for the passengers and giving ample water ballast.

A great feature is the grand promenade-deck space for the use of passengers, and the arrangement of the fore part of the vessel shows that she has been built with an eye to the heavy weather frequently met with off the coast of Australia. She has a well deck forward, with permanent bridges running along the bulwarks in place of the breakneck flying bridge from the upper deck to the forecastle. The stanchions are moveable, and a section of the bridge on the port and starboard sides is hinged so that it can be dropped down to permit of cargo being loaded or discharged, while the high bulwarks and her grand bearings make it unlikely that she can ever be a wet ship in any weather.

The new ship has all the good looks and attractive elegance of an express boat in the passenger service between these colonies, and it is safe to predict for her a great future.

In the *Sydney Morning Herald* the same day, Huddart, Parker & Co., Ltd promoted their new ship and its service thus:

TO HOBART

SUMMER RESORT OF THE SOUTHERN HEMISPHERE

S.S. TASMANIA, 3,000 tons
Leaves Huddart Parker's Wharf

This magnificent steamship, unequalled in this trade, is
fitted with cooling chambers, duplicate electric lighting,
and all modern sanitary arrangements.
Her cabins are all on the main deck, with a promenade
deck above, which gives passengers ample accommodation, and makes the passage most enjoyable.

Tasmania departed Sydney on 2 August 1892 on its first voyage to Hobart, and remained on this trade for just over a year before being transferred to the Tasman trade.

Instead of following the circular route operated by the New Zealand & Australasian Steamship Company, Huddart Parker Limited decided to send their ship from Sydney to Auckland, Napier and Wellington, then across Cook Strait to Lyttelton. The voyage back to Sydney would call at the same ports in reverse order. This was somewhat unusual, as Huddart Parker was based in Melbourne, and the southern port was a popular destination for people from New Zealand.

The Union Line clearly saw the entry of Huddart Parker into the Tasman trade as a major threat, and countered by arranging to have *Rotomahana* depart Sydney the same day as *Tasmania*, and follow exactly the same route.

On 29 November 1893, *Tasmania* left Sydney bound for Auckland, passing through Sydney Heads at 3.20 pm, closely followed by *Rotomahana*. The Union Line vessel soon passed *Tasmania*, and arrived in Auckland at 10 am on 3 December. *Tasmania* did not reach the New Zealand city until 8.30 pm the same day, leaving the next day for Napier, with *Rotomahana* in close attendance. The two vessels remained together for the passage down the east coast to Wellington and on to Lyttelton, with *Rotomahana* arriving first at each port. The same situation applied on the voyage back from Lyttelton to Wellington, Napier and Auckland.

On 12 December, *Tasmania* departed Auckland at 5 pm, followed two hours later by *Rotomahana*, which again steamed past the Australian ship. *Rotomahana* arrived in Sydney on the morning of 16 December, with *Tasmania* trailing twelve hours behind. It was not an auspicious start, but Huddart Parker Limited were determined to persevere, and a rate war broke out between the two companies. The one-way fare from Wellington to Sydney, a seven-day trip which included calls at Napier and Auckland, eventually could be had for as little as £2-10-0 saloon class or £1-10-0 steerage.

The Union Line seemed to expect the low fares would soon force the Huddart Parker ship off the route, as had happened with *Warrimoo* and *Miowera*. This time, however, the Australian company was in a much stronger financial position, and could offset any losses incurred on the New Zealand trade with income derived from its Australian coastal services.

When *Tasmania* departed on its second voyage to New Zealand, it was again shadowed by *Rotomahana*, but on future voyages the Union Line replaced *Rotomahana* with the larger *Mararoa*,

Mararoa provided strong competition to Tasmania.

which did not suffer from vibration when travelling at high speed. The intense competition between the two companies generated considerable interest, particularly in New Zealand, and stories about the ships often appeared in local newspapers. The *New Zealand Herald* published in Auckland on 7 March 1894 carried the following item:

> The Queen Street wharf presented a very animated appearance at 5 o'clock last evening when the steamers *Mararoa* and *Tasmania* took their departure for Sydney. Both vessels were taxed to their utmost capacity to find accommodation for their passengers. As the two boats were timed to depart at 5 the crowd collected to witness their departure was very large. The *Mararoa* was first to draw away from the wharf being immediately followed by the *Tasmania*. The decks of the vessels were lined by those on board and there was a great waving of handkerchiefs for some little time.

With its superior speed, *Mararoa* easily beat *Tasmania* to Sydney. Despite the fact that their sole ship on the Tasman trade could not match the Union Line vessels in size or speed, Huddart Parker was determined to persevere, and in 1894 increased their presence on the Tasman trade with *Elingamite*, which joined *Tasmania* on the service from Sydney to Auckland, Wellington, Lyttelton and Dunedin.

Built by C. S. Swan & Hunter at Newcastle-on-Tyne, *Elingamite* had been launched on 6 August 1887 and completed the following month. On arriving in Australia the vessel operated between Newcastle and Melbourne as a collier. Although primarily a cargo vessel, it also had accommodation for 150 passengers in cabins, while a further 80 could be carried in rather basic steerage quarters.

The cabins on *Elingamite* comprised one or two berths, a small chest of drawers and wardrobe, and a washbasin. Toilet and shower facilities were shared by the passengers. The steerage quarters, however, were extremely basic, being in a 'forecabin' located under the forecastle head, near the bow.

The single large room was fitted along either side with rows of lower and upper berths, which were fitted with curtains for privacy. Each bunk had a mattress filled with straw, but no blankets, these having to be supplied by the passengers themselves. Males were on the port side, with females and children on the

Elingamite joined Tasmania on the Tasman trade in 1894 (Fred Roderick collection).

starboard side. Along the midship bulkhead there was a long table for meals, with a bench seat along each side. For washing there were two large enamel basins on a bench-top at one end of the cabin.

In October 1889, *Elingamite* was placed on the passenger trade across Bass Strait from Melbourne to Launceston, but withdrawn the following month. To better suit it to the passenger trade, the ship, which had cost £50,000 to build just three years earlier, was withdrawn from service in April 1890 and given a major refit, costing £20,000. *Elingamite* was then placed on the passenger trade between Sydney and Hobart, and remained on this service until being transferred to the Tasman route.

Later in 1894, Huddart Parker Limited decided their New Zealand service could sustain three ships, but they did not have a suitable vessel in their fleet to transfer to the Tasman trade. As a result, the company decided to purchase a ship, and eventually settled on *Anglian*, which was twenty years old, and had an iron hull, probably viewing it as a stopgap until a new ship could be built.

Anglian was built by Aitken & Mansel in Glasgow for the Union Line, which operated a regular service from Britain to South Africa. Launched on 3 March 1873, the vessel had been handed over to the Union Line on 2 July the same year, at which time it was fitted with a compound vertical direct-acting steam engine, could carry 94 first, 50 second and 100 third class passengers, and operated on the mail service to South Africa. In 1886 the original engine was replaced by triple-expansion machinery, and then the vessel was relegated to a coastal service between South African ports, acting as a feeder ship for the larger liners then operating the mail service. In 1894, *Anglian* returned to Britain, and was offered for sale.

In September 1894, Huddart Parker bought the *Anglian*, and secured a cargo to be carried on its delivery voyage to Australia. *Anglian* went to Barry in Wales to load coal, departing on 25 October and enduring a very rough passage around South Africa before reaching Melbourne on 17 December. The vessel's port of registry was changed to Melbourne, but under the regulations of the day its name could not be changed.

Following a refit in Melbourne, during which the accommodation was increased to about 200 in two classes, *Anglian* entered service in January 1895 from Sydney, going to the same ports as *Tasmania*. At 2159 gross tons, *Anglian* was smaller than both *Elingamite* and *Tasmania*, offered a lower standard of accommodation, and proved to be not as popular with passengers as the other vessels. However, Huddart Parker was now able to offer frequent departures from Sydney to New Zealand, and provided serious competition to the Union Steam Ship Company, who continued to schedule their ships to depart at the same time as the Australian vessels. The fare war continued in earnest, with the cost of a trip between Sydney and Auckland reducing to just £2 saloon and £1 steerage. By June 1895 the rival companies had reduced their fares further, so that it was possible to travel between Sydney and Auckland for just £1 in saloon class and 10/- steerage.

In the March 1959 issue of *Sea Breezes* magazine, there was an interesting record of a trans-Tasman voyage of this time in a letter by G. E. Arundel, who wrote:

In the 'nineties I made a voyage in *Te Anau* from Sydney to Gisborne, Poverty Bay, New Zealand, leaving the former port on December 26, 1894; I was then 15.

At the time there was particularly keen competition on the Australia–New Zealand route for Huddart Parker had entered into competition with the Union Steam Ship Company. Fares at this time were cut ridiculously low

Anglian was purchased by Huddart Parker for the Tasman trade (WSS Victoria).

and at one period saloon fare from Sydney to Auckland (1,233 nautical miles) was 20s. and steerage 10s.

When I made the crossing the opposition steamer was Huddart Parker's *Anglian*. She had no yards. The *Te Anau* was rigged as a barquentine then and on the voyage set a fore course, fore topsail and fore topgallantsail and fore and aft mainsail and main topsail as well as staysails including a jib. The ship was not then fitted with electric lighting. She was later put on the cargo/passenger service from Auckland to Dunedin via Gisborne, Napier, Wellington and Lyttelton. Her passenger accommodation was subsequently taken out and she ran with cargo only.

The cost of operating the ships was seriously affected by the determination of the two companies to compete directly whenever possible, with same day departures, and extra coal being poured into the furnaces to build up more speed in an attempt to reach port first. This not only created a positive news story, but also gave the victor first call on available wharf labour to move cargo, which enabled the ship to leave port first.

Some voyages across the Tasman were affected by adverse weather. In July 1895 the *Anglian* was on a voyage from Sydney to Auckland when it steamed into a massive storm. Despite a reduction in speed, huge seas broke over the bow, smashing the skylight over the saloon, which was flooded along with nearby staterooms, and washing overboard nine occupied horseboxes that were being carried on deck.

For several hours the *Anglian* was assailed by the full fury of the storm. Hatch covers were damaged, allowing water to enter the holds, and fears were held that the vessel might founder under the weight of water. Eventually the *Anglian* fought its way through the storm, and was able to continue its voyage to Auckland, which in the end took six days. The passengers were so thankful to have survived the ordeal that before the ship docked they presented Captain P Le Neveu with a testimonial in appreciation of the gallant efforts of himself and the entire crew during the voyage.

In August 1895, the Union Line reduced their fares even more, with passages between Sydney and Auckland being available at just 15/- saloon and 7/6 steerage. This time Huddart Parker did not follow them, leaving their fares at 20/- and 10/-. By now both companies were suffering major financial problems as a result of the low fares, which made their entire trans-Tasman operations totally uneconomic. It was time to call a truce, and the two companies sat down to negotiations.

On 31 August 1895 came an announcement that arrangements had been agreed by both companies to terminate the fare war, and the direct competitive voyages. Instead, weekly departures would be offered from Sydney on a four-weekly basis, to be operated alternately by two ships from each company, while the Union Line would be allowed to operate an extra steamer on the coastal trade between Auckland

and Dunedin. This was the start of a cooperative relationship between the two companies which would continue for over half a century.

However, the rivalry between the two companies to attract passengers remained intense, and their advertising reflected this. Huddart Parker included in their sailing schedules for *Tasmania* and *Anglian* a statement that 'The attention of the public is drawn to the fact that the low rates of freights and passenger fares now ruling in this trade are due to the competition of these steamers, and by supporting them the public protect their own interests'.

At that time the Union Line was operating what they referred to as 'The Magnificent Passenger Steamships' *Manapouri* and *Tarawera* in competition with the Huddart Parker pair, departing on alternate weeks to *Tasmania* and *Anglian*. However, the Union Line sailing schedule also included the statement that 'Special attention is drawn to the superior saloon and steerage accommodation of this steamer, and passengers are requested to make an inspection before booking elsewhere'.

It was also in 1895 that John Traill, the last of the original directors still involved with Huddart Parker, became chairman, a position he would retain until his death at in 1916 at the age of ninety-two. Although he was a major figure in the Melbourne business scene, Traill was unusual in that he lived quietly with his family, and did not become involved in Melbourne's demanding social whirl. The Traills never owned a carriage, coach-house or stables, and John Traill walked each day to the office until he was ninety.

During the final years of the nineteenth century, the discovery of gold in Western Australia created a boom in the passenger trade from Sydney and Melbourne to Fremantle. In 1895, Huddart Parker ordered a ship to be built by Sir James Laing & Sons at Sunderland for the coastal trade. Named *Westralia* when launched on 23 September 1896, the vessel was completed in January 1897, and went to London to load cargo and embark passengers for the delivery voyage to Australia. *Westralia* left London on 28 January, and after calling at Cape Town for bunkers, steamed to Albany, where it arrived on 10 March. The next six days were spent discharging cargo, then *Westralia* steamed directly to Sydney, arriving on 22 March.

At 2884 gross tons, *Westralia* was the largest vessel under the Australian flag, a distinction it would hold until 1902. Comfortable accommodation was provided for 180 first class passengers, all in cabins, while dormitory accommodation was available for about 200 steerage passengers. The ship was powered by triple-expansion machinery driving a single propeller, with a service speed of 14 knots. The overall design of *Westralia* would prove so successful it would form the basis of a series of passenger ships built for Huddart Parker over the next ten years.

The day after *Westralia* arrived in Sydney, a reporter from the *Sydney Morning Herald* went down to the Margaret Street wharf to inspect the new vessel, and the following story was published on 24 March under the headline, 'Arrival of a Handsome Passenger Steamer':

Who, a year or two ago, would have predicted that the word Westralia would become a word to juggle with for gold, a talismanic sign at the sight of which the owners of millions of golden shekels would shed their wealth in joyous expectation of seeing it return tenfold? Who indeed! ... Lloyds' register of shipping now for the first time records the word as having passed into the mercantile marine history of British steam vessels, and the handsome vessel now lying at the foot of Margaret Street has the name emblazoned over her counter, '*Westralia*, Melbourne'. She arrived yesterday with the flag of the old house of Huddart, Parker, and Company flying at the main, and here incidentally it may be mentioned that she represents in her cost perhaps as much gold as some of the good Westralian mines have as yet produced.

When a *Herald* reporter stepped up the gangway yesterday afternoon he was welcomed by an officer who asked whether he 'would care to look through the most beautiful ship under a colonial flag?' and at once the two started on a journey over this 3000 ton floating hotel, a trip that lasted for nearly two hours. The ambitious query of the officer led our representative to climb to the lofty summit occupied by the commanding officer when the *Westralia* is under steam. Here on the flying bridge 40 feet above the water line one obtains a better idea of the ship's proportions – her length and beam. Just underneath is a wheelhouse and close handy there are business places for the commander (a suite), chart room, and private cabins.

On the boat deck midships is the smoke stack, an oval-shaped tall chimney perhaps 30 feet [9 m] in circumference. It hasn't, perhaps, 'rake' enough to give the necessary smart appearance wanted now-a-days. Surrounding this deck are automatically worked life boats (the upper decks are thick with boats), and the officer here remarks 'We can drop you down if you wish in one of those with twelve hands aboard in 43 seconds. Would you like to see it?'

Taking his word for the deed, a remark was passed by the reporter as to the rolling and pitching qualities of the ship, and how many seconds margin would be allowed for lowering automatically in, for example, a

Dandenong gale. 'Oh, that's where we haven't come to yet. This ship doesn't roll. That's what I was going to show you. Now, up here, with all this top hamper on, as you call it, and, say, 30 feet above the sea, if any place would feel it it would be here; but just come into this cabin (the captain's). There is nothing there lashed. Even the trinkets, the little photos of his friends, are standing on the photo stands, just as they would be ashore in one's parlour. There hasn't been much rolling or pitching about that lot.'

The officer pointed out that the *Westralia* has tremendous flanges of steel (called rolling chocks), which on both sides of the vessel extend like the flappers of, say, a whale, just for keeping her upright. These are unusually large in the *Westralia*, as compared with some merchantmen, 'reducing the angle of stability,' said the officer, 'by half, or from 20° to 10°, the biggest roll the ship made in the Bay of Biscay.'

Comparatively with, say, the liners, the comforts to be obtained aboard a big steamer are abundantly present on the *Westralia*, and there is this in addition; they are an improvement upon some of the steamers running round the Australian coast today. 'Just let us stroll through the promenade deck,' said the officer. 'In this deckhouse is the main saloon. There is no diving down to get your meals, and then coming up to breathe,' and the reporter was ushered into an attractive dining hall with tables for four, all round, and down the port and starboard centres, sideboards, and lavishly furnished – an admirably finished saloon, one which would do credit to any liner.

Scarcely had we left the saloon when a notice 'Private entrance to the engine-room' over a door was noticed. 'Ah, that is the chief's private entrance to those tremendous engines, the machinery of the ship; triples that drive us along at 15 knots in any weather, and have brought us to Sydney at 11½ knots every hour since we started, without a stop anywhere, excepting, of course, landing passengers at the Cape and at Albany. I may tell you that when leaving London Mr. James Huddart and our commander fixed the times for each port, and yesterday we made Sydney Heads within two hours of the original time given, and, remember, this our maiden trip.'

We passed on to the social hall (on upper deck), a pretty place and next to the smoking room. These are aft, handsome and substantially furnished apartments. Marble panels, granite pilasters, carved oak (beautifully hand-carved) and mahogany abound here, and in the social hall is a Collard and Collard [piano].

'By the way,' said the officer, 'I forgot to show you an innovation,' and we went back to the saloon. 'Just come in here,' he said. 'What do you think of this? After coming from dinner instead of going promenading the deck here is a lounge where a fellow can have a chat.' This is in fact a sort of open 'den', with a bar adjacent,

Westralia was the first of a series of similar vessels (WSS Victoria).

where friends can forgather either before or after dinner, but 'all lights are extinguished at 10 pm,' said the officer, 'so that you have the advantage of us ashore by an hour in that respect. The licensing laws at sea are more rigid than in even Sydney.'

We were still on the promenade deck, and had to see the haunts and abodes of the *Westralia*'s citizens, in all 50 upper second and 200 lower, the distinction to be explained. We entered this part of the ship from aft, and came up by a similar staircase forward, after looking into a lovely boudoir and a music hall, in which Beethoven, Handel, Wagner, Mozart, Verdi, Bach, Gounod and Schubert's memories are appropriately commemorated in illuminated panels, the interspacing being in hand-cut solid oak emblems of the history of music, since the days of Solomon. It is here that music and song find adequate acknowledgement to a degree not found on many floating music halls.

The passengers' deck, on which we are now looking from aft, on the starboard side is all for ladies, on the port for the male sex. Baths and lavatories abound, with cabins for either two or four, roomy, well-furnished places, with big ports – 'which can always be open,' said the officer, 'as no sea finds it way up here' – and double-folding washhand-stands in the four-berthers, a real blessing to the suffering landsman. Besides, the stationary washstands are connected with pipes for the outlet – no emptying of pans underneath. 'This is Collins Street,' said the officer, as we went along an open space for many yards forward (an alley-way, the reporter suggested), and found our way to the fore cabin of the *Westralia*.

As already mentioned there are but two classes, first and second, and the second upper that is on the saloon deck just described contains cabins for married people on one side and single women on the other. There are bathrooms, good table accommodation, and the berths are well fitted, enclosed, and as private in every respect as the first-class cabins. For single men the accommodation is similar to what is found in the third class of the large ocean-going steamers. It is down forward on the main deck and extends well aft. It is lighted from ports and from a skylight. The berths, which are open of course, are all what would in a lodging-house be called single iron bedsteads with spring mattresses, and of these there are 200. Nothing better is to be found on the coast in that respect.

By the time *Westralia* arrived in Sydney, the demand for passages to the west had greatly diminished, so instead of entering this trade, *Westralia* was advertised to operate only between Sydney and Melbourne. Huddart Parker placed this special advertisement in the *Sydney Morning Herald*:

STEAM TO MELBOURNE

S.S. WESTRALIA
2,500 tons

This magnificent new steel steamship will leave
SYDNEY FOR MELBOURNE
on
SATURDAY, APRIL 10, AT 4 PM

The attention of the public is drawn to the superb accommodation of this steamship. Hot and cold water
baths. Electric lights throughout. Dining Saloon situated on upper deck, with seating accommodation
for 80 passengers.
Ship will be open for public inspection on
SATURDAY, 10th April.

For the next three months *Westralia* made regular round trips on this route, then was transferred to the trans-Tasman trade, then being operated by *Tasmania* and *Anglian*. *Westralia* made its first departure for New Zealand from Sydney at 4 pm on Wednesday, 7 July 1897, going to Auckland, Gisborne, Napier, Wellington, Lyttelton and Dunedin.

With the introduction of *Westralia*, *Anglian* was taken off the Tasman trade, its final departure from Sydney being on 24 June, and began operating between Sydney and Fremantle. It had been intended that *Westralia* would be on the Tasman service for only a short time, partnered by *Tasmania*, but this arrangement came to a sudden early end.

On 23 July 1897, *Tasmania*, under the command of Captain M'Gee, left Sydney for Auckland, arriving there four days later, then on 28 July left for the next port of call, Gisborne. While proceeding down the east coast of North Island, the ship ran into stormy weather, with a southerly gale raising a very rough sea. When *Tasmania* arrived off Gisborne on the afternoon of Thursday, 29 July, the captain concluded it was too rough to attempt an entry to the port.

Deciding to bypass Gisborne and continue on to Napier, the captain set a course that would take the ship well clear of the coast during the night. Shortly after nightfall, the weather became even worse, and unbeknown to the captain, the officer of the watch changed the course to bring the ship nearer land. About 11 pm, the lookout sighted land dead ahead, but before any action could be taken to alter course, *Tasmania* ran onto rocks. Immediately water began to pour into the ship, and the lifeboats were lowered away, containing all 35 saloon and 33 steerage passengers, as well as the entire crew. In less than an hour, *Tasmania* had sunk. The lifeboats struggled through high seas to reach the nearby shore, but such a huge surf was pounding onto the beach that one boat capsized and another was swamped, eleven persons losing their lives from these two boats. The survivors were able to drag themselves ashore, and report the sinking.

First news of the disaster did not appear in Sydney newspapers until Saturday, 31 July, in a series of stories in the *Sydney Morning Herald*:

> The wreck occurred a little to the westward of Table Cape. The third officer was on the bridge at the time. Shortly before 11 o'clock on Thursday night he reported to the captain that land was in sight. It was then, however, too late to prevent her striking. There was no great crash, and excellent order was maintained on board. Fortunately no seas broke over the vessel, and this no doubt reassured the passengers, to whom lifebelts were served out. The quietness and the absence of panic were most marked. 'It was,' said one of the passengers in describing the disaster, 'the quietest wreck you can possibly imagine. Not even women screamed.' While the boats were being got out one of the passengers sat down at the piano, and played a lively tune to keep the spirits of the ladies up. No hitch occurred, and as the boats were lowered they were filled by the passengers. The ladies were taken off first. The night was pitch dark, and a heavy sea was running. All the boats were equipped with water and food. They hung alongside on the leeward side, where the water was comparatively smooth. The captain was the last man to leave the vessel. After he left the boats shoved off, and shortly afterwards the steamer's lights disappeared. Orders were then given to make for a landing place. The first and third officer's boats landed at Mahia, and the captain and second officer's at Gisborne. Two other boats – the gig and the yawl – contained the members of the crew, in addition to those in other boats. It is these two boats regarding whose safety doubt exists. All the cargo and passenger's luggage have been lost, and also the mails, but the Post Office authorities are arranging to recover the latter.

Captain M'Gee, on being interviewed, said:

> 'We arrived at Gisborne soon after 4 o'clock yesterday afternoon, having met with dirty weather all the way from East Cape. On arrival we stood off for a time waiting to see if we could get communication with the shore. We did not drop anchor, but kept the vessel going slow with her head on to the sea. At 9 o'clock I decided to go on to Napier, and started at full speed. The weather was very dirty and thick. As I had been up all day I went and lay down for a little while, leaving the third officer in charge of the bridge. Shortly before 11 o'clock he called me to say that land was in sight, and that he had kept the vessel out of her course a bit. As soon as he called me I hastened on the bridge, and immediately ordered the wheel to be put over to turn the vessel's head out to sea, but it was too late. The vessel immediately took the ground. There was no sign of light on land, which looked a long way off. The point where we struck was, I reckon, to the westward of Table Cape, and we were scarcely far enough ahead to have seen the light on Port land Island.'

Asked as to the nature of the impact, Captain M'Gee said, 'It was not much of a sensation. She just bumped, and you would think there was really nothing much the matter. I do not think there was a hole torn in her. It did not seem to be a pinnacle rock, but more like a level bottom than anything else, but I presume that when the *Tasmania* disappeared she listed clean over.'

Captain M'Gee continued, 'Immediately the vessel struck I gave the order "Out boats" and all hands promptly went to their stations, every man behaving splendidly. There was a very heavy sea running, but it was not breaking over the steamer, which was lying almost broadside on. There was some little difficulty in launching the boats on the weather side, and as soon as they were in the water they were passed round the stern of the steamer to the lee-side, which was fairly sheltered. The passengers were by this time assembled on deck, and all were supplied with lifebelts. Our first care, of course, was for the ladies, who were the first to be passed down into the boats by means of the accommodation ladder.

'There was no sign of panic; in fact I never saw ladies and people generally behave as well. There was never a suspicion of a hitch, everyone simply doing as they were told. The men were all at their stations and worked splendidly, and there was really no more hitch than there would have been if we were lying in the roadstead. We hung alongside the vessel, all the boats being on the leeward side, attached by light lines. I stayed on deck for some time, and walked about to see that there was no one left behind, and I was the last to leave the ship. Before doing so I passed oranges and biscuits down into the boats, all of which were properly equipped and supplied with water and food. Water had been flowing rapidly into the steamer, and when I left there must have been a depth of 12 feet in the stokehold, and the water was just reaching the saloon on the main deck. Prior to our leaving the vessel she had been lying pretty steady and fairly upright, just taking a slight list to starboard. We could just feel her roll and work a bit, but nothing to alarm anybody. After hanging on about a quarter of an hour we shoved off, and lay to within sight of the vessel. The electric light had gone out some time previously, and I left a flare-up near the ladder, and this and the masthead light were to only ones remaining. Suddenly the lights disappeared, and we supposed then the ship had turned over. I don't know for certain, but one of the officers tells me he was close to the steamer, and saw her disappear. Three of the officers had their instructions to go to Happy Jack's and land there if possible, but of course they had to use their own discretion, and in fact the second officer came on and landed in Gisborne before me. The first and third officers, I learn, have landed at Mahia, and that leaves two small boats, containing the members of the crew, the gig and the yawl, in charge of the carpenter and the quartermaster respectively, to be accounted for. I do not think they have any of the passengers, because my object was to get all the passengers into the lifeboats, and as a matter of fact I had two or three passengers who had got into the small boat put into the larger ones before we left the ship's side.

'When we left the ship there was a very nasty sea running, and we could feel the full force of it before we had gone 50 yards. I feel very pleased that everything was done that possibly could be done, and that there were no hitches. Of course it is a very great loss, but still under the circumstances I feel very pleased that things have so far turned out so well. I have often heard people say that on occasions such as this there was no fuss or trouble of any sort, and I did not quite understand it, but last night it was possible for such a state of things to be. I never saw women so quiet, and take things so easily. They just did as they were told, and I never heard them cry or sing out. It is really fine to think that such coolness and courage were displayed. The stewards and stewardesses behaved remarkably well, and I heard them cheering up the passengers.'

Another short item referred to the two small boats that had mostly been carrying members of the crew:

Further information from Muriwai is to the effect that the carpenter's boat capsized off Kawakawa beach, a few miles away. Its occupants, eight in number, had a great struggle to reach the shore. Two, one a passenger and the other a member of the crew, were drowned, and their bodies were washed up on the beach. The sailor had a deep gash evidently inflicted by the rocks. The six survivors are being sheltered by the settlers. They are in a terribly exhausted condition, and mentally and physically unfit at present to give any particulars. The two bodies will be brought to Gisborne tomorrow for identification.

It is now thought that there is no doubt that the second small boat containing eight of the crew capsized, and that all the occupants have been drowned. This makes the total loss of life 10. The names cannot be ascertained. It is not considered likely that any of the passengers but the one mentioned have been drowned.

More information on the wreck was reported in the *Sydney Morning Herald* on Monday, 2 August, following the arrival of many of the survivors in Auckland the previous day on the Union Line vessel *Tarawera*, which had picked them up at Gisborne, and was going to bring them on to Sydney. Among the new details was a report on happenings in the engine room:

When the vessel struck the chief engineer was in the engine-room. The telegraph immediately rang 'Stop'. The firemen in the stokehole reported that the stokehole plates had been thrown out of place, but that no water was coming in. Soundings showed that no water was making in the boiler room tank. The fourth engineer was then sent on to the bridge to report to the captain that the stokehole plates had been thrown up by the concussion. At this moment the telegraph rang 'Full speed ahead' and a quarter of a minute later 'Stop' was rung. Almost immediately they felt the plates rising up beneath them, and at the same time the main steam pipe carried away. Orders were then given to keep the electric light running so long as there was steam. Lifebelts were then served out to the engineers. At this time the water was making in the engine-room, and when the chief engineer left the ship there was 13 feet of water in the engine-room.

Mr. Neville, a passenger from Sydney, states that when the boats left the steamer instructions were given to follow the captain's boat, but owing to the strong wind extinguishing the light in the leading boat they became separated. The boat in which Mr. Neville was was pulled under the *Tasmania* for shelter, lying off about two cable lengths. About 2 o'clock the horses, of which there were 17 on board in the forehold, began whinnying, and almost immediately the steamer plunged down stem first, and the stern also began to settle, finally disappearing. Being on a lee shore it was decided to keep the boat's head to sea, those on board taking alternate turns at the oars. At daybreak the sail was hoisted, and despite a heavy sea the boat was brought safely to the boat harbour at Mahia, landing at half-past 10.

It is not often a person has the good and bad fortune to be born and shipwrecked on the same day. That was the experience of a little stranger on the *Tasmania*, one of the steerage passengers giving birth to a child on the day of the wreck. Both mother and the child were landed in safety at Mahia.

The day after the sinking, the steamer *Dingadee* arrived at the wreck site, and the captain sent the following message to the Collector of Customs: 'Passed close to the steamer *Tasmania* at 9 am, sent out a boat and took soundings, and found her perfectly upright in from 15 to 16 fathoms of water, heading SSW, bearing Table Cape SE half south, four miles. No wreckage was seen. The mastheads are 8 feet above the water. I attached a red flag to the foremast.' The Huddart Parker representative was also reported to have sent a message stating that the vessel had struck an uncharted rock on a safe course.

Divers were sent down to try and retrieve the bags of mail being carried by the ship, but the water was too murky for them to find anything, and mud was already beginning to fill the ship. After several dives the recovery attempt was abandoned. Gradually the wreck of the *Tasmania* sank into the muddy bottom, and the masts disappeared under the water. At the subsequent court of inquiry into the sinking, both the captain and the third officer, who had been on watch, were found guilty of careless and negligent navigation, and their licences were suspended for six months.

The loss of *Tasmania* left Huddart Parker one ship short on their Tasman trade, so *Anglian* had to be brought back to the trade once more, departing Sydney on 15 September for New Zealand, and *Westralia* remained on the Tasman service too. At the same time, an order was placed for the construction of a new ship, which would be a virtual repeat of *Westralia*.

Meanwhile, in August 1897 some new competition appeared on the Tasman trade. The New Zealand Government had offered a £20,000 annual subsidy to James Huddart if his vessels *Warrimoo* and *Miowera*, now operating as the Canadian-Australasian Royal Mail Line, would include a call at Wellington on their voyages between Sydney and Vancouver. In August 1897 the new service commenced, the ships going from Sydney to Wellington, then Suva and Honolulu and on to Victoria and Vancouver, following the reverse route on the return trip.

As well as *Warrimoo* and *Miowera*, with which he had commenced operations in 1892, James Huddart now owned a third vessel, *Aorangi*, which he had purchased in 1896 from the New Zealand Shipping Company. Built in 1883 by John Elder & Co. in Glasgow, *Aorangi* had accommodation for 60 first class, 40 second class and 200 third class passengers, with extra temporary quarters provided for emigrants in the holds when possible. For ten years *Aorangi* operated regular voyages between London and New Zealand, but was withdrawn and laid up in Britain during 1894. In 1896, James Huddart arranged to charter the ship, but then decided to purchase it outright.

The ship was sent to the Swan & Hunter shipyard at Newcastle-on-Tyne for an extensive refit. The original compound engine was replaced by triple-expansion machinery, with four new boilers, while the funnel was heightened by ten feet to increase the draught to the boilers. The interior was also rebuilt to carry 100 first class and 50 second class passengers.

Aorangi entered service for James Huddart in May 1897, with a voyage from Vancouver to Sydney. *Warrimoo* and *Miowera* had also been refitted since leaving the Tasman trade in 1893, and now provided less crowded accommodation for 112 first class and 60 second class passengers. However, as the three ships could only offer a voyage to and from Wellington every few weeks, they did not constitute

Aorangi was operated by James Huddart (Fred Roderick collection).

major opposition to the services being provided by Huddart Parker and the Union Line.

Unfortunately, the expense incurred in refitting *Aorangi* caused James Huddart to go bankrupt in January 1898, and the company he had founded went into liquidation. In February 1898 the New Zealand Shipping Company, which was the chief creditor, was appointed receiver, and took over the Canadian-Australasian Royal Mail Line and its three ships when Huddart defaulted on payments for *Aorangi*. The failure of the company broke James Huddart completely. He was still a director of Huddart Parker as well, but he severed his ties with the company he had helped to found and returned to England, where he died in 1901.

The New Zealand Government did not renew their subsidy with the Canadian-Australasian Royal Mail Line for 1899, and the Wellington call was dropped from April that year. However, the Queensland Government then offered a subsidy, so a call at Brisbane was instituted. In 1900 the Fijian subsidy was also terminated, and the Suva call omitted.

Meanwhile, the ship Huddart Parker had ordered as a replacement for the *Tasmania* was built by Gourlay Bros at Dundee in Scotland, being launched on 29 March 1899 and completed in May 1899, being named *Zealandia*. Leaving Britain in June, *Zealandia* steamed out to Australia via Cape Town, Fremantle and Melbourne, arriving in Sydney for the first time on the evening of Saturday, 26 August. The day before, *Westralia* had also arrived in Sydney from New Zealand, and the two ships berthed side by side.

On Monday, 28 August 1899, the following report appeared in the *Sydney Morning Herald*:

Lying abreast of each other at Messrs Huddart, Parker and Co.'s wharf are two of their newest steamers – the *Westralia*, which has proved a fast and comfortable ship under the popular flag of her owners, and the *Zealandia*, which reached the wharf on Saturday evening, direct from the builder's hands. This brings the company fleet now up to 17 steamers, the largest of which are the two steamers just mentioned, and the *Elingamite* and *Burrumbeet*, *Anglian*, *Lindus*, *Nemesis* and *Wendouree*. The owners for many years have enjoyed the confidence and liberal patronage of ocean travellers, and it is by the introduction of that fine type of vessel embodied in the *Zealandia* that the high reputation of the H.P. flag in Australian waters is maintained.

The new ship is almost sister to her predecessor *Westralia*, almost a counterpart. She is better described as an improved *Westralia*. The latter vessel first took the water a little over two years ago, and now the *Zealandia* launched this year comes along, only that brief interval having elapsed, but having many later improvements introduced in her construction or fittings. Whatever was capable of improvement in the *Westralia*, the *Zealandia* has it. They are ships of nearly 3,000 tons, and the space devoted to promenades, berths, social halls, smoking-rooms, and dining saloons takes in more than the 327ft of length and 42ft of breadth, the dimensions of the main deck, but also of an upper deck of almost equal area. Employing an experience in the Australia–New Zealand passenger trade covering many years, the owners in designing their new ship have had produced a shapely steamer of 14½ knots speed, charmingly fitted up in every part.

Upon going over the vessel after her arrival it was at once seen that no expense has been considered in her equipment. And what will be much appreciated in the

Zealandia was built to replace Tasmania on the Tasman trade (Fred Roderick collection).

design is the flush deck which secures to the passenger a 'free leg' over the greater part of the steamer. Upon this upper deck is the first class dining saloon, a most attractive room fitted with chairs for 75 guests, and lighted up by a dome-shaped transom, gorgeously flowered. The steward explained that when the electric light is turned on the brilliancy of this dome is quite bewitching, and certainly the surroundings within this part of the ship are so picturesque that one can readily believe that a fairy-like scene is in store for the saloon traveller when those highly cut glass globes are all shedding the Swan-Edison ray upon the gay colours of the furnishings.

The panelling is in oak emblematic of Australian life and of British life or history. The British lion is well in evidence; the rose, the shamrock and the thistle each have a place; and the kangaroo, the wallaby, and the moa are depicted in the panelling, which appears to have been cleverly executed. A tattooed Maori chief and a dusky maiden, also an aboriginal mother with her babe slung a la native, are also remembered in the decorations.

Just off this delightful saloon is a smoke lounge and a bar, but not so near to the saloon as to risk annoyance, and the place is very private though commodious. There is besides this on the upper deck, and right aft, a large smoke saloon, fitted up with marble tables and substantially upholstered, and furnished with bar and lavatory abutting. Pretty well aft is situated the social hall, in which is a Brimsmead [piano], and which is an altogether roomy place furnished in green plush, the stained glass ports or windows surrounding it adding to the attractiveness of the place. An air of luxuriousness is apparent here, as the lady passengers will find who travel by the *Zealandia*.

Upon this upper deck, which is elevated far above the reach of sea spray, except in exceptionally bad weather indeed, deck lounges and settees abound. Then conspicuously from the social hall leads a grand staircase with polished cedar and carved oak panelling. This staircase brings the passenger into the vestibule, from which leads the alleyways to the staterooms, berths for 150 passengers being provided. The library and writing desks will be found here – everything very complete, with softly-cushioned settees all round the compartment. It is a place which will be much resorted to in wet or stormy weather.

The staterooms do not call for special notice. There are some with two berths in them and others with four berths, but two berths is the rule. A companionway or staircase to the upper deck brings the visitor back on the spacious promenade, whence he may find his way back into the main saloon, the social hall, or the smoking department. The alleyways, off which are staterooms, are wide and lofty, with ample provision for ventilation.

A word is necessary as to second cabin. This is forward, and is remarkably fine for the steerage. Recently owners have shown a desire to cater for the second-class passenger to such an extent that as one moves about the *Zealandia* it is almost difficult to say when you merge from the first into the second. The berthing cabins are fitted up with mirrors and lavatory arrangements apparently equal to those in the first class. There is a well furnished dining room with revolving chairs in it and stylish sideboards. There are bathrooms for ladies and gentlemen, and admirable cabins for families. It is certain, in short, that a trip by the *Zealandia* to New Zealand can be made with as much comfort as by one of the liners.

Zealandia provided accommodation for a maximum of 180 saloon class passengers in cabins, while up to 200 persons could be carried in cabins and dormitories in steerage. The vessel left Sydney on 13 September on its first voyage to New Zealand, going south as far as Dunedin. With the arrival of the new vessel, *Elingamite* was temporarily taken off the New Zealand trade, and placed on the shorter service from Sydney to Melbourne and Geelong.

The arrival of *Zealandia* enabled Huddart Parker to expand their services to New Zealand, and begin operating in competition with the Union Line on the horseshoe route between Sydney and Melbourne. At noon on 4 November 1899, *Zealandia* departed Sydney on the first Huddart Parker voyage to Wellington, Lyttelton, Dunedin and Bluff, then back across the Tasman Sea to Hobart and on to Melbourne.

With *Zealandia* maintaining the horseshoe route on its own, *Elingamite* was brought back to the Tasman trade to again partner *Westralia* on the service from Sydney to Auckland, Gisborne, Napier, Wellington, Lyttelton and Dunedin, with a departure every second week.

During the final years of the nineteenth century several vessels owned by the Union Steam Ship Company were taken out of service to carry troops from New Zealand to South Africa and the Boer War. One of the vessels affected in this way was *Monowai*, which left Port Chalmers on 24 March 1900 for Durban, carrying 239 officers and men and 220 horses. When the vessel returned to New Zealand it resumed its place in the horseshoe service.

4

Into a New Century

The first decade of the twentieth century would see both Huddart Parker Limited and the Union Steam Ship Company of New Zealand introduce a succession of new liners of increasing size on the Tasman trade. Although the two companies were no longer engaged in fare wars, and operated their ships on a joint schedule, there was still considerable competition to attract passengers.

As the nineteenth century came to a close, Huddart Parker Limited was maintaining its presence on the trans-Tasman trade with three vessels, *Zealandia*, *Elingamite* and *Anglian*, but only *Zealandia* was of a standard to compete seriously with the vessels being operated on the trade by the Union Steam Ship Company of New Zealand.

To overcome this situation, Huddart Parker decided to build another new vessel, which would be the first addition to their fleet in the twentieth century. The order was placed with Gourlay Bros of Dundee for a ship that was specifically designed for the route, whose general appearance was very similar to *Westralia*, though slightly larger than that vessel.

Launched on 21 June 1902, the new vessel was named *Victoria*, which was surprising, as there was already a ship of that name on the British register, a liner owned by the P&O Line and operating on a regular basis to Australia.

Victoria departed London on 3 October 1902 on its delivery voyage to Australia. Going around South Africa, with a stop at Cape Town, *Victoria* called at Fremantle on 14 November, and arrived in Melbourne on 25 November. The vessel stayed there for two weeks being prepared for its first voyage to New Zealand. However, the celebrations of its arrival were considerably tempered by the tragic sinking of *Elingamite* just a few weeks earlier, with considerable loss of life.

On the afternoon of 5 November 1902 *Elingamite* had departed Sydney for Auckland. On board were 136 passengers and 59 crew members. In command was Captain Ernest Atwood, who had held his master's ticket for nineteen years, but had only been on *Elingamite* for four months.

Among the passengers was a group of eleven Sydney tram drivers and their families on their way to drive the newly installed trams in Auckland. There was also a group from Dalmatia on their way to the New Zealand goldfields to seek their fortunes, while other passengers included some Australian families going for holidays, businessmen, and New Zealanders returning home. These included Agnes Robb, whose 6-year-old son had been receiving treatment in Sydney for spinal tuberculosis, and they were now returning home. The mixed cargo in the holds included 52 boxes of gold and silver coins consigned by the head office of Bank of New South Wales in Sydney to its branches in Lyttelton and Dunedin.

During the first three days at sea the weather held fine, and this continued on the morning of 9 November, as the vessel neared the northern tip of North Island, Cape Reinga. Some 40 kilometres north of this point lies a group of islands known as the Three Kings, and it was standard practice for *Elingamite* to pass between Cape Reinga and the Three Kings. This particular stretch of water is where the waters of the Pacific Ocean and the Tasman Sea meet, and is notorious for treacherous currents and storms.

As *Elingamite* neared land, it was enveloped in a dense sea haze, so Captain Atwood ordered a reduction in speed, lookouts posted, and the fog horn sounded at regular intervals. At the same time, Atwood also ordered a slight change of course, heading more north-east to keep clear of Cape Reinga. This was to prove disastrous for, unknown to mariners, the Three Kings were wrongly located by three nautical miles on the charts of the day. Instead of heading through the open channel, *Elingamite* was now on a collision course with West King Island.

Approaching midday the Three Kings came into view, and passengers thronged the decks for their first sight of New Zealand. One of the tram drivers, Stephen Neill, later recalled, 'I saw one of the most beautiful sights I have ever witnessed. A thick heavy bank of fog had come down the side of a hill. Charmed I stood looking it at it for seconds then it struck me we were making straight for it.'

Suddenly the bells on the bridge telegraph rang as the officers on duty realised what was happening, and ordered the engine put in reverse, but it was too late, and *Elingamite* grounded on rocks on the south-west side of West King Island. Immediately water flooded into the forward parts of the ship, while passengers and crew scrambled to launch lifeboats and rafts. Six lifeboats were lowered, and in the mayhem No. 3 boat smashed against the hull of the *Elingamite* and was too badly damaged to be used, while No. 6 boat capsized and sank. Two rafts were also lowered into the water, but most people tried to get into one of the four surviving lifeboats. As *Elingamite* filled with water the decks sank lower into the water, and soon waves were washing people overboard. About twenty minutes after striking the rocks, *Elingamite* sank.

Seven lives were lost at the time of the sinking, leaving 188 survivors spread through four lifeboats

The Three Kings Islands (Manawa-tawhi or Nga Motu Karaka in Maori) are a group of thirteen islands about 55 kilometres (30 nautical miles) north-west of Cape Reinga, the northernmost point of the North Island of New Zealand where the South Pacific Ocean and Tasman Sea converge. They have a combined area of about 4.86 square kilometres and are at the same latitude as southern Sydney. (Courtesy GNS)

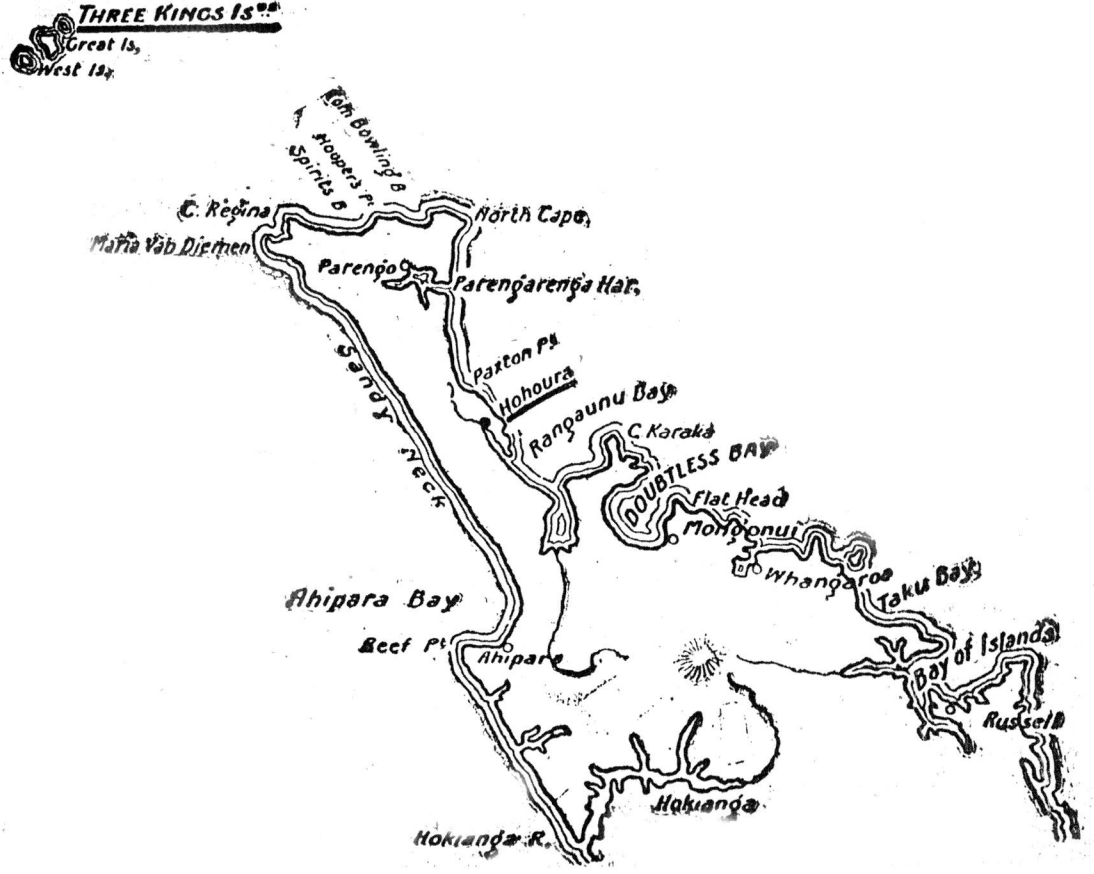

This map of the wreck site appeared in the *Sydney Morning Herald* on 12 November 1902.

and two small rafts. In accordance with the safety regulations of the day, only one of the lifeboats, No. 4, contained provisions and a compass, it being the expectation that lifeboats would stay together after a vessel sank. However, in the thick fog that blanketed the area at the time of the sinking, the four surviving lifeboats and the two rafts soon lost contact. Agnes Robb later recorded, 'Boats quickly drifted apart in the fog. Now and again the fog lifted and we would see another boat and then lose sight of it again as the fog closed around us.'

Several hours after the *Elingamite* sank the lifeboat Agnes Robb and her son were in managed to make a landing on the dangerous shores of Middle King Island. With almost sheer cliffs rising out of the water, it was only possible for the survivors to clamber up a short way to a ledge, where they huddled together. Later another two lifeboats managed to reach the same location, and eventually there were 73 survivors crammed together on the ledge, where they spent a terrifying night. Meanwhile, one of the rafts with 11 survivors on it managed to reach Great King Island about 7 o'clock the same evening.

Agnes Robb recorded:

> We had landed about 5 o'clock and by ten that night we thought it must be morning. Alas there was an eternity to be gone thru ere that. Imagine, the seas roaring on three sides, the spray dashing up on the ledge and the sea birds screaming and screeching all night long. With the fog and rain in addition, I never wish to hear these sounds again. Dreary, cruel, desolate, eerie!

On the day after the wreck some sailors among the survivors on Middle King took a lifeboat back to the wreck in a desperate bid to find food, but because of the heavy seas could not get back to Middle King, and landed on Big King instead. Those left on Middle King survived on crabs and shellfish collected from the rocks as they faced a second night stranded on the ledge. Agnes Robb recalled, 'There was a good deal of fainting and hysteria on the part of some women that night and much wailing on the part of the children for the food that might not be had.'

Lifeboat No. 2 was commanded by Chief Officer L. J. Burkett, who decided to try and make it to land, despite not having a compass. Later an unidentified passenger gave the following account, which was reported in the *Sydney Morning Herald* on 13 November, of how he came to be in that lifeboat:

> I went on board the *Elingamite* with my wife and child at Sydney. Nothing happened until Sunday morning about half-past 10 o'clock. I felt no shock when the vessel struck, being at the time in the cabin. My wife and child were on deck. On leaving the cabin I saw a lady crying and she informed me that we had struck on the Three Kings. The first thing I noticed was the cliffs towering high above the masts, and partially obstructed by the fog which was very dense. They were then launching the first boat, and I went to the stern to find my wife and child. The boat commenced to be filled, and I decided not to put them in the first boat, fearing the rush. I intended putting them in the second boat, and to wait my chance after all the women and children were safe.
>
> I got away in the fifth boat. That boat had to be launched between the wreck and the cliffs. When picking up the others in the water the boat capsized, throwing us all out, and afterwards another boat got clear and picked us up. After being about half an hour in the water the first and second mates were also picked up. At the time the only provisions we had in the boat were a few oranges and loquats, with a case of schnapps, all of which were picked up out of the water. There was no time to provision the boat, as the fore part of the vessel sank about 20 minutes after she had struck, the seas going right over the vessel as we got away. I did not notice the others get away, but they left before us. We had 52 people and one dead body in the boat; but the officer stayed some time to try and pick up anyone floating about. There was a large number of women and children on the vessel, but they were all taken off, some of them being on rafts. They were not all fully clothed when they left the vessel. It was raining slightly during the night, but not heavily.

Also in Lifeboat No. 2 was Second Officer Renaut, whose account of his experience was reported in the same issue of the *Sydney Morning Herald*:

> The *Elingamite* struck the Three Kings about a quarter to 11 am on Sunday. The weather was very thick for the previous 36 hours and very thick at the time of striking. We were going dead slow, about four and a half knots, for about three quarters of an hour before striking. No breakers were seen at all, and the first intimation that anything was wrong was when we saw the cliffs towering above us. The engines were immediately put full speed astern, but without avail. When she struck there was no sign of panic, the passengers behaving splendidly. All the boats and rafts were launched immediately.
>
> The women and children were the first care, after which the male passengers and crew were attended to. Our boat was the last that left the scene of the wreck. All the boats got completely separated in the fog. One boat was sighted just before dark about three miles to the southwards, but before we could make anything of her, the fog closed down, and we lost sight of her. There was a moderate sea running when we left the wreck. One boat capsized, but I believe all the occupants were

saved by our boat. No officer was in charge of this boat until I was picked up, the captain, officers and engineers staying on board until the boats were launched. Then, as the ship was settling down, we were washed off, and were picked up by the boats that were standing by. One lady passenger was picked up dead (Mrs. Sully).

After I was picked up we stood by and picked up all the persons we could find floating about, including the chief officer. When we could find no more we pulled clear of the wreckage, and then set sail, steering to the eastward to pick up the North Cape. The weather being still very thick throughout the night, we thought it advisable to stand on as we were till daylight, when we altered our course to the southward. We had 37 passengers and 13 of crew, with Mrs. Sully's dead body.

At half past 6 on Monday morning the weather gradually cleared, and we sighted the mainland at 8 o'clock, and steered for it, beaching our boat at half-past 12. Shortly after landing the Maoris found us and took us to their settlement, and treated us with great kindness and hospitality, bringing not only food but clothes as far as they were able. We stayed there all night, and they brought us over here to Hohoura, where we are being treated with the greatest kindness by all the settlers. I am thankful to say all are now in good health, and there is no serious sickness from exposure.

As there were no direct communications from Hohoura to the rest of the country, whaleboats were manned by local fisherman, and rowed out to sea in the hope of meeting up with a passing ship and diverting it to the site of the disaster.

On 11 November, another Huddart Parker steamer, *Zealandia*, under the command of Captain Wylie, who had been transferred from the *Elingamite* only four months previously, had departed Auckland on its way back to Sydney, and it met up with the whaleboats on 12 November. *Zealandia* then steamed at top speed to the Three Kings. The survivors on the ledge on Middle King saw the steamer approaching and waved frantically. They were sighted from *Zealandia*, which sent boats over to rescue them, along with other survivors from Big King Island. In the end there were over 90 survivors on board when *Zealandia* turned around and headed back to Auckland.

The Auckland correspondent for the *Sydney Morning Herald* sent the following report on the Wednesday afternoon:

A dense crowd thronged Queen Street wharf this afternoon as the steamer *Zealandia* with 92 more survivors from the wreck of the *Elingamite* came slowly steaming to berth.

It appears that the first news those on board the *Zealandia* got of the wreck was about 6 o'clock on Tuesday morning, when they were hailed by whaling boats which had put out from Hohoura with the intention of intercepting them. The whaling boats had been out all night flying signals of distress to attract the attention of the *Zealandia*. They communicated to the captain news of the landing of the boat at Hohoura, and that other survivors were possibly on the Three Kings. The *Zealandia* at once set a course for the Three Kings, to which, without the information supplied by the whaleboats, they would not have got near enough to see the signals of distress which the shipwrecked party had managed to put up. The *Zealandia* got off the Three Kings about half-past 3 on Tuesday afternoon. She went as near as possible and launched a boat, in which the chief officer went with provisions. It took the boat an hour to row to a landing place.

Passengers and crew were in a most pitiable condition, many being badly clad and without shoes. The passengers on the *Zealandia* at once put everything they had at the disposal of the shipwrecked people, and made them as comfortable as possible. Then the story of their shipwreck, and their subsequent experiences came out.

The *Elingamite*, it was learned, sank 23 minutes after she struck, all hands having succeeded in leaving the ship except Captain Atwood and Mr. Vine, the chief steward, who were washed overboard, the captain not even having a lifebelt on. On one of the rafts there were 16 people and on the other 11, the former having three oars and the latter two. The raft with 11 on board reached the Great King at 7 pm on Sunday, while the three boats reached Middle King some two hours earlier. The raft with 16 persons on board is, unfortunately, still missing.

When the shipwrecked party from the three boats got ashore on Middle King a covering was made of sails to provide shelter for the women and children. The men had to sleep – if such it could be called – on the rocks, having nothing but their life preservers to keep them off the sharp rocks. The party had no provisions, and at 4 o'clock on Monday morning Captain Reid (superintendent of Mercantile Marine in Auckland), who was one of the saloon passengers on the *Elingamite*, got together the crew and went with one of the boats to the wreck in search of provisions. They found two cases of gin and two dozen bottles of champagne, but were unable to get food, the *Elingamite* having sunk completely out of sight. They had only crabs and cockles to eat till Tuesday morning, when some of the passengers made fishing lines out of the strings of the ladies' corsets and cords of life preservers. Fishhooks were made from ladies' hatpins, and some fish were caught and boiled in a tin pannikin, which had been used to bale out the boat. A fresh water spring was found about a mile distant. There were men, women and children in this party. They had managed to get some brandy, which was served out only to the women. The women of the party speak in terms of the highest praise of the gallantry of the men, who did all they could for the women and children.

When the survivors first saw the smoke of the *Zealandia* they all joined in making as big a fire with brushwood as they could, realizing that if they failed to attract the attention of the distant steamer all hope was gone. They hoisted some white shirts as a flag of distress on oars, planting these on the highest pinnacle the sailors could reach.

The arrival of *Zealandia* in Auckland was met with a mixture of joy and grief, as those waiting on the wharf for loved ones received either good or bad news. It was known that another lifeboat and a raft were still out at sea somewhere, so a search was started, though the area to be covered was huge.

The missing raft had fifteen men and one woman on board, but no compass, and their only food was two apples. The raft was so low in the water that the survivors were constantly sitting in water, being circled by sharks as they were scorched by the sun during the day and very cold at night. One of the men on the raft was Stephen Neill, who later stated, 'We were terribly hungry, but the agonising thirst was even harder to endure. We strained our eyes through the fog hoping against hope to pick up a light.' During the first day they shared one of the apples.

On the first night one man died, and two more next morning. Those left decided to push their bodies overboard to lighten raft. Some of them were starting to lose their minds. As Stephen Neill later said, 'The desire for water was overpowering and some of the people on the raft began to drink salt water despite all that can be said of the terrible consequences. It was very hard indeed to resist the temptation and several times I had to shut my eyes and hide from the tempting sight.'

On the third evening a steamer came close but did not sight the raft or hear their shouts. One man was so disappointed he jumped overboard and swam away. On day four the second apple was shared between the twelve left alive, but that night two more men jumped overboard. Stephen Neill had tried to dissuade one man from jumping, but to no avail. 'I threw a lifebelt to him,' he said later, 'but he pushed it away and was singing a tune as he drifted away to his death.'

By the morning of day five the raft had drifted 60 nautical miles north-east of the Three Kings. During the morning another man died, as did the sole female, in the arms of Stephen Neill. By the afternoon of day five there were only eight people left alive on the raft.

One search ship, HMS *Penguin*, was in the same area as the raft, but due to return to Auckland that evening. Late in the afternoon of day five, someone on the raft saw the *Penguin*. Only one man had the strength to stand up and wave. As Stephen Neill recalled, 'A wild hope throbbed within us, and when we found that we were sighted and that the vessel was making towards us our joy was unspeakable.' The eight survivors were taken aboard and the ship made top speed to Auckland, where Stephen Neill was reunited with his wife and daughter.

This left only Lifeboat No. 4 missing, under the command of Third Officer Watson with 30 survivors on board, it being the only one to have contained a compass and provisions. Surprisingly it was never found. When the search for further survivors was called off, it was found that 45 persons had lost their lives in the sinking, including 28 passengers.

Almost immediately attempts began to try and retrieve the gold and silver coins that had been carried by *Elingamite*, which were worth £17,000 at the time. However, the isolated location of West King Island, and the heavy seas that continually pounded the area in which the wreck lay, caused immense difficulties. The salvage work continued off and on for over five years, but none of the bullion was recovered. In 1907 a diver lost his life, and the following year another diver was killed, which brought salvage attempts to a halt.

It was not until sixty years later that more divers tried to recover the sunken treasure. After many attempts, in January 1968 they did succeed in retrieving 120 pounds/54.5 kg of bullion. However, the constant danger ended further attempts to recover the bulk of the gold and silver coins, which will probably remain on the ocean floor for ever.

The Court of Inquiry into the disaster released a finding on 19 January 1903 blaming Captain Atwood, whose master's certificate was suspended for one year. In March 1911 it was discovered that the Three Kings were wrongly charted by three miles, and in December 1911 the Inquiry was reopened, and found in favour of Captain Atwood.

On 9 December 1902, *Victoria*, commanded by Captain W. Waller, departed Melbourne on its first voyage to New Zealand, following the usual horseshoe route to Hobart and Bluff, then up the east coast to Dunedin and Lyttelton before reaching Wellington, then crossing the Tasman Sea directly to Sydney, arriving there for the first time on 23 December. Next day the following item appeared in the *Sydney Morning Herald*:

Victoria joined the Tasman trade in December 1902 (WSS Victoria).

The new steamship *Victoria*, the latest addition to the fleet of Messrs Huddart, Parker and Co., which has been specially designed and built for the passenger and cargo trade between Australia and New Zealand, paid her first visit to Sydney yesterday and was greatly admired. She has been built on the lines of the well-known New Zealand trader, *Zealandia*, but is larger than that vessel by about 200 tons. The *Victoria* is 335 ft in length with a beam of 43 ft and her gross tonnage is 2,979.

No expense has been spared by the company in fitting up and furnishing the *Victoria*. She has accommodation for 150 first-class and 112 second-class passengers. The spacious saloon, which is situated on the upper deck, has seating accommodation for 90 persons and is luxuriously fitted, the walls being decorated with carved panels of oak. A cosy and elegantly furnished drawing room has been provided for the ladies below, and there is a large and airy social hall on the main deck. The smoking room is a comfortable compartment situated on the upper deck where also may be found a lounge room with a bar attached. A staircase leads from the smoking room to the poop deck, where passengers may promenade without being annoyed or inconvenienced by the work of loading and discharging cargo. Excellent accommodation has also been provided for second-class passengers.

The *Victoria* arrived at Melbourne on her maiden voyage from London on 25th ultimo, and after being docked proceeded to Hobart, Bluff, Dunedin, Lyttelton and Wellington. She sailed from the last-named port for Sydney at 10 pm on Friday last, and arrived here before 9 o'clock yesterday morning. The passage was therefore accomplished in the excellent time of three days 10¾ hours, or at an average speed of upwards of 14 knots.

Captain Waller (formerly of the steamer *Westralia*), who has been given command of the new vessel, states that but for the fact that heavy weather, lasting 20 hours, was encountered in the Tasman Sea, the run would have been made in three days and seven hours.

In a separate item in the same issue, a further description of the ship was provided, though it varied in some of the details. There was also special attention paid to the life-saving facilities aboard the ship, no doubt the writer being mindful of the recent sinking of the *Elangamite*.

The *Victoria* displaces 5,000 tons of water, and her principal measurements are:- Length 335 ft; breadth 43 ft, and depth 21 ft 5 in when loaded. She is equipped with triple expansion engines, which enabled her to steam at the rate of 15½ knots per hour on her trial trip. The accommodation for passengers leaves nothing to be desired. Travellers will appreciate the placing of the saloon on deck. She can carry 162 first-class and 102 second-class passengers. The cabins, bathrooms etc are extremely roomy and comfortable, whilst the utmost attention has been devoted by the designers of the vessel to the important element of ventilation. The saloon is tastefully fitted, and capable of seating 72 persons in comfort. It is panelled in oak, and set off by a handsome stained-glass dome, which while adding to the ornamentation of the apartment, ensures an ample supply of light.

The *Victoria* is equipped with eight lifeboats, each capable of accommodating 50 persons. They are built of yellow pine, with copper fastenings, and with proper handling would probably live in any seas. The apparatus in use for lowering these boats is simplicity itself. With fall-away chocks and a wheel working on cogs on the davits they can be successfully and rapidly launched by the manipulation of a lever, operated by one man, and which is somewhat on the principle of those used for turning the points on the railways. During the maiden voyage from London the utility of this invention was demonstrated on several occasions, not a hitch occurring.

It is worth noting here that shortly before the new *Victoria* arrived in Sydney, the P&O liner *Victoria* had been in port, departing Sydney on 18 December for London. The new *Victoria* departed Sydney on 27 December on her second voyage, going directly to Wellington, then Lyttelton, Dunedin, Bluff and Hobart on her way back to Melbourne, and this would be her regular route for the next few years.

With the sudden loss of *Elingamite*, *Westralia* was quickly withdrawn from the Tasmanian trade and returned to the Tasman service, partnering *Zealandia* on the route from Sydney to Auckland, Gisborne, Napier, Wellington, Lyttelton and Dunedin. *Zealandia* had left Sydney on 19 November, and the *Westralia* followed only three days later, on 22 November. However, this now left Huddart Parker one ship short on their Tasmanian service, so an order was soon placed with Caird & Co. at Greenock for a new ship to be built for the trans-Tasman trade, which would be a virtual repeat of *Victoria*.

Apart from the loss of *Elingamite*, the arrival of *Victoria* was also somewhat overshadowed by the arrival of the latest addition to the fleet of the Union Steam Ship Company of New Zealand, *Moeraki*, which also entered the Tasman trade in December 1902. At 4392 gross tons, *Moeraki* was considerably larger than *Victoria*, in fact the largest passenger vessel yet in the Union Line fleet, and provided excellent accommodation for 230 first class and 135 second class passengers. *Moeraki* arrived in Sydney for the first time on 16 December, a week before *Victoria*, and next day the following appeared in the *Sydney Morning Herald*, giving an idea of the type of competition being provided to the Huddart Parker ships by the latest Union Line vessels:

The magnificent new steamship *Moeraki*, built for the Union Steam Ship Company of New Zealand, and for the service between Sydney and Wellington, paid her first visit to Sydney yesterday, and was throughout the day an object of great admiration. The *Moeraki* left Wellington at 6.30 pm on Friday last, and entered Sydney Heads at 2.30 am yesterday, the trip having thus occupied but three days and eight hours. Throughout the voyage she averaged a speed of 15 knots, the best day's steaming being 381 miles. In this, as in other respects, the *Moeraki* has fulfilled expectations, for on her official trial trip prior to her departure from London she maintained a speed of 15.3 knots.

The saloon is a spacious and elegantly furnished compartment situated on the upper deck, and is surmounted by a dome. Seating accommodation has been provided for 112 persons; electric fans have been fitted; and the room is brilliantly illuminated at night by electricity. The social hall, which is above the saloon,

Moeraki provided serious competition for the Huddart Parker ships.

is panelled in highly polished mahogany with an ivory enamel finish. The smoking room, which is on the upper deck, is a well-furnished and comfortable compartment, and an elegant drawing room has been provided for the use of the ladies. The accommodation for second-class passengers is all that can be desired. The dining hall has seating for 82 persons, and the comfort and convenience of the passengers has been carefully studied in every detail.

Twenty of the first-class cabins are situated on the deck, and are roomy and exceedingly comfortable. The remainder of the saloon cabins are of course below. Berthing space has also been provided for 124 second-class passengers. In every part of the ship the most modern improvements have been introduced ... Needless to say the electric light has been installed throughout the vessel.

The engine-room is replete with all the latest inventions and a remarkable feature of her official trial trip was the fact that while she maintained a speed of over 15 knots there was a complete absence of vibration.

The *Moeraki* was thrown open to the public between the hours of 7 and 10 o'clock last evening, and a large number of interested persons availed themselves of the opportunity of inspecting the new vessel. The visitors were conducted over the ship, and expressions of admiration were heard on every hand. The *Moeraki* left for Newcastle at 2 o'clock this morning to replenish her coal bunkers, and will return to Sydney tomorrow. She sails for Wellington on Friday afternoon next.

At the start of 1903 the trans-Tasman trade was being operated for Huddart Parker by a fleet of recently-built ships, while the Union Line services were being maintained by the brand-new *Moeraki* and two older vessels, *Mararoa* and *Waikare*.

In January 1904 the Union Line presence on the trans-Tasman trade was further enhanced when *Moeraki* was joined by a slightly larger sister ship, *Manuka*, of 4534 gross tons. Also built at the Denny shipyard, *Manuka* arrived in Melbourne from Scotland on 2 January 1904, and went straight into the horseshoe service, departing on 6 January. A few months later, in May, *Manuka* was transferred to the longer service from Sydney to Vancouver.

Meanwhile, the new ship being built in Scotland for Huddart Parker Limited was given exactly the same hull design as *Victoria*, but a slightly larger superstructure, and was named *Wimmera* when launched on 19 August 1904. Completed in late September, *Wimmera* departed Glasgow on 6 October on its delivery voyage to Australia. Going around South Africa, *Wimmera* called at Durban for bunkers, then steamed non-stop to Melbourne, arriving on 29 November.

Wimmera was fitted with accommodation for 160 first class and 100 second class passengers. The vessel was powered by a coal-fired triple-expansion engine driving a single propeller, providing a service speed of 14 knots. At 3022 gross tons, *Wimmera* was slightly larger than *Victoria*, but still smaller than the Union Line ships operating across the Tasman at that time.

Wimmera was placed on the horseshoe service, replacing *Victoria*, which had departed Melbourne on 9 November for the last time on that route. *Victoria* then joined *Zealandia* on the shorter service from Sydney to Dunedin via Wellington, her first departure on that service being on 26 November.

Wimmera was placed on the horseshoe service in 1904.

Maheno was the fastest ship on the Tasman for many years (Fred Roderick collection).

Wimmera, under the command of Captain J. B. Rainey, entered the Tasman trade with a departure from Melbourne on 14 December, passing through Wellington on 24 December, and arriving in Sydney for the first time on 28 December. The return voyage departed Sydney on 31 December, while the next departure from Melbourne was on 18 January 1905. *Wimmera*'s schedule was integrated with that of the Union Line to provide regular departures by ships of both companies from both Sydney and Melbourne.

Late in 1905, the Union Line introduced yet another new liner on the Tasman trade, this being one of the most notable ships they would ever own. At 5282 gross tons, *Maheno* was much larger than any previous vessels on the trade, and provided superior accommodation for 234 first class, 116 second class and 60 third class passengers. It was also the first liner on the Tasman trades to be given two funnels.

Built by Wm Denny & Bros at Dumbarton, *Maheno* was fitted with direct-drive turbines connected to three propellers, and achieved 17.5 knots during trials, though its service speed was 16 knots. Arriving in Sydney on 13 November 1905 on its delivery voyage, the ship immediately broke all records for the Tasman service. On its maiden voyage, *Maheno* crossed from Sydney to Wellington in three days and three hours, creating a record that stood until November 1930, when it was bettered by the much larger and newer American liner *Malolo*. *Maheno* then continued down the east coast of South Island before crossing to Hobart and on to Melbourne, at every port of call creating a sensation with its beautifully appointed accommodation. Later in 1905, *Maheno* set a new record by crossing from Wellington to Sydney in 2 days 23 hours, which was not bettered until March 1933 by *Monowai*.

In April 1906, *Maheno* was taken temporarily off the Tasman service to make two voyages to Vancouver. On completion of these trips, *Maheno* returned to the Tasman service in September, but now followed the longer route to Auckland, Gisborne and Napier before arriving in Wellington, then continuing to South Island ports, Hobart and Melbourne. In 1907, *Maheno* set a record for the passage between Sydney and Auckland of 2 days 21 hours and 36 minutes that stood for the next 25 years.

At the end of 1906, Huddart Parker was operating *Zealandia* and *Victoria* on the service from Sydney to Wellington and Dunedin, while *Wimmera* was on the horseshoe route. In January 1907, *Zealandia* was taken out of service for overhaul, and Huddart Parker took their newest liner, *Riverina*, off the Australian coastal trade and placed it temporarily on the Tasman horseshoe service in place of *Wimmera*.

Built by J. Laing and Sons at Sunderland, *Riverina* was launched on 16 May 1905, being delivered to Huddart Parker in October 1905, and at 4758 gross tons was an enlarged and improved version of *Wimmera*. Entering service in January 1906, *Riverina* was placed on the major coastal service between Sydney and Fremantle, and soon proved to be the fastest liner on that route, being nicknamed the 'Coastal Express'. *Riverina* arrived in Sydney for the first time on 19 January 1906, and the same day the *Sydney Morning Herald* gave the following description of the new vessel:

The new steamer *Riverina*, which will make her first

appearance in Sydney today, is built generally on the lines of *Wimmera*, but is much larger, and affords even greater attraction for passengers than that vessel.

There are three separate classes for passengers, accommodation being provided for 160 first class, 116 second class and 100 third class travellers. One of the most striking features of the vessel is the spaciousness of the promenade decks, both for the first and second class passengers. The first saloon accommodation is placed amidships, and embraces all the comforts and conveniences that ingenuity and money can ensure. Marble-fitted lavatories and bathrooms, with hot and cold water, are conveniently scattered among the staterooms, whilst the latter are unusually high, roomy, and well ventilated.

The first class dining hall, a magnificent apartment, capable of seating 120 persons, is situated on the shelter deck. It extends the full width of the vessel, and is fitted in polished Austrian oak, with richly carved panels and pillars of Corinthian design, the ceiling being white, picked out with gold lining. A double staircase leads to the social hall above. This apartment is especially inviting, the fittings, upholstering etc being of a most elaborate kind, and so arranged that passengers may rely upon a maximum of comfort. Light is supplied by a large and handsome dome of stained floral glass. The smoking room is at the after end of the promenade deck. It is a spacious and comfortable apartment, upholstered in red morocco, and with all the seats partitioned off.

On the upper deck and abaft the first saloon stands the second class accommodation, which, excepting that its situation is not so favourable, is little inferior to that of the first class, the dining hall, social hall, smoking room, staterooms, lavatories etc, all being arranged almost on the same liberal and costly plan which marks the first class. It is certainly of a much higher standard than is to be found generally on coastal traders.

The steerage accommodation is placed on the upper deck, near the bows of the ship. It consists of open berths, with a plain but well ventilated dining room, entirely apart from the sleeping space, neat lavatories and bathrooms also being provided in suitable situations.

In the *Sydney Morning Herald* on 31 December 1906, the following item appeared under the Huddart Parker shipping advertisement on the front page:

NOTICE TO PASSENGERS

PASSENGERS booked per S.S. WIMMERA are requested to note that this vessel will not sail as previously advertised, the new steamship RIVERINA taking her place, sailing SATURDAY, January 5, noon. Passengers are requested to call on the undersigned regarding accommodation.

HUDDART, PARKER and CO. PROPRIETARY, LTD

The Huddart Parker advertisement also referred to a 'New Zealand Exhibition, Specially reduced fares, as arranged with New Zealand Government'. *Riverina* departed Sydney as scheduled on 5 January, following the horseshoe route via Wellington and Lyttelton, Dunedin, Bluff and Hobart to Melbourne. *Wimmera* left Sydney on 9 January for Auckland and east coast ports as far south as Lyttelton, being followed by *Victoria* on 23 January.

Wimmera had previously been scheduled to depart Melbourne on 16 January 1907 on the horseshoe route, but this departure was taken a week later, on 23 January, by *Riverina*, the voyage including an excursion into Milford Sound, arriving back in Sydney on 9 February. *Riverina* remained on the horseshoe service throughout February and March, departing Sydney on 9

Riverina arriving in Sydney.

February, Melbourne on 27 February and Sydney again on 16 March.

Riverina departed Melbourne on its last voyage on the horseshoe service on 3 April, the same day as *Wimmera* left Sydney on its final round trip to Dunedin. On arriving in Sydney, *Riverina* resumed its place on the trade to Western Australia, while *Zealandia* returned to service with a departure from Sydney on 17 April for Wellington and Dunedin, and on 20 April *Wimmera* left Sydney to resume its place on the horseshoe service.

The Tasman Sea could be a very dangerous ocean, and any ship encountering problems could quite easily be lost unless another vessel came to the rescue. In October 1901, *Monowai* was two days out of Bluff, bound for Hobart, when the boss and two blades were lost from the single propeller, which left the ship drifting helplessly. Emergency sails were rigged, and *Monowai* drifted for six days until another Union liner, *Mokoia*, chanced upon her, and towed the disabled vessel back to Port Chalmers. Had the *Monowai* not been sighted, the vessel could have drifted south, well out of the regular shipping lanes, and never been found.

In September 1907, when the *Monowai* was on a voyage from Wellington to Sydney, the rudder shaft broke, leaving the vessel drifting helplessly once again. At the time *Monowai* was 220 miles (350 km) from the Australian coast and, as happened before, emergency sails were rigged. *Monowai* was posted missing after being posted overdue in Sydney, and several ships were sent to search, but in an amazing coincidence it was *Mokoia* that again located *Monowai*, and towed the disabled vessel to Sydney.

In November 1907, the Union Line introduced another new liner on the Tasman service. Built by Caird & Co. at Greenock, at 6437 gross tons *Marama* was larger than *Maheno*, but had only one funnel, older style triple-expansion machinery, and twin propellers, with a service speed of only 15 knots. Accommodation was provided for 229 first class, 79 second class and 153 third class passengers, with the emphasis on comfort rather than luxury.

Voyaging from Glasgow by way of Cape Town and Melbourne, *Marama* arrived in Dunedin on 4 November, where the final touches were added before the liner went to Wellington on 20 November. Six days later *Marama* left Wellington for Sydney, and then joined the horseshoe service. However, after only three months on this trade, *Marama* was transferred to the service from Sydney to Vancouver. At the same time, Huddart Parker also introduced a new liner on the Tasman trade.

Marama only served briefly on the Tasman trade for the Union Line.

5

Ulimaroa

In the three years since *Wimmera* was built, the Union Line had brought out two larger and faster liners on the same trade, so in 1906 Huddart Parker also ordered a new liner, to be built by Gourlay Bros at Dundee. An enlarged version of *Riverina*, the new vessel would be the first Huddart Parker steamer to be fitted with twin propellers.

The new liner was given the name *Ulimaroa*, which is usually claimed to be derived from an ancient Maori name for Australia, and translates as 'blue and distant'. It was also the name of the house in which John Traill, who was still chairman of Huddart Parker, had lived since 1890. 'Ulimaroa' was an eighteenth century name for Australia, being shown as an alternative to 'New Holland' on several maps published in Germany in 1795. The name clearly derives from Watkin the geographer, educated in Auckland and respected for his knowledge of early Australian and Polynesian history. It appears to be Polynesian in origin, possibly Hawaiian, but not Maori, as there is no 'l' in the Maori language.

Ulimaroa was launched on 20 July 1907, but delays were encountered during fitting out, as Gourlay Bros were in serious financial trouble. *Ulimaroa* was finally completed at the end of December 1907, and during the morning of 2 January 1908 departed the builder's yard on sea trials. Returning the same afternoon, it had the misfortune to run aground off West Ferry, and remained stuck fast for two days before being pulled free. The vessel had to go to the Tyne for drydocking and survey, but no damage was found, so on 5 January *Ulimaroa* left Dundee on its delivery voyage, under the command of Captain Thomas Free. In 1908, Gourlay Bros was wound up, their demise being partly due to the delays in the building of *Ulimaroa*, described in official documents as 'a source of considerable expense to the builders'.

Ulimaroa provided comfortable accommodation for 292 first class passengers in two and three berth cabins located midships on the upper, shelter and promenade decks. The 121 second class passengers had three and four berth cabins located in the after sections of the ship. The vessel was powered by triple-expansion engines driving twin propellers, with a service speed of 15 knots. After calling at Glasgow, *Ulimaroa* steamed non-stop to Cape Town, then Durban, arriving on 29 January to take on bunkers. Leaving the next day, *Ulimaroa* then steamed directly to Melbourne, arriving on 16 February. The next day the following report appeared in the *Sydney Morning Herald*:

The magnificent new twin-screw passenger steamship *Ulimaroa* – the latest addition to the extensive fleet of Huddart, Parker, and Co. Proprietary, Limited – which was recently launched at Dundee for the trade between the Commonwealth and New Zealand, arrived at Melbourne yesterday from Scotland, via Durban, and may be expected in port at Sydney very shortly. The *Ulimaroa*, which was constructed in the well-known shipbuilding yards of Messrs Gourlay Brothers, at Dundee, is a vessel of 5,770 tons gross, and is 400 ft long between perpendiculars, her breadth being 52 ft. Features of the new vessel are a high forecastle head and bulwarks half her length, to ensure dryness even in the heaviest head seas.

Accommodation has been provided for 292 first-saloon and 121 second-class passengers. The first class apartments are situated amidships, and consist principally of two and three berth cabins on the upper, shelter and promenade decks. The dining saloon seats 124 persons, and an overflow saloon, to seat 80, has also been built. The music hall, on the promenade deck, is a magnificent room, furnished with luxurious divans and comfortable chairs. The dome and stained glass ports add to the elegance of the furnishing, and a grand piano completes the equipment. The smoking room, also on the promenade deck, is panelled in oak and upholstered

Ulimaroa in Sydney Harbour.

with morocco, and card tables are comfortably arranged. A smaller smoking-room and ladies morning room, with piano, are on the shelter deck.

The second-class passengers are accommodated forward of the first-class, on the upper and shelter decks, in roomy cabins. Plain but comfortable dining saloon, smoking room and ladies sitting room are provided for these passengers.

The vessel is driven by two sets of triple-expansion engines driving twin screws, and indicating 6,000 horse-power, capable of maintaining a speed of 16 knots. Steam is supplied by seven single-ended boilers.

The *Ulimaroa* will take the place of the *Wimmera* in the Sydney to Melbourne via Wellington, Lyttelton, Dunedin, Bluff and Hobart trade, the *Wimmera* replacing *Zealandia* in the Sydney, Auckland, Dunedin trade.

Ulimaroa remained in Melbourne for only two days then went on to Sydney, arriving for the first time on 19 February. That day the following report on the voyage to Australia appeared in the shipping section of the *Sydney Morning Herald*:

The magnificent new twin-screw passenger steamer *Ulimaroa*, the latest addition to Huddart, Parker, and Co.'s fleet, and specially built for the New Zealand trade, will arrive at Sydney on her maiden voyage today, from Scotland, via Durban and ports. Captain Thomas Free, who is in charge, reports that for 40 hours after leaving Glasgow the vessel encountered bitterly cold weather and frequent snowstorms, which made life on deck extremely disagreeable. Then strong head winds and seas prevailed the whole way down to Las Palmas. There, however, an improvement set in, and a fine run was made to the equator. Upon crossing the line the ship met with the S.E. trades, which blew with great strength, and raised high head seas, greatly retarding progress. Cape Town was reached and left on January 26, and Durban on 30th. Thence down to lat. 45 deg. south misty weather prevailed, but subsequently a favourable trip was experienced to Port Phillip.

At no stage of the voyage was the *Ulimaroa* asked to exert herself, only five of her seven boilers being in use. Her best day's run was 350 miles, but she nevertheless accomplished the trip across from Durban in the creditable time of 17½ days. An endless round of amusements was maintained among passengers, finishing up with a fancy dress ball prior to arrival on the coast. The *Ulimaroa* brought no general cargo, but shipped 2,500 tons of coal before commencing her voyage. The *Ulimaroa* is the sixth vessel that has been brought out to Australia for the Huddart, Parker line by Captain Free, the others being the *Zealandia*, *Wimmera*, *Victoria*, *Riverina* and *Barwon*.

On 29 February 1908, *Ulimaroa* departed Sydney on its maiden voyage across the Tasman Sea, following the usual route to Auckland, then down the east coast to Wellington, Lyttelton, Dunedin and Bluff before crossing to Hobart and on to Melbourne. Her first voyage to New Zealand from Melbourne departed on 18 March. When the Union Line transferred *Marama* to the Vancouver trade, *Ulimaroa* became the largest liner engaged on the horseshoe service, a position it would retain until February 1912, when *Maunganui* arrived.

With the arrival of *Ulimaroa*, *Wimmera* was taken off the horseshoe service to join *Victoria* on the shorter route from Sydney to Auckland, Gisborne, Napier, Wellington, Lyttelton and Dunedin, returning via the same ports in reverse.

Zealandia was sold to the Union Line, and is shown here as Paloona.

Zealandia departed Sydney on 19 February 1908 for its last voyage to New Zealand, returning to Sydney on 13 March. *Zealandia* was then withdrawn from the Tasman trade, and laid up, as Huddart Parker did not require the ship on any other route.

In April 1908, *Zealandia* was chartered to the Union Steam Ship Company, and placed on their service between Sydney and Hobart. In September 1909, the Union Line bought *Zealandia* outright, and it was renamed *Paloona*. The ship was given an extensive refit, during which the funnel was heightened, and it then returned to the trade between Sydney and Hobart.

For the remainder of 1908 *Ulimaroa*, *Wimmera* and *Victoria* maintained the New Zealand service with regular departures. After a year in service, on 13 February 1909 *Ulimaroa* departed Sydney on a regular voyage to New Zealand, being due to commence the return voyage from Melbourne on 7 April. However, on the morning of Saturday, 20 February, *Ulimaroa,* when arriving in Dunedin, was caught by the ebbing tide and pushed onto Quarantine Rock at the entrance to Port Chalmers. The ship was able to free itself quickly, but was found to be leaking badly through damaged plates. *Ulimaroa* managed to dock in Dunedin, where temporary repairs were made, but the vessel then had to make a fast trip up the coast to Lyttelton, where it was immediately placed in drydock for repairs.

On 22 February the Christchurch newspaper, *The Press*, reported, 'The *Ulimaroa* struck Quarantine Island coming up the harbour on Saturday, and damaged several plates. She will probably be sent to Lyttelton for docking, and the *Talune* will probably take up her running, leaving for Melbourne on Monday night.' The shipping movements column in the same paper on 24 February showed that *Ulimaroa* arrived in Lyttelton at 7.30 am on 23 February from Port Chalmers. On 25 February, the following more extensive report appeared in *The Press*:

The Huddart Parker Company's large steamer *Ulimaroa*, which grounded in Otago Harbour last Saturday morning, and which was badly damaged, was docked at Lyttelton on Tuesday evening. A survey of the vessel's bottom was held yesterday morning, and it is understood that tenders will be called at once and a contract let for the work of repairs.

An inspection of the vessel in dock shows that she has sustained very serious damage through contact with the rocks. The first dent shows under the bottom of the vessel on the port side, about 60 feet from the bow. The plates are badly dented and the rivets are started. Going aft, numerous bad dents can be seen, and then for about 120 feet or more the plates and frames are very seriously buckled and 'set up'. The damage seems to be confined to the two rows of plates extending from the keel outwards for about eight feet, and fore and aft for well over 100 feet amidships. The plates at the after end of the damaged section are badly cracked, and water was streaming through in numerous places.

A number of the cracks were so bad that they had to be plugged at Port Chalmers by a diver, with canvas and wood wedges. It is understood that the contract for repairs will involve the removal of 18 plates, each about 22 feet in length ... Permanent repairs to the vessel will be carried out at Lyttelton, and she will be in dock for some weeks.

Shipmasters say that the mishap to the *Ulimaroa* has emphasised the need for a light being placed on Goat Island in such a position that it will become visible when a ship coming up the Dunedin harbour at night time has reached the fairway between the islands. A vessel, after passing Port Chalmers, steers for the light on Quarantine Island overlooking the gut between it and Goat Island. At present a shipmaster has to depend on his own judgement as to when he has approached near enough to this light to justify him in putting the helm over and striking through the tide-swept gut. A light on Goat Island, placed so that it became visible when a ship had approached near enough to the Quarantine Island light to be in the fairway, would simplify the navigating of the 360ft channel that separates the islands.

The accident created a major problem for Huddart Parker, as *Ulimaroa* had been scheduled to call at Hobart and arrive in Melbourne on Saturday, 27 February, and commence its return trip to Sydney via New Zealand ports on 3 March, and then from Sydney again on 20 March. In the short term there was not a lot Huddart Parker could do, as the only vessel immediately available to them was the veteran *Anglian*, which was at that time laid up in Sydney, but was not really suitable as a replacement. The passengers who had been aboard *Ulimaroa* were transferred to the Union Line vessel *Talune* to complete their journey. *Riverina*, which at that time was on its way back to Sydney from Fremantle, was due in Sydney on 8 March, and was then due to go into drydock for maintenance before commencing its next voyage west on 10 April.

In the *Sydney Morning Herald* of Monday, 1 March, the Huddart Parker advertisement still listed *Ulimaroa* as being scheduled to depart Melbourne on 3 March, with the veteran *Burrumbeet* departing Sydney on 23 March, replacing *Riverina* for one round trip to Fremantle. On 2 March, the Huddart Parker advertisement showed *Riverina* taking the 20 March departure on the horseshoe service, and *Ulimaroa* being due to depart Melbourne on 7 April.

Amazingly, the only mention in an Australian newspaper of the *Ulimaroa* having been involved in an accident appeared in the Melbourne newspaper, *The Argus*, in a short item in their shipping news section on Monday, 1 March:

In consequence of a mishap to the *Ulimaroa*, she was unable to make her trip from New Zealand ports to Melbourne as intended, and a substitute had to be found in the *Talune*. The latter vessel, which is rarely seen in this port nowadays, arrived alongside the wharf yesterday afternoon, having made a satisfactory run of 35½ hours from Hobart. She is to leave here on a return trip next Wednesday at 10 am. Shippers are notified that no cargo will be received on sailing day.

On 3 March a further item appeared in the Christchurch newspaper, *The Press*:

Work at the damaged steamer *Ulimaroa* in dry dock is being pushed on with all despatch, a large number of men being engaged in drilling and removing the plates from the bottom of the vessel. A number are also engaged in taking out the blocks from under the keel and replacing them by 'built up' blocks placed further out. As the vessel will be in dock for some considerable time, a large proportion of her crew, comprising those not actually required to work about the steamer while she is under repairs, have been paid off, and will return to Australia in the *Victoria* today. The *Riverina* is being withdrawn from the Australian inter-state service to take up the running of the *Ulimaroa*.

On the morning of 8 March *Riverina* arrived in Sydney from Fremantle, with a large number of passengers on board, and was immediately prepared for a quick turnaround. The same afternoon, *Riverina* left Sydney for Wellington, arriving on 12 March, and embarking a large number of passengers previously booked to travel on *Ulimaroa*. That evening *Riverina* left Wellington, and endured quite a rough trip back to Sydney, where it arrived on the morning of 16 March. The next day, *Riverina* entered the Woolwich Dock in Sydney for cleaning and painting.

On 20 March, *Riverina* departed Sydney on the horseshoe service, but by then the full extent of the damage that had been suffered by *Ulimaroa* was known to Huddart Parker, as well as the fact the vessel would be out of service for many weeks. There was no mention of the accident that befell *Ulimaroa* in Sydney newspapers until 18 March, when the following item appeared in the shipping section of the *Sydney Morning Herald*:

Our New Zealand correspondent, writing under date Wellington, March 12, says 'A telegram from Christchurch states that the work of repairing the Huddart Parker Company's fine steamer *Ulimaroa*, which was seriously damaged in Otago Harbour a couple of weeks ago, and is now in dock at Lyttelton, will be a long and very costly one, and will rank as one of the biggest ship-repairing jobs ever undertaken in New Zealand. The work of "stripping" the damaged plates from the vessel's bottom was carried out by Messrs Anderson Limited, who had a very large number of men working night and day. This extensive preliminary work was completed on Saturday morning. Altogether ten steel plates, each about 22 ft in length, were taken out, after which a survey was held.

'The plates having been removed, it was then possible to form a good idea of the damage to the vessel's frames, angle bars, and floor plates, a large number of which are badly buckled and twisted. Five of the plates in the garboard strake, seven in the second strake, and two in the third strake are to be renewed; two plates in the second strake and three in the third strake are to be straightened and put back in their places.

'By far the most serious damage is that which has been done to the floor plates, angle bars, and frames in the No. 2 tank; fourteen floor plates and angle bars and four angle bars and the lower half of the after-bulkhead are to be cut out and renewed. Where the angle bars are cut out, "hacking pieces" of the same thickness are to be riveted on to the new angle bars. In the No. 3 tank, five floor plates and angle bars and one angle bar are to be straightened in their places; fifteen floor plates, angle bars, and frames are to be cut out and renewed from where marked to the keelson; the lower half of the after-bulkhead and the angle bars are also to be cut out and renewed. In the No. 4 tank twenty-three floor plates and angle bars and frames are to be cut out and renewed. The after-bulkhead is also to be cut, and the lower half with the angle bars are to be renewed. In the No 5. tank four floor plates and angle bars and frames are to be cut out and renewed; one length of the port rolling chock, which is buckled, is to be straightened, while eight butts on the garboard strake on the starboard side of the vessel are to be caulked and the rivets to be renewed where required.

'Tenders are being called by Huddart Parker & Co for these repairs and it is understood that a number of big engineering firms are tendering. The terms of contract require tenderers to include the coast of dry dock accommodation in the amount of their tender and it is anticipated that this will run into about £43 per day. In the event of the contract time being exceeded, the contractor agrees to a deduction of £50 per day for every day he exceeds his time.

'A practical engineer has expressed the opinion that the whole work will take eight or ten weeks, and the cost will be from £5,000 to £10,000. The plates to be renewed in the vessel's bottom may have to be specially imported, because of their unusual size.'

By then, Huddart Parker had ceased advertising *Ulimaroa*, and showed *Riverina* being due to depart Melbourne on 6 April. This meant that the voyage to Fremantle originally scheduled for *Riverina* on 10 April had to be taken by *Yongala*, chartered from the Adelaide Steam Ship Company. In the hope that the repairs to *Ulimaroa* would be completed by the end of April, Huddart Parker began advertising that *Riverina* would be departing Sydney on 8 May on a voyage to Fremantle, with *Ulimaroa* leaving Melbourne on 12 May to resume its regular service. In the meantime *Riverina* was scheduled for a second voyage from Sydney to New Zealand departing on 24 April, resulting in the cancellation of the planned 8 May departure for Fremantle.

Fortunately *Ulimaroa* was able to depart Melbourne as scheduled on 12 May, arriving back in Sydney on 25 May, at which time it was reported that repairs had cost between £10,000 and £12,000. *Riverina* resumed its place on the Fremantle trade with a departure from Sydney on 22 May, while *Ulimaroa* left Sydney for New Zealand on 29 May.

Not long after *Ulimaroa* first entered service, Huddart Parker had ordered another vessel to be built for them, with the intention that it, too, would be placed on the trans-Tasman trade. Built by John Brown & Co. in Glasgow, when the new liner was launched on 20 November 1909 it was named *Zealandia*, the second Huddart Parker ship to carry the name, and was completed in May 1910. Departing

A fine view of *Ulimaroa* departing Sydney.

the Clyde on 14 May 1910, *Zealandia* steamed non-stop to Durban, berthing there on 8 June to take on bunkers, then proceeding directly to Melbourne, arriving on 25 June, and Sydney on 2 July.

The next day the *Sydney Morning Herald* carried a report on the new vessel, including the fact that, instead of going into the Tasman trade as planned, it would be operating between Australia and Canada:

> The first vessel built for Australian owners which is fitted with a wireless telegraphy installation, the *Zealandia* (owned by Huddart, Parker Proprietary Limited) arrived in Sydney yesterday from Glasgow and Durban, via Melbourne. She maintained communication with England for some days. When 1,100 miles off Durban a message was sent to the Postmaster-General of the South African Federation, and was duly acknowledged.
>
> The vessel maintained an average speed of 13½ knots using only five boilers out of seven, and burned only 63 tons of coal per day. This was before reaching Melbourne. From Melbourne to Sydney she made 14.1 knots, using three boilers. Captain Free says the vessel is equal to a speed of 16½ knots loaded, and to 17 knots half loaded. The steamer is intended for the Canadian–Australian trade, in substitution for the *Manuka*, which is to go into the interstate and New Zealand trade. 'The size, capacity, and equipment of the *Zealandia*,' says a London shipping expert, 'will undoubtedly give her a foremost place among the vessels of 1910 constructed for colonial owners.'
>
> Accommodation is provided for about 200 first-class passengers, 120 second-class, and 120 third-class. The officers and crew number about 130. The first-class accommodation, consisting of two and three-berth staterooms and public rooms, is arranged amidships on the upper shelter and promenade decks. The second-class accommodation is arranged at the aft end on the upper and shelter decks, and comprises staterooms, dining saloon, music room, and smoking rooms. The dining saloon, placed on the upper deck, occupies the full width of the vessel, and seats 90 persons. The third-class accommodation is arranged forward on the main, upper and shelter decks. The cabins are arranged for from two to six passengers.

Zealandia's charter to Canadian-Australasian Line came about due to the Union Line being one ship short on this route following the withdrawal of the veteran *Aorangi* in February 1910. In May 1910 James Mills, chairman and managing director of the Union Line, made a special trip to Melbourne for talks with Huddart Parker Limited regarding this situation.

John Traill had been chairman of Huddart Parker & Co. Ltd since 1895, but in 1910, the last survivor of the original four partners who had formed the company, he handed over the chairmanship to Mr. W. T. Appleton, who had become a director the previous year.

Mills made an offer to Appleton that if Huddart Parker would refit *Zealandia* to suit it for the Canadian trade, and take a one-third stake in Canadian-Australasian Line, the Union Line would take a one-quarter interest in a reconstructed Huddart Parker, and extend the current agreement on the Tasman trade for a further five years.

Huddart Parker agreed to the last two terms, but refused to take an interest in Canadian-Australasian Line, instead offering to charter *Zealandia* to the company at a favourable rate. This was agreed to by both parties, and *Zealandia* was refitted with space for 500 tons of refrigerated cargo in the holds..

Zealandia was built for the Tasman trade, but served elsewhere.

The Huddart Parker Tasman service continued on a regular basis until towards the end of 1910, when all the passenger ships operated by the company were each given a thorough overhaul, as noted in the *Sydney Morning Herald* on 4 November 1910:

With a view to coping with the expected large passenger traffic to New Zealand, Tasmania and the other States during the forthcoming Christmas and New Year holidays, Messrs Huddart, Parker and Company are having their express steamers placed in dry dock for cleaning and painting, the accommodation for passengers receiving special attention. On arrival last voyage from Western Australia the steamer *Riverina* was floated into Woolwich Dock, sailing again from Sydney on October 22. She will be followed by the steamer *Victoria* next week. This ship has been undergoing a thorough overhaul since her arrival from Auckland on October 21, the *Westralia* relieving her in the New Zealand trade meanwhile. The *Victoria* will take up her running again this month, leaving here on the 23rd inst. The *Westralia* will go into dock on arrival from the Dominion on the 18th instant, and after being cleaned and painted, will sail for Hobart on 26th. Mort's Dock has been engaged for the *Ulimaroa* for December 7, and she is time-tabled to leave Sydney again for Wellington December 10. The *Wimmera*, which will arrive from Auckland on December 2, will dock on the 3rd, and take her departure for New Zealand on the 7th.

That the Tasman Sea can be a very dangerous stretch of water was vividly illustrated during a voyage from Auckland to Sydney by *Maheno* in March 1911, about which the following report appeared in the *Sydney Morning Herald* on 1 April, commencing with comments on the problems that had been encountered by a number of steamers along the New South Wales coast during recent bad weather, then continuing:

The Union Company's steamer *Maheno*, from Auckland, had the worst experience of all. After having moderate to fine weather up till Thursday, the wind changed to an increasing gale from the south-west. At midnight on Thursday, and until 2 am on Friday, a heavy sea broke on board, doing considerable damage to deck fittings and cabins. It was believed to be a tidal wave. Some 50ft to 60ft of the wooden taffrail was carried away, and the iron stanchions were torn asunder, bent and twisted. This same sea, in its wild fury, found its way into the saloon smoking-room, and smashed woodwork and glass mirrors. It also got in between decks, and washed an invalid lady passenger out of her bunk.

Wirth's circus people, who were on board, found their baggage floating in several feet of water. Skylights, with a thickness of an inch and a half, were broken in all directions. Pieces of glass were mixed with panels of doors in the debris, which was piled up on deck when the vessel arrived with a heavy list to port.

The horses and elephants had a bad time. The latter were forward on the main deck exposed to the elements. The horses were between decks. During the continuance of the storm the circus staff were all kept on duty. The opinion was expressed by one authority that if another sea had struck the vessel she would probably have gone under.

In 1911 it was decided to change Huddart Parker into a public company, with a capital of £1 million divided equally between preference and ordinary shares. Subscriptions were invited from residents of both Australia and New Zealand. Such was the public response that the offer was oversubscribed, a total of 2 448 996 shares being applied for. On 1 January 1912 the new entity, Huddart Parker Limited, came into existence.

The changes within the company structure did not affect the operation of the vessels at all, but in February 1912 *Ulimaroa* found herself operating in friendly competition with *Maunganui*, another new Union Line vessel. It appears that initially it was planned that *Maunganui* would enter the trans-Pacific service, while the chartered *Zealandia* would be returned to Huddart Parker and placed on the Tasman trade, as noted in this item that appeared in the *Sydney Morning Herald* on 9 August 1911:

The new steamer *Maunganui*, now under construction in Scotland, will probably be used by the Union Company for the Pacific Royal Mail Line pending the completion of the 10,000 tons steamer which has been specially ordered for the Sydney, Auckland and Vancouver service. The latest order provides for a speed of from 16 to 17 knots. The vessel will be used in conjunction with the *Makura* and *Marama*, the *Zealandia* reverting to the New Zealand service, for which she was specially constructed.

As events panned out, the Union Line decided to place *Maunganui* on the horseshoe service, and continue the charter of *Zealandia* on the Canadian service. The '10,000 tons steamer' referred to in this item entered service in 1913 as *Niagara*, at which time it did replace *Zealandia*.

At 7527 gross tons, *Maunganui* was considerably larger than *Ulimaroa*, and also of a more attractive design. On 10 October 1911 the *Sydney Morning Herald* carried the following description of *Maunganui*:

Maunganui was a superb addition to the fleet of the Union Line.

Accommodation is provided for 244 first-class, 175 second-class and 80 third-class passengers, and for a crew of 136 men. There is a spacious entrance hall which contains the main stairway leading to the upper deck, and the lounge and music room and smoking lounge are on the promenade deck. Forward of the main stairway there is a dining saloon over 50ft in length, and extending the full width of the vessel. The tables are arranged on the café principal [sic], and are capable of sitting 144 persons. The second class dining saloon has seated accommodation for 110 persons. The first-class staterooms are on the Bibby system, with berths for one, two or three persons. Forward of the main saloon is the third-class saloon, with seating accommodation for 58 persons, and staterooms adjacent.

Maunganui arrived in Melbourne on 2 February 1912 on her delivery voyage, continuing to Sydney, where she arrived on 5 February, and was prepared for entry into the horseshoe service, replacing the veteran *Warrimoo*, which had originally been managed by Huddart Parker.

Throughout this period, Huddart Parker maintained regular services across the Tasman without major interruption, with *Wimmera* and *Victoria* providing a departure from Sydney every second week to Auckland and North Island ports, while *Ulimaroa* departed Sydney every fifth Tuesday, and Melbourne every fifth Saturday on the horseshoe route.

Each year the vessels had to be withdrawn for brief periods to allow for maintenance and survey. For example, on 8 June 1912 a brief item appeared in the *Sydney Morning Herald* shipping notes, advising that Huddart Parker would be withdrawing 'several of their well-known passenger steamers at Sydney during the winter months for the purpose of putting them through a thorough overhaul'. The first vessel to be withdrawn would be *Westralia*, at that time on the Hobart trade, which would be replaced by *Burrumbeet*, followed by *Wimmera* and *Ulimaroa*. On Thursday, 13 June the following item appeared:

> The *Burrumbeet* leaves Sydney on Saturday for Hobart, and she will remain in the service until she arrives at Sydney on July 21. She will take up her usual coastal running on July 23. The *Westralia* will go into dock, and afterwards will replace the *Wimmera* in the New Zealand service, sailing from Sydney for Auckland on June 19. She will return to the Sydney-Hobart running on July 27. On the arrival of the *Ulimaroa* in Sydney from New Zealand on June 18, she will lay up for survey. She will leave Sydney for Melbourne direct on July 6, to take up her usual running in the Melbourne-Hobart-New Zealand-Sydney service, leaving Melbourne on July 10. The *Wimmera*, which replaces the *Ulimaroa* while she is in dock, leaves Sydney for Wellington on June 22, then to Melbourne, via Hobart, arriving at Melbourne on July 5, and sailing for Sydney direct on July 6, to take up her usual service to New Zealand, leaving for Auckland on July 17.

On 24 July, the *Sydney Morning Herald* shipping

report included a brief mention that '*Wimmera* and *Ulimaroa* have resumed their regular services between New Zealand and Sydney'. On the same day the following item also appeared, referring to the latest employment for one of the original Huddart Parker Tasman ships:

> Arrangements have been made for the Huddart Parker steamer *Anglian* to be pressed into service at Sydney as a depot for about 100 Asiatics who have been employed on two of the Clan liners taken up for time charter in the Australian trade. The Asiatics will be kept on board the *Anglian* pending arrangements for their return to their own country.

Early in 1910, Huddart Parker and the Union Line found themselves facing serious competition from an unexpected source. The major operator of passenger liners between Britain and Australia was the P&O Line, with a departure from London and Sydney every two weeks. To maintain a service of this regularity required a large fleet, with the vessels usually remaining in Sydney for a week or more before commencing the return trip back to London. In February 1910, the P&O Line began extending every second voyage from London across the Tasman Sea to New Zealand on a seasonal basis, and also offered passengers the opportunity to travel on these voyages between Sydney and Auckland.

The first of the P&O trans-Tasman voyages was taken by the *Malwa*, which departed Sydney on 12 February 1910, followed by *Mongolia* on 12 March, and *Morea*, which left Sydney on 9 April. This was the last of these trips to be conducted for the next seven months.

From 19 November 1910 to 10 April 1911, P&O liners made six return voyages from Sydney to Auckland, offering a departure every four weeks. The same schedule was followed the next summer, with *Moldavia* departing Sydney on 20 November 1911, and *Mongolia* closing out the season, leaving Sydney on 6 April 1912

These summer extensions were also operated from November 1912 to April 1913, the first being *Mongolia* on 18 November. However, the departure from Sydney by *Macedonia* on 7 April 1913 was the last time P&O extended their service across the Tasman Sea for a number of years.

It was also in April 1913 that the charter of *Zealandia* to Canadian-Australasian Line ended, and *Zealandia* was handed back to Huddart Parker. Instead of placing the vessel on the Tasman trade for which it had originally been built, *Zealandia* joined *Riverina* on the service between Sydney and Fremantle.

This only continued for three months, as on 16 July *Riverina* left Sydney on its final voyage to Fremantle, then was transferred to the Tasman trade, replacing *Wimmera*, which made its last departure for Auckland on 16 July, then on 13 August began operating between Sydney and Hobart.

On 13 August 1913, *Riverina* made its first departure from Sydney for Auckland, and east coast ports as far south as Dunedin, operating a fortnightly service in conjunction with *Victoria*. Unfortunately, this coincided with the outbreak of a smallpox epidemic in New South Wales, and the New Zealand Government introduced a regulation that all passengers from Australia had to be in possession of a vaccination certificate.

Riverina made one round trip per month over the next two months, but in early November a national strike, which included waterside workers, began in New Zealand. The departure of *Riverina* scheduled for 5 November was cancelled, and the ship laid up in Sydney, being joined by *Victoria* when it returned to Sydney, but *Ulimaroa* continued to operate on the horseshoe route, along with the Union Line vessels, until New Zealand seamen joined the strike in December.

The strike continued until just before Christmas. On 24 December *Riverina* returned to service with a departure for Auckland, followed by *Victoria* on 31 December. Going into 1914 a normal service was resumed, and initially *Riverina* and *Victoria* were scheduled to operate one round trip per month from Sydney to Auckland, Gisborne, Napier, Wellington, Lyttelton and Dunedin.

On 19 February Huddart Parker announced that after *Victoria* departed Sydney on 25 February, *Riverina* would begin operating a fortnightly service from Sydney starting on 11 March, and connect in Auckland with *Victoria*, which was operating a feeder service for passengers and cargo bound for other New Zealand ports as far as Dunedin.

6

World War I

In the weeks leading up to the outbreak of war in Europe in August 1914, the Huddart Parker services across the Tasman continued as they had over recent years. *Riverina* and *Victoria* were maintaining a regular fortnightly service between Sydney and Auckland, in conjunction with *Maheno* of the Union Line to provide a weekly departure schedule. *Ulimaroa* was the Huddart Parker representative in the horseshoe route from Sydney to New Zealand ports, Hobart and Melbourne, with a departure every fourth week. This service offered weekly departures from each terminal port, the other three ships being used at that time being *Manuka*, *Maunganui* and *Moeraki* of the Union Line.

At this time, *Wimmera* was being used by Huddart Parker on their regular service between Sydney and Hobart, while *Zealandia* was on the coastal trade between Sydney, Melbourne, Adelaide and Fremantle, but *Westralia* was not included in any advertising.

On 4 August 1914, the day Britain declared war on Germany, *Riverina* was in Auckland, and due to depart from Sydney again on 12 August, while *Ulimaroa* was on its way from Wellington to Sydney, being due to depart again on 8 August. Of the Union Line ships, *Maheno* was in Sydney, and left next day as scheduled for Auckland, while the horseshoe service departures were listed as *Warrimoo* on 15 August, followed a week later by *Manuka* and then *Maunganui* on 29 August, with *Manuka* due to leave Melbourne on 5 August on its northbound trip.

Both *Riverina* and *Ulimaroa* left Sydney as planned on the regular routes, with *Ulimaroa* scheduled to leave Melbourne on 26 August for the return trip to Sydney. At first it was thought the war would have no major effect on these trades, but within a few weeks there were some major alterations.

Instead of following the usual horseshoe route back to Sydney, when *Ulimaroa* left Melbourne on 26 August the vessel came up the east coast to Sydney, arriving on 28 August, and leaving the same afternoon for Wellington and Lyttelton only. On the return trip, *Ulimaroa* went back to Wellington, then across to Sydney and down the east coast to Melbourne, departing from there on 15 September for Sydney, Wellington and Lyttelton. This would be the route *Ulimaroa* would operate for the next few months.

Riverina completed its round trip to Auckland as planned, but on 26 August left Sydney bound for Auckland, Gisborne, Napier, Wellington, Lyttelton and Dunedin. Two weeks later, on 9 September, *Westralia* departed Sydney on the same route, enabling *Riverina* to return to the Auckland trade again, with a departure on 23 September. It is surprising that, despite the country being at war, shipping advertisements containing full sailing schedules continued to appear in local newspapers.

The Union Line operation was to be affected to a far greater extent by the start of the war, but at first they were able to maintain most of their services. *Maheno* departed Sydney on 19 August for Auckland as planned, while *Manuka* left on 21 August on the same route as *Ulimaroa*, going to Wellington and Lyttelton only.

With both the Australian and New Zealand governments offering to send troops overseas to assist Britain, it was necessary to find the ships to transport them. The Australian Government opted to requisition British vessels as they arrived in Australian ports, but the New Zealand Government decided to use local vessels, and as a result the Union Line saw both *Maunganui* and *Tahiti* requisitioned for service as troop transports in October 1914; a month later *Willochra*, an Australian liner on charter to the Union Line, was also taken over. This meant the Union Line had to juggle their fleet to be able to maintain not only their trans-Tasman services, but also those across the Pacific to Vancouver and San Francisco.

Ulimaroa (WSS Victoria).

By May 1915 the Huddart Parker ships were operating a variety of services across the Tasman. *Riverina* departed Sydney on 20 May and again on 2 June for Auckland, Wellington and Lyttelton. Meanwhile, *Westralia* left Sydney for Hobart on 18 May, then on 27 May departed for Auckland, Wellington and Lyttelton, and on 16 June left on a round trip to Auckland. *Riverina* then made two round trips to Auckland, departing on 15 July and 29 July.

Ulimaroa left Sydney on 17 June for Wellington and Lyttelton, but on returning to Sydney did not continue to Melbourne instead departing on 29 June on a round trip to Hobart, which was followed by a voyage from Sydney on 8 July to Wellington and Lyttelton. On 20 July *Ulimaroa* again left Sydney for Hobart.

There was also a service being operated from Melbourne to New Zealand by *Wimmera*, with a departure every third week for Hobart, then Wellington, Lyttelton, Dunedin and Bluff, back to Hobart and Melbourne.

At the same time, the Union Line had *Moeraki* and *Manuka* operating in conjunction with *Ulimaroa* on the route to Wellington and Lyttelton. The service to Auckland was being advertised for *Niagara* and *Makura*, on the first leg of their route to Vancouver, while *Maitai* was going to Wellington on its way to San Francisco.

Of other Union Line ships, *Maheno* had been requisitioned and converted into the first New Zealand hospital ship, leaving Wellington on 15 July in this role for Egypt and Britain. A few weeks later *Marama* was also taken over for duty as a hospital ship, and over subsequent months more Union Line vessels would be taken over for military service, apart from those operating on the routes across the Pacific, which were considered to be of national importance.

As 1915 drew to a close, *Riverina* remained permanently on the service between Sydney and Auckland, with the Union Line having offering this route on the first and last legs of the voyages by *Makura* and *Niagara* between Sydney and Vancouver. *Ulimaroa* was on the route from Sydney to Wellington and Lyttelton, with a round trip from Sydney to Hobart between each voyage to New Zealand.

The two Union Line ships, *Manuka* and *Moeraki*, were also operating a round trip to Hobart from Sydney in the middle of their round trips from Lyttelton and Wellington. From Melbourne the Union Line was operating *Mokoia* to Bluff, Dunedin, Lyttelton and Wellington.

On 1 December 1915, Huddart Parker advertising for their trans-Tasman services showed that both *Riverina* and *Ulimaroa* were due to leave Sydney on 2 December. The advertisement included the following statement:

All male passengers to New Zealand between the ages of 18 and 45 years, inclusive, per S.S. *Riverina* and *Ulimaroa*, sailing hence for Auckland and Wellington respectively on Thursday next, Dec 2nd, and following voyages, are notified that Permits must be obtained from the Department of External Affairs to enable them to leave the Commonwealth

A few days later this wording was modified to state that men in the age bracket identified would be 'required to obtain passports from the Department of External affairs before booking passages'.

Going into 1916, both *Riverina*, under the command of Captain Entwhistle, and *Ulimaroa*, with Captain Wyllie in command, were due to depart Sydney on 13 January on regular voyages to New Zealand. Both ships left as scheduled, with *Ulimaroa* arriving in Wellington on 17 January, and due to continue to Lyttelton as usual. However, *Ulimaroa* was requisitioned suddenly while in Wellington, and the voyage terminated.

On 19 January 1916, in the Huddart Parker advertisement in the *Sydney Morning Herald*, *Ulimaroa* was shown as being due to leave Sydney for Hobart on 25 January, then on 3 February departing again for Wellington and Lyttelton, and on 15 February for Hobart, while *Riverina* was scheduled to make its next departure for Auckland on 27 January, and again on 10 February.

In the next day's *Sydney Morning Herald*, the Huddart Parker sailing schedule showed *Riverina* making the voyages previously arranged for *Ulimaroa*, while *Victoria* was now to operate the voyages previously to be made by *Riverina* to Auckland. Beneath was the following statement:

Passengers booked per *Ulimaroa* to Hobart on Jan. 25th and to New Zealand on Feb. 3rd are notified this vessel has been withdrawn and the *Riverina* substituted. The sailing for Auckland on Jan. 27th will be undertaken by the *Victoria* in lieu of *Riverina*.

A brief report in the shipping section of the same issue stated that *Ulimaroa* had been taken over in Wellington by the New Zealand Government, and the return voyage to Sydney was cancelled. The vessel was repainted in camouflage colours, and allocated pennant number HMNZT 42, though this number would change with every voyage the ship made.

Still under the command of Captain W. J. Wyllie, over the next three years *Ulimaroa* made seven trips from New Zealand to either Egypt or Britain. The vessel also made one trip from Egypt to India and back, carrying Indian soldiers.

On its first voyage with New Zealand troops,

Ulimaroa as HMNZT 42 (Dallas Hogan collection).

Ulimaroa departed New Zealand on 5 February 1916, stopped at Albany on 15 February for coal, departing two days later on the way to Egypt, the troops disembarking at Suez on 12 March. The vessel then voyaged back to New Zealand, stopping at Albany on 11 April.

A second voyage to Egypt, with *Ulimaroa* as HMNZT 51, departed New Zealand on 1 May 1916, calling at Albany on 10 May, with the troops disembarking at Suez on 9 June. On its way back to New Zealand, *Ulimaroa* stopped at Albany again on 7 July.

The third voyage with New Zealand troops was made by *Ulimaroa* as HMT 17, departing on 29 July 1916, with a stopover at Albany on 8 August, leaving two days later. The troops disembarked at Plymouth on 28 September.

During 1917, *Ulimaroa* made two more trooping voyages from New Zealand, the first, as HMNZT 74, leaving Wellington on 19 January and Lyttelton on 21 January, with a call at Albany on 1 February. *Ulimaroa* then crossed the Indian Ocean to Cape Town, where it remained in port until a convoy was assembled, departing on 24 February. The other vessels in the convoy were the *Orcoma*, *Omrah*, *Miltiades*, *Anchises* and *Walmer Castle*.

The convoy stopped at Freetown in Sierra Leone for coaling on 9 March, leaving on 12 March for England, arriving at Plymouth on 27 March. *Ulimaroa* again stopped at Albany on 5 August on its next voyage to Britain with New Zealand troops.

On 8 February 1918, *Ulimaroa* departed New Zealand on another trooping voyage to Britain, this time as HMNZT 100, arriving in Liverpool on 29 March. The vessel did not depart Liverpool until 1 May, bringing a contingent of troops back to New Zealand, where they arrived on 14 June. *Ulimaroa* left New Zealand again on 27 July on its final voyage to Europe with troops.

The Tasman services being operated by the Union Line were also affected by the withdrawal of ships for military duty. With *Mokoia* being requisitioned in January 1916, the Union Line placed *Paloona*, originally the *Zealandia* of Huddart Parker, on the service from Melbourne to Hobart, Bluff, Dunedin, Lyttelton and Wellington, her first departure being on 26 January.

In order to move the passengers and cargo that had been booked on *Ulimaroa*, Huddart Parker sent *Victoria* to Wellington, from where it departed on 22 January, arriving in Sydney on 26 January. The same day the following item appeared in the shipping section of the *Sydney Morning Herald*:

Messrs Huddart Parker Limited notify that on and after January 28 their steamers *Westralia* and *Victoria* will leave Sydney fortnightly for Auckland, and thence via ports to Dunedin. Thursday as sailing day will be discontinued, and these vessels in future will sail hence on Wednesday.

In the sailing schedule published that day, *Victoria* was shown as scheduled to depart Sydney on Friday, 28 January, one day later than originally scheduled for *Riverina* to go to Auckland, followed by *Westralia* from Sydney on Wednesday, 9 February. Meanwhile, *Riverina* had left Sydney on 25 January on a round trip to Hobart, then on 3 February began operating from Sydney to Wellington and Lyttelton.

In April 1916, Huddart Parker again altered their service to the North Island of New Zealand, with the two ships only going from Sydney to Auckland, Gisborne and Napier. The first departure on this shorter route was taken by *Victoria* on Wednesday, 20 April, but *Westralia* left Sydney on Tuesday, 3 May, for the same ports. *Riverina* continued to operate from Sydney to Wellington and Lyttelton, and also made a round trip to Hobart between voyages. From Melbourne, *Wimmera* remained on a service to Hobart, then Wellington and South Island ports, with a departure every third week.

In January 1917, Huddart Parker was still able to maintain most of their passenger services on a regular basis. On the Australian coast, *Zealandia* was running between Sydney and Fremantle, with a departure every fourth week, the first for the year being on 5 January. *Riverina* left Sydney for Hobart on 16 January, and continued to make a return trip to Hobart from Sydney every third week between its voyages to Wellington and Lyttelton, the next departing on 25 January. *Westralia* and *Victoria* were operating a service from Sydney to Auckland, Gisborne and Napier, with a departure every second week, with *Westralia* leaving on 11 January and *Victoria* on 24 January. *Wimmera* was on a circular route from Melbourne every third week, being due to depart on 6 January and 27 January, but now omitting Hobart, going directly to Wellington, then Lyttelton, Dunedin and Bluff, and directly back to Melbourne.

For the first ten weeks of the year the various schedules were advertised daily in local newspapers. On 13 March it was advertised that *Wimmera* would be leaving Sydney on 21 March, *Riverina* on 29 March and *Victoria* on 4 April on their various routes to New Zealand. However, on 14 March this changed, with the New Zealand trades being advertised only as 'steamer early', though the departure dates for *Zealandia* to

Fremantle continued to be shown, as well as the trips by *Riverina* to Hobart.

For the rest of 1917 the schedules of the ships trading to New Zealand ceased to be advertised, and their arrivals and departures were no longer reported in the shipping section, though the movements of coastal vessels continued to be shown.

On Saturday, 11 August 1917, crew members aboard the coastal liner *Indarra*, owned by the Australian United Steam Navigation Company, also members of the Seamen's Union, refused to allow the ship to leave Melbourne due to non-union volunteers doing some of the work on board. The strike quickly spread to other coastal vessels in Melbourne, and when the ship owners tried to replace the strikers with non-union workers, the strike spread nationally, and members of more unions involved in shipping became involved. Eventually the entire waterfront around Australia came to a standstill, and as Australian-owned vessels arrived in port their crews joined the strike.

Zealandia, which had left Sydney on 4 August, became strikebound in Fremantle, and as each of the Huddart Parker vessels operating services across the Tasman Sea arrived back in Australia, their crews also walked off. From Monday, 13 August, the advertisements for Huddart Parker stated 'All steamer sailings cancelled meantime owing to strike'. The strike was not resolved until 18 October, and by the following day Australian flag ships were starting to move again. Just when the trans-Tasman service resumed is not certain, as there was no notification in the local papers.

Going into 1918, Huddart Parker was still able to maintain a three-ship service across the Tasman Sea, with *Wimmera* operating between Sydney and Auckland, *Riverina* running to Wellington from Sydney, and *Westralia* on the route from Melbourne to Wellington. Despite the war still being in progress, the sailing schedules for all three ships were again advertised regularly in the daily newspapers. The company also had *Zealandia* operating regular voyages between Sydney and Fremantle.

Victoria, another passenger vessel owned by Huddart Parker, was sold in January 1918 to the recently formed company, China-Australia Mail Steamship Line, being delivered to them on 25 April 1918. At that time the vessel was registered in Australia under the ownership of W. J. Lumb Liu, an Australian Chinese who was managing director of the China-Australia company. The new owners had intended to operate the vessel, without a change of

Victoria was sold by Huddart Parker in 1918 (Dallas Hogan collection).

name, on a service from Australia to Hong Kong, but before this could happen *Victoria* was requisitioned by the Australian Government, and operated under their control on various Australian coastal trades until October 1919.

With *Ulimaroa*, *Zealandia* and *Victoria* already removed from their passenger fleet, the likelihood of losing one of the remaining ships engaged in the Tasman trade probably was not uppermost in the minds of the Huddart Parker management, as the area continued to seem quite remote from the major war zones. It was therefore an enormous shock when, in August 1918, news was received that *Wimmera* had sunk after striking a mine laid by a German surface raider.

Wimmera departed Sydney on 17 August on a regular voyage to Auckland, arriving there on 21 August. At 11.30 on the morning of Tuesday, 25 August, *Wimmera* left Auckland on the return voyage to Sydney, having on board 158 persons, both passengers and crew. Several days earlier, a German minefield had been detected off the northern tip of North Island, a fact of which Captain H. J. Kell of *Wimmera* must have been aware. The vessel headed north to round Cape Reinga, but at 5.15 the next morning, 26 August, struck a mine and quickly sank.

News of the sinking was not released in Australia until 28 August, when the Navy Department issued a statement, published in the *Sydney Morning Herald* on 29 August, that commenced:

> Early on the morning of the 26th inst. the steamer *Wimmera*, on a voyage from Auckland to Sydney, was sunk by striking a mine. It is known that there are 85 survivors out of a total of 158.

Huddart Parker released a statement on the evening of 28 August, also reported the next day, which began:

> The *Wimmera* left Auckland, bound for Sydney, at 11.30 am on Tuesday, 25 inst., with 80 passengers, mails, 400 tons of cargo, and five horses. From reports received she struck a mine, and sank shortly afterwards at 5.15 am on Wednesday, 26th inst.

Information had reached the owners in Melbourne at 11.40 on Wednesday evening, and was to the effect that the *Wimmera* had been sunk by a mine at 5.15 am on that day; 85 persons, it was stated, 'were known to have landed, but whether there has been loss of life or not is not yet known. Trawlers are searching for the other boats'.

Apart from considerable speculation regarding finding more survivors, and details of the captain and some officers on *Wimmera*, and a full list of the crew, no extra news was provided that day. On a lighter note, the following small item also appeared:

> The latest advices concerning Desert Gold, the champion New Zealand mare, are to the effect that she will most likely leave New Zealand in August for the spring meetings. It is improbable that she was on the *Wimmera*.

On Monday, 1 July 1918, the *Sydney Morning Herald* carried the following, and also created some confusion as to the actual number of persons that had been on board the doomed ship:

> At an early hour this morning the Department of the Navy received the following cable message from the Naval Department of New Zealand: 'Thirty-one additional persons have been rescued, making a total of 116 in all. The remainder, about 25 in number, are presumed to have been lost. The search for them has so far been fruitless.'

It will be noted that the total number of passengers and crew obtained by adding the total number of rescued given in the latest message to those supposed to have been lost is 141, which is 17 short of the 158 stated in the earlier messages to have been on the vessel.

According to advices received by Huddart Parker, there were 70 passengers and 78 members of the crew on the *Wimmera*: 'A list of the officers and crew received from Sydney contains 72 names'.

There was a list of the names of those known to be missing, which comprised eight female passengers, two of whom had infants also posted as missing, and sixteen members of the crew, including the master, Captain Kell, the chief officer and third officer, the wireless operator, two engineers, the chief steward, three stewards and three stewardesses, two seamen and a fireman.

In the same issue of the *Sydney Morning Herald*, it was noted that the *Wimmera* had been carrying '56 bags and 19 hampers of mail', and the following small item also appeared:

> S. Henderson, who is one of the saved, is a leading New Zealand cross-country jockey. He was coming to Melbourne to ride Glue Pot in the V.R.C. Grand National Steeplechase, and John Bunny in his engagement. Glue Pot died at Flemington on Thursday. Henderson won the Great Northern Steeplechase at Auckland in 1917 on Glue Pot.

On the evening of 8 July, the Union Line passenger vessel *Manuka* arrived in Sydney, and among the passengers on board were many members of the crew of *Wimmera*, along with some of the passengers. It was only then that the full story of the sinking became known in Australia, being reported next day in the *Sydney Morning Herald*:

The *Wimmera* left Auckland for Sydney at 10 am on Tuesday, June 25, having on board about 76 passengers and a crew of 75 all told. Early the following morning there were two explosions at an interval of a few seconds. The social hall was smashed to pieces, and the mainmast carried away, the latter carrying with it the wireless apparatus, thus shutting off all chances of calling for help. The operator, however, persevered in his endeavours to send out the S.O.S., and lost his life.

Two minutes after the explosion the ship was in total darkness. For some time she rode on an even keel, and then listed to port. The heavy seas almost immediately righted her, and then, pausing momentarily, she threw her bows 50 ft in the air, and made her plunge, stern first, into the depths. With her went her commander, Captain Kell, the first officer, chief steward, and others. It was an awesome spectacle for those of the passengers and crew who, in boats, were near enough to witness it.

There was not the slightest panic when the explosion awoke the sleeping passengers. They and the crew are reported to have acted quickly, but quietly, and without confusion.

The verdict of the men who were also saved was that the behaviour of the women was excellent. They acted with coolness; in the hour of supreme danger they showed no signs of panic, but did what they were directed to do. One lady, Mrs. E. R. Dunn, of Melbourne, took the bearings of her cabin when she went on board at Auckland. The explosion extinguished all the lights, but Mrs Dunn groped her way along the corridors until she found an exit to the deck, and also piloted another lady to safety. She had saved some clothing from her cabin, and on reaching the deck gave her woollen coat to a little child who was with her mother waiting for a boat. The child and her mother are among the missing, and it is believed they got into the boat which was stove in against the ship. One of the things Mrs. Dunn saved was a Military Cross awarded to her son, the late Captain F. H. Dunn.

This was followed by several eyewitness accounts from survivors

Mr. William Francis Sedgebeer, commercial traveller representing C. Crowley and Sons, Queen Victoria Markets, Sydney, who was returning to Sydney on the Wimmera, was one of the passengers to arrive on the Manuka.

'There were two distinct explosions,' he said, 'just at 5.17 am. They occurred under the stern of the vessel, and the dense fumes that rose immediately were so extremely nauseating that they made nearly all the passengers ill. Though naturally there was commotion, there was no confusion; there was not the least panic, though the ship was in complete darkness two minutes after the explosions. There was no rushing for the boat, and the crew behaved magnificently.

'With the first explosion the mainmast was carried away, displacing the aerial. The wireless operator, however, knowing nothing of what had happened, continued to the last his endeavours to send S.O.S. signals, and went down with the ship. When last seen he was entering his office as the ship made her final plunge, stern first, beneath the waves less than twenty minutes after the explosion.

'A very high sea was running, which made the launching of the boats very difficult. Five were launched, but one of them – the third – was swamped, and all who were in her were drowned. I was in one of the three boats that landed in Tom Bowling's Bay. We had been ten hours in the boats. The fourth boat, after being afloat for 30 hours, landed north of Maunganui Bay.

'We who landed at Tom Bowling's Bay had further trying experiences before we reached comfortable quarters. We landed at the foot of a precipitous cliff, 10 ft to 20 ft high, and up this we had to climb – men, women and children – and every one of us was barefooted.

'A Maori who saw our boats approaching took us for Germans about to take possession of New Zealand. It was fortunate for us that he made that mistake, for he raced off to inform Mr. Murdoch Munro, a large pastoralist, who lived 15 miles inland. Mr. Munro, however, ridiculed the idea of a German invasion, and induced the Maori to accompany him to the beach. Had it not been for this it is impossible to imagine how long the castaways would have been awaiting help.

'However, we had a difficult walk on our bare feet to Mr. Munro's station homestead, and there were treated in a manner I shall not easily forget. The women and children behaved splendidly through it all; their fortitude was magnificent

'Captain Kell,' Mr. Sedgebeer continued, 'with the chief officer, the third officer, and the chief steward, went down. None of them attempted to get into a boat; they elected to go down with their ship.'

The ordeal suffered by the survivors in the boat that was at sea for over thirty hours was graphically described by one of the passengers.

The ill-fated *Wimmera* departing Melbourne (WSS Victoria).

'When the explosion came,' said Mrs. W. G. Giblin, a Wellington lady who was coming to Australia on a holiday trip with her husband and two children, 'we were all thrown out of bed. We knew at once that something dreadful had happened, and made for the deck. I had gone to bed partially dressed. The children were only in their night clothes, and I did not wait to dress them. After we got on deck my husband went back and got two rugs, and these were a veritable Godsend afterwards. There was no panic or confusion as the boats were being lowered, although Mr. Giblin, who was carrying the little girl, slipped and nearly went overboard. The children were wonderfully good, and as for the women, I never saw anything like it. They were as calm and self-possessed as if being wrecked were a common occurrence. We pushed off from the side of the ship and had hardly got clear when the *Wimmera* went down. The moon was just setting, and there was light enough for us to see, but the cries of the horses were terrible.

'There was a strong wind, and every now and again cold showers of rain. There were six women and my two little ones in our party, besides the men, and we lay in the bottom of the boat all that day and night, shivering with cold. There was water in the boat and we got wet. I tried to rest on a pile of ropes but it was very hard.' Mrs. Giblin bared her arm, showing the flesh chafed and bruised. 'But there were others much worse off than I,' she observed. 'There was one old lady with nothing on but her nightdress. We gave her one of our rugs, and she took my little boy and crouched in the locker at the head of the boat with him. The crew took turns at the oars and one of them had only a thin coat on. His feet were bleeding and his head had been hurt, and I gave him my raincoat.'

The refugees kept watch all that day, praying for rescue, but night fell without relief. 'I do not know how we lived through the cold and misery of that night,' said Mrs. Giblin. 'I was aching all over with stiffness and cold, and a lot of us were seasick. One of the crew had some tobacco. He shared it with the men, and next morning, when there was only a tiny bit left, he rolled it into a cigarette, and they all had a few whiffs. All the next day we kept on the lookout, and it rained and blew until we were almost frozen. Biscuits were passed round, but none of us seemed to have the heart to eat, although the men tried to cheer us up. There was plenty of water, but we did not drink much.

'At last, in the middle of the afternoon, when we were almost in despair at the thought of having to spend another night in the boat, we came to land. The waves were breaking high on the rocks, and for a while I felt afraid, but then we struck a bay where it was not so rough and the men brought the boat in safely. They built a big fire on the beach, and we stood round it and tried to dry our clothes. Four others climbed up the hill and found their way to a Maori settlement, and in the evening between seven and eight, some Maoris came back for us.

'We were so thankful that when someone started "Praise God from Whom All Blessings Flow", we all joined in, and sang as we never had before. Two of the Maoris carried my little ones, and the girl was so tired she went to sleep on his shoulder. I do not know how far we had to walk, but it seemed a long way. The path was only a goat track cut in the cliffs, and most of us had bare feet. The pain was almost unendurable, and we half-dead from exposure and exhaustion. Someone had found a quilt, and with this they bandaged the cut feet of the steward, so he managed to get along.

'We got to the Maori settlement about ten o'clock, and I shall never forget the wonderful kindness of the natives, who had a fine meal of hot coffee and tea, and cakes and scones ready. The Maori women took the clothes off their backs and gave them to those of our party who had so little. Mr. and Mrs. Stacey, the schoolmaster and his wife, were also most kind. We got to bed about midnight, sleeping in one of the native houses.'

This was the end of the story of two days and a night in the boat. They landed at Okitunia Bay, near Manganui, late in the afternoon of June 28. Next morning the party, after a Maori breakfast and gifts of tobacco from the Maoris for the men, were taken on board a launch and carried to Manganui. 'All the town turned out to welcome us,' said Mrs. Giblin, 'and there were dinner, hot baths and clothes for all. We women went to bed, and rested all the afternoon, the people at the hotel and boarding-house, as well as private residents, showing us great kindness.'

The courage of Captain Kell and the others who lost their lives in the sinking was reported by Mr M'lean, a member of the crew, who was in No 2 boat, the last to get away from the ship:

When we launched her there were only nine remaining on the ship, as far as I could see. Amongst them were the captain, the chief officer, the third officer, and one male passenger, the rest being firemen and seamen. Someone had to remain on the ship to lower the boat, but we were ordered into the boat by the captain, who, with the chief and third officers, refused to leave the ship. I could not see in the darkness, but they evidently lowered the boat, which was launched successfully. We expected the captain and officers to slide down the falls to the boat, and we called up to them. In reply we heard the captain call out, 'Get away and pick up anybody you can'. This was the last we saw or heard of the captain or chief officer. The third officer evidently jumped off the steamer, for we heard him calling from the water. We tried to find him, but could not do it in the darkness. We were drifting to leeward, and could not pull against the heavy sea and wind. We cannot sufficiently express our admiration of the heroic conduct of the captain and these officers. We remained in the vicinity for some time, but found no sign of survivors. Looking around we saw No. 3 boat signalling to us. We pulled after her, and Jones, the seaman in charge, asked us to stand by in

This painting of *Wimmera* sinking was sold as a postcard (Dallas Hogan collection).

order to render any assistance if his boat, which had 37 people on board, got into difficulties. It was impossible to transfer any of them to our boat in the heavy seas.

There were many stories of individual acts of courage by members of the crew and some passengers, including that of one elderly lady:

When the passengers were being taken off, Mrs. Gould, an old lady of nearly 70 years, offered to stay on board so that some of the younger women might be saved. 'I have lived my life,' she said. She also remarked that the lives of younger women were more valuable than hers.

Her offer was not accepted. She was taken on board No. 3 boat, and landed. On the rough journey along the track to Wachuahua, without boots, and with very little clothing, she bore up wonderfully, and her spirits helped to keep up those of the party.

A total of 27 persons lost their lives in the sinking, including the captain, chief officer and chief steward, six female passengers and three stewardesses. In addition all the mails and cargo was lost, as well as five thoroughbred horses being sent to Australia for the racing season.

An official report released later by Huddart Parker Limited stated, 'The records show that fine discipline on the vessel at the time of the disaster, the comparatively small number of lives lost, and the fact that Captain Kell remained with his ship till the last and gave his life in so doing, were in accordance with the best traditions of the British Mercantile Marine'.

After the war it was ascertained that *Wimmera* had run into a minefield laid by the German commerce raider *Wolff*, a vessel that caused considerable problems in the waters around Australia and New Zealand until it was captured.

The sinking of the ship was a particularly severe blow for Huddart Parker Limited, as they were not able to claim compensation from the Commonwealth Government, which had only recently introduced a new scheme covering war risks, under which merchant vessels were only covered against loss by enemy action when within Australian territorial waters. At the time it sank, *Wimmera* was valued at about £150,000, and a major portion of the insurance was carried by the company itself. So on top of losing their ship, the company had to carry a considerable financial loss.

The sudden loss also created a problem for Huddart Parker as far as maintaining a service between Sydney and Auckland was concerned, for there was no ship available as a replacement. *Wimmera* had been due to depart Sydney again on 3 July, but for some time the company only stated there would be a 'steamer early' in the advertisements. In fact, it would be almost three months before Huddart Parker would be able to resume their service to Auckland, and then on a much reduced schedule.

Riverina was operating a combined schedule of services to both Wellington and Hobart from Sydney, with a departure roughly every twenty days on each route. It was not until 1 September 1918 that Huddart Parker began advertising that *Riverina* would be making a voyage to Auckland, departing Sydney on 26 September. On 8 September, *Riverina* departed Sydney for Wellington, followed by a departure on 17 September to Hobart, then the vessel made its first voyage to Auckland in several years, followed by another trip to Wellington, departing Sydney on 17 October.

On 11 November 1918, the day the Great War, as it was then known, came to an end, *Riverina* arrived in Auckland on a voyage from Sydney, and was due to leave there on 17 November to return to Sydney. *Riverina* was then scheduled to leave Sydney for Hobart on 19 November and 23 November, and depart for Wellington on 28 November. *Westralia* had been due to leave on a voyage from Melbourne to Wellington on 14 November, but was now only advertised as due to leave Melbourne again for New Zealand 'early'.

7

The 1920s

The end of World War I did not bring about an immediate resumption of regular passenger services across the Tasman Sea. It would be some time before the surviving liners taken over for military duty were all returned to their owners and able to resume commercial service.

Of the four vessels Huddart Parker Limited had been operating to New Zealand in August 1914, *Ulimaroa* had been taken over by the New Zealand Government in 1916 for duty as a troop transport, *Victoria* was sold in January 1918, and *Wimmera* had been sunk in June 1918. *Riverina* had not been affected, and remained on the Tasman trade throughout the conflict, being joined by *Westralia*.

However, there were to be major changes on the Tasman trade soon after the war ended. On 15 November 1914, *Riverina* was advertised as leaving Sydney 'early' for Auckland and Wellington, while the next day it was shown as due to leave Sydney for Wellington on 28 November. On 20 November, the advertisements showed only a 'steamer' due to leave for Wellington 'early', while *Riverina* was shown as departing Sydney on 29 November for Fremantle.

Riverina arrived back in Sydney from Auckland on 20 November, made two voyages as scheduled to Hobart, and on 29 November left Sydney on a voyage to Melbourne, Adelaide and Fremantle. This was followed by a second departure from Sydney on 4 January 1919 to Fremantle, and a further voyage in March. At the same time, *Westralia* was also taken off the Tasman trade, and on 22 November arrived in Sydney to take over the trade between Sydney and Hobart, departing on 27 November and again on 7 December. This left Huddart Parker with no representation at all on the trans-Tasman trade.

Several months later, on 22 March 1919, Huddart Parker again began advertising services across the Tasman, with *Riverina* due to depart Sydney on 5 April for Wellington, and for Auckland on 25 April, while *Westralia* was due to leave Melbourne for Wellington on 27 March and again on 23 April. However, a special note attached to the advertisement stated, 'Passengers must attend at Quarantine Department two days before sailing and obtain Quarantine Permits in addition to ordinary Permits'.

This notice was due to the influenza epidemic then raging through Europe, which had been brought to Australia and New Zealand by returning soldiers, and was beginning to affect people in both countries. The New Zealand Government was particularly concerned about preventing its spread through the Dominion, and decided to impose restrictions on passengers arriving from Australia.

Riverina completed its voyage to Wellington in early April as planned, but the 25 April voyage to Auckland was cancelled. In their advertising on Tuesday, 29 April, Huddart Parker included the following statement: 'Owing to the New Zealand Government's action in regard to passengers from Australia landing in the Dominion, Messrs Huddart Parker & Co have decided to divert the steamer *Riverina* from the Sydney–Wellington run and despatch her for Hobart. She leaves for that port at 2 pm on Thursday. No passengers will be carried.'

Riverina left Sydney on 29 April to go to Newcastle to take on coal bunkers, then returned to Sydney two days later to make the scheduled departure for Hobart, carrying only cargo.

Just when it seemed that things could not get any worse, a mass meeting of Australian seamen in Sydney on 20 May 1919 decided to call a strike to support their claim for better working conditions and pay on the coastal services. As Australian-manned ships began arriving at their home port, their crews walked off, and the ships were laid up. Among the vessels affected by this action were *Riverina* and *Westralia*, which were left idle in Sydney and Melbourne respectively.

Riverina remained on the Tasman trade in the early 1920.s

For over two months no headway was made in attempts to settle the strike, but in the middle of August 1919 there were signs that the parties were about to reach a settlement. At one time there was even an announcement that all ships would be manned again on 18 August. This did not happen, as there were several issues still to be sorted out, but at mass meetings held on 25 August the men agreed to an immediate return to work.

Huddart Parker decided to send *Riverina* on a special trip to Hobart, departing Sydney on 30 August, after which, with the influenza threat now passed, the vessel would resume its place on the trade across the Tasman Sea. There was no regular schedule in place for several weeks, and departures were subject to change. For example, *Riverina* was first advertised to depart Sydney on 9 October for Wellington, but this was put back to 15 October. The next departure was not until 6 November, followed by 27 November and then 17 December, all going only to Wellington.

The service between Melbourne and Wellington was also able to recommence, with *Westralia* departing about every four weeks. The ship left Melbourne on 10 October, then 1 November, 27 November and 18 December.

Although almost all of the vessels the Union Steam Ship Company of New Zealand had been operating across the Tasman in 1914 were taken over for military duty, none were lost. During 1919, as their passenger liners were gradually released from government service and refitted for commercial trades, the Union Line was slowly able to resume regular services across the Tasman between New Zealand and Australia. However, one pre-war route that was not resumed was the famous 'horseshoe service'; the Union Line opted instead to run several direct services from Sydney or Melbourne to Auckland and Wellington.

The Union Line service from Lyttelton and Wellington to Sydney was being operated by the sister ships *Moeraki* and *Manuka*, whose schedule worked in conjunction with *Riverina*. In between each voyage, *Moeraki* and *Manuka* were also programmed to make a voyage from Sydney to Hobart and back, thus providing a weekly service on that route.

One of the Huddart Parker vessels that had been taken over for military duty, *Zealandia*, was also able to return to commercial service at the end of 1919.

In November 1918, *Zealandia* departed Liverpool with returning Australian troops, arriving in Sydney on 10 January 1919. Departing on 22 February, *Zealandia* steamed to Bombay, where British troops were embarked and transported home. On 6 May 1919, *Zealandia* departed Plymouth with a full complement of Australian troops returning home, arriving in Sydney on 1 July, and shortly afterward returned to Huddart Parker. After being reconditioned for a return to commercial service at Cockatoo Island in Sydney, *Zealandia* departed Sydney on 13 December 1919 on her first post-war voyage to Fremantle, the route on which she would primarily serve for the next years.

On 20 December 1919, a strike involving marine engineers began in Victoria and soon spread to other states. With no immediate resolution in sight, the Australian coastal trade began to grind to a halt as engineers walked off their ships when they arrived in their home port. The strike soon spread to include Australian-flag ships operating on overseas trades, with the result that *Riverina* had to be laid up, and the Huddart Parker service across the Tasman Sea came to a halt yet again.

The Tasman service was maintained through to the end of 1919, and into the early months of 1920, by the two New Zealand ships on their own, as they were not affected by the strike in Australia.

As the strike dragged into January 1920, more and more Australian-owned vessels were forced out of service, and on 3 February the *Sydney Morning Herald* was reporting that 101 vessels, or 303 090 gross tons of coastal shipping, were sitting idle in ports around the country. The strike was not resolved until 26 February, following which crews were quickly signed on and ships began moving again.

The day the strike was settled, Huddart Parker was able to secure a crew and reactivate *Riverina*, which departed Sydney for Wellington on 27 February. A few days later, Huddart Parker was able to return *Ulimaroa* to the Tasman trade.

Ulimaroa had made a number of voyages to Egypt and Britain with New Zealand troops during the war, and after the Armistice was used to repatriate both Australian and New Zealand troops. Departing Britain on 13 March 1919, the vessel arrived in Fremantle on 8 April, and Albany two days later, departing the next day for Sydney, where it arrived on 25 April, still in dazzle paint.

Ulimaroa made its final departure in this capacity from Suez on 30 June 1919, calling at Colombo before steaming directly to Albany, where it arrived on 27 July. After taking on coal, *Ulimaroa* left Albany the next day, arriving in Auckland on 8 August. The vessel went on to Wellington to land more returning troops, and was then released from military duty. *Ulimaroa* arrived back in Sydney on Tuesday, 26 August, immediately being sent to the Cockatoo Island Dockyard for refitting, work commencing on 1 September. During its war career, *Ulimaroa* steamed 225 000 miles/360 000 km and carried 16 000 troops.

After her refit, *Ulimaroa* entered the Woolwich Dock in Sydney for final painting on 25 February 1920, and the next day was handed back to Huddart Parker. On 27 February *Ulimaroa* left the Woolwich Dock, and voyaged up the coast to Newcastle to take on bunkers, returning to Sydney on 3 March. *Ulimaroa* departed Sydney on 4 March 1920 on her first post-war voyage, to Auckland.

Huddart Parker returned to the Hobart trade when *Riverina* departed Sydney on 10 March 1920 for Tasmania, but on her return to Sydney resumed

Ulimaroa, still in camouflage colours, in Sydney Harbour in April 1919.

her place on the Tasman trade, with a departure for Auckland on 19 March.

On 18 March, *Ulimaroa* departed Sydney on her first post-war voyage to Wellington and back, which was followed by a voyage to Hobart, leaving Sydney on 29 March. Subsequently *Ulimaroa* operated this combined service once every three weeks, in conjunction with *Moeraki* and *Manuka*. These three vessels now maintained a combined schedule that provided a weekly departure across the Tasman to Wellington from Sydney, and also a weekly return trip to Hobart, departing Sydney every Tuesday.

Riverina continued to operate regular departures from Sydney to Auckland. Very occasionally *Riverina* would also make a voyage to Hobart between her Auckland voyages.

In August 1920 *Manuka* was taken off the trans-Tasman service for overhaul, being replaced by *Moana*, which also made the round trip to Hobart from Sydney between trips to New Zealand. *Manuka* returned to the trade in early September, and was partnered by *Moana* while *Moeraki* was taken off the route. These two and *Ulimaroa* continued the three-weekly schedule until the end of the November, at which time *Moeraki* returned and *Moana* was transferred to other routes.

On Wednesday, 15 December 1920, members of the Marine Stewards & Pantrymen Union decided to start an immediate strike, which affected Australian-owned ships only. *Ulimaroa* had just left on a voyage to New Zealand, but on returning to Sydney had to be laid up when the crew walked off. The ships operated by the Union Steam Ship Company were not affected, so *Manuka* and *Moeraki* were able to continue operating through December 1920 and January and February 1921. It was not until after the strike was settled on 25 February 1921 that *Ulimaroa* was able to return to service.

Ulimaroa, *Manuka* and *Moeraki* continued to provide a weekly connection between Sydney and Hobart between their Tasman trips over the next few months, but major changes were happening on the Australian coastal trades. The introduction of the *Navigation Act* would eventually prevent non-Australian ships from carrying passengers between Australian ports. This would have a major effect on the Union Line operation to Hobart, which was terminated on 30 June 1921.

Moeraki took the last Union Line sailing from Sydney, on 28 June, leaving Hobart on 2 July. When *Ulimaroa* departed Sydney on 5 July it marked the end of the combined Huddart Parker/Union Line weekly service to Hobart. Subsequently *Manuka*, *Moeraki* and *Ulimaroa* operated a combined service across the Tasman from Sydney, though *Ulimaroa*, being under the Australian flag, could have continued making voyages between Sydney and Hobart.

In November 1921 Huddart Parker transferred *Riverina* from the Tasman service to run between Sydney and Hobart on a regular basis. *Riverina* departed Sydney on 22 October on its final voyage to Auckland, arriving there four days later, leaving Auckland for the last time on 29 October, and returning to Sydney on 1 November.

The final trans-Tasman voyage to be made by *Riverina* departed Sydney on 5 November, arriving in Wellington on 9 November and departing two days later, terminating in Sydney on 15 November. On 22 November *Riverina* left Sydney for Hobart, replacing *Westralia* on that route. This left *Ulimaroa* as the sole Huddart Parker representative on the trans-Tasman trade, on which it would now be serving both Auckland and Wellington. *Ulimaroa* departed Sydney on 19 November on its first voyage to Auckland, followed by a 3 December sailing to Wellington, and this pattern of alternate voyages to each port would be followed for the next decade.

Riverina remained on the Hobart service for six years, her career coming to a sudden end when, on the evening of 17 April 1927, the vessel ran aground south of Gabo Island on a trip from Hobart to Sydney. *Riverina* could not be refloated, and was eventually declared a total loss. The upper sections were broken up during 1928 where she lay on the beach, and what remained of the wreck was used as target practice by military aircraft during the Second World War.

Through the rest of the 1920s, *Ulimaroa* was the sole Huddart Parker vessel on the Tasman trade, while the Union Steam Ship Company also operated a reduced number of vessels. *Ulimaroa* seldom made news, but one rough voyage to New Zealand was reported from Auckland in the *Sydney Morning Herald* on 12 July 1928 as follows:

THE ULIMAROA
A Rough Voyage
ARRIVES WITH LIST
Passengers Alarmed

The Huddart Parker steamer *Ulimaroa* arrived 24 hours late as a result of stormy weather experienced all the way from Sydney.

After clearing Sydney Heads on Friday last she encountered a strong south-westerly gale with a high seas on the quarter. This lasted until Cape Maria Van Diemen was reached. Thereafter a southerly gale was experienced to Auckland.

In the early stage of the voyage, the vessel developed

Ulimaroa in the 1920s.

a decided list to port, due to the draining of water from the ballast tanks on the leeward side. This, and the difficulty of firing the boilers, owing to the tossing of the vessel, caused slow steaming. The ship was severely buffeted by tumultuous seas. An unusually heavy sea swept over the promenade deck on Friday, causing havoc and consternation. Port holes on the windward side were burst open, causing the flooding of all cabins along the shelter deck.

There was great alarm among the passengers. Suitcases and other belongings floated in at least a foot of water. Much clothing was spoiled or damaged, one man estimating his loss at £20. The cabins were dried and new bedding was supplied as soon as possible. The rail of the shelter deck was frequently level with the sea, while waves washed over the promenade deck above. The vessel rolled so much on Friday night that there was difficulty in keeping crockery on the tables, and a great quantity was smashed. On arrival today some of the passengers had their first full meal for four days. The engines were stopped for 1½ hours on Sunday, and an hour yesterday for minor repairs. The trouble was not serious. The vessel hove to for an hour off North Cape last night.

Captain Wylie had a most anxious time, with little sleep since leaving Sydney. "It is the worst trip I have had for years," he said. 'Fortunately nothing gave way except a steam pipe casing and a canvas screen.'

A passenger said; 'I was glad when daylight came after the first night. We were all very frightened.'

On Friday night heavy seas washed a sailor against the rails. He was bruised severely, and was unconscious for several minutes. The carpenter and the boatswain narrowly escaped being washed overboard.

On arrival the port ballast tanks were filled, and the vessel regained an even keel. All the passengers arrived well, though weary.

On 20 November 1931 *Ulimaroa* attracted considerable media attention when the most famous racehorse in Australia, Phar Lap, was loaded on board, to be taken to New Zealand for several weeks rest before being put on the *Monowai* and transported to the United States. On 21 November, the *Sydney Morning Herald* reported:

Mr. Tom Woodcock, who has been in charge of the horse for some years, is taking care of him during the trip. Everything possible was done to make Phar Lap comfortable. Padding lined the stall, and sawdust was spread thickly over the floor. Among his travelling companions were two small donkeys.

By this time *Ulimaroa* was nearing the end of its career. On 11 March 1932 it departed Sydney on its final voyage to Wellington, leaving there on 17 March for the return trip. On 24 March the vessel left Sydney on its last eastbound Tasman Sea crossing, arriving in Auckland on 28 March. Leaving Auckland on 1 April, *Ulimaroa* arrived in Sydney

Zealandia joined the Tasman trade in April 1932 (Dallas Hogan collection).

at the end of its final voyage across the Tasman on April 1932, and was laid up in Sydney.

Zealandia was now taken off the Hobart service to begin operating between Sydney and New Zealand ports, the first time this vessel actually ran on the service for which it had been built. Her first voyages departed Sydney on 8 April for Wellington, and on 22 April to Auckland. *Zealandia* maintained the New Zealand service for the rest of the year.

Huddart Parker did not have a replacement passenger vessel available for the Hobart service, so through the winter months it was operated by one of their cargo ships, *Yarra*.

The weather was particularly bad in the Tasman Sea for lengthy periods during September 1932, one storm affecting the *Zealandia*. The vessel left Sydney on 17 September bound for Wellington, and its arrival was reported from Wellington in the *Sydney Morning Herald* on 21 September:

> The steamer *Zealandia* arrived at 9.15 pm yesterday from Sydney, 14 hours late, the voyage having been the worst the vessel had ever encountered in the Tasman Sea. Head winds and huge seas were experienced throughout the trip and the passengers had a very uncomfortable time. The speed was frequently reduced to prevent the propellers racing.
>
> After arrival a fire broke out in Captain Wyllie's room owing to the fusing of a wire. The woodwork was damaged.

With the coming of spring and summer it was essential that a passenger vessel be placed on a regular service between Sydney and Hobart, so *Ulimaroa*, which had been laid up in Sydney through the winter, was reactivated to operate the Hobart trade. Her first departure from Sydney was on 29 October 1932, and she operated two further trips the following month, departing Sydney on 12 November and 26 November. *Ulimaroa* maintained a weekly service to Hobart, departing Sydney every Wednesday through December, and on 4 January 1933, her final arrival in Sydney being on 9 January.

Meanwhile, *Zealandia* had arrived back in Sydney on 27 December 1932 from its last voyage to Wellington, and departed on Friday, 30 December on its final voyage across the Tasman Sea, to Auckland. *Zealandia* arrived back in Sydney on 10 January 1933, and the next day left for Hobart, a trade on which the vessel would be employed permanently for the next seven years.

Zealandia was replaced on the trans-Tasman route by the brand-new *Wanganella*.

8

Wanganella

Wanganella had such a long and successful career on the trans-Tasman trades for Huddart Parker Limited that it is sometimes forgotten the vessel was designed and built for another company to operate a totally different service. The order for the vessel was placed in 1928 by the British & African Steam Navigation Co., which operated as Elder Dempster Line, and had a fleet of passenger liners and cargo ships running between Britain and British outposts in West Africa.

Elder Dempster Line had come under the control of Alfred Jones in 1884, when the founders, Alexander Elder and John Dempster, retired. Jones built the company up into a major operator, but on his death in 1909 the firm was converted from a private to a public company, and in 1910 passed into the control of the Kylsant group of companies. It thus became part of a shipping empire owned by Lord Kylsant, which included Royal Mail Line.

The new owner immediately ordered three new liners for Elder Dempster, with *Abosso* being delivered in 1912, *Appam* in 1913 and *Apapa* in 1914, the first and last both being sunk in 1917. After the war several more ships were built, culminating with the sisters *Accra* and *Apapa* (the second of that name) in 1926 and 1927.

At 9350 gross tons, this pair was much larger than previous vessels owned by the company, but business seemed to be booming, so in 1928 an order was placed for a slightly larger and faster liner with Harland & Wolff at Belfast, which at that time was also part of the Kylsant empire. The new ship would have a more imposing appearance than the previous vessels, with two funnels and a classic modern motorship profile, and provide superior accommodation.

It was intended the new liner would replace the veteran *Appam* and operate in conjunction with *Accra* and *Apapa* on the primary Elder Dempster passenger service from Liverpool to the West African ports of Freetown, Takoradi and Lagos.

In 1926, Lord Kylsant had added the famous White Star Line to his group of British shipping companies, and by 1930 the Kylsant group owned about one-sixth of the world's liner tonnage. However, they were also encountering major financial difficulties, having paid too much for White Star, and now struggling to repay loans obtained from the British Government.

Meanwhile, construction of the new ship had commenced in Belfast, and it was announced the vessel would be named *Achimota*, after an outer suburb of Accra, the capital of the Gold Coast, which today is known as Ghana. Building proceeded on schedule until an unexpected delay occurred. The two Burmeister & Wain 8-cylinder oil engines to be fitted into the vessel, rated at 1305 horsepower, were built under licence by the Harland & Wolff yard at Govan, near Glasgow in Scotland. When completed they were to be loaded onto a small cargo ship operated by Burns & Laird Line for transporting to Belfast.

It has been claimed by some sources that this vessel sank during the voyage to Belfast, but in April 1930 the following item was published in the British magazine *The Motor Ship*:

> The double-acting Harland-B&W machinery which was being transported from Harland & Wolff's works at Glasgow to Belfast for installation in the liner *Achimota*, was lost overboard in handling and it has not been found possible to salvage it. Consequently, the *Achimota*'s completion will be delayed.

What this story indicates is that when the engines were either being loaded in Glasgow or unloaded in Belfast something went terribly wrong, and they went over the side into the water.

Achimota was launched on 17 December 1929, but while it was in the final stages of fitting out the Kylsant financial empire collapsed. Despite this, work continued, with the vessel being completed in

Achimota on sea trials in September 1931.

September 1931, and painted in the Elder Dempster colours, light grey hull and light yellow funnels. Sea trials were run under the supervision of Captain A. H. Crapper, of Elder Dempster Line.

As completed, *Achimota* measured 9576 gross tons, 6526 net tons, with a deadweight capacity of 6238 tons. Hull dimensions were 474 feet/144.4 m length, with a beam of 63.9 feet/19.4 m and a depth of 29.1 feet /6.7 m. The hull was subdivided by seven main bulkheads. There were two full-length decks, with a lower deck in the holds, a long open forward well deck, and a short well decked over aft. The promenade and boat decks in the midships superstructure were both 213 feet/64.9 m long. There were four cargo holds and hatchways, with a small hatch and two derrick posts between the funnels for ship's stores.

The forward funnel was a dummy, with the engine room below the aft funnel. The machinery that drove the twin propellers comprised two Burmeister & Wain type 8-cylinder 4-stroke oil engines, with airless injection and Buchi superchargers, the blowers driven by exhaust-gas turbines. The crankshaft was chain driven. At 105 rpm the engines developed 8500 bhp and gave the ship a maximum speed of 17 knots, with a service speed of 15 knots.

A report on the ship published in the January 1930 issue of *The Motor Ship* included this:

> The public rooms include a first class lounge and reading room in modern Spanish style, and there is a smoking room designed in the Italian manner. A first class smoking lounge – a new feature – is also provided, where a Spanish treatment has been adopted. The general standard of the accommodation was described by another source as 'up to Union-Castle standards'.

The final cost of building the ship came to £520,000, but due to their financial situation Elder Dempster was unable to pay the final instalment, amounting to £300,000, and take delivery of the vessel. *Achimota* was laid up at the Harland & Wolff shipyard in Belfast.

Initially the builders hoped that Elder Dempster would be able to overcome their financial problems and still buy the ship. Alternatively, it could be arranged for Elder Dempster to charter the new liner from them, and place it in service, but the creditors refused to agree to this, as the value of the ship in a brand-new state was greater than the likely return on revenue and possible sale as a second-hand vessel. As a result, *Achimota* remained idle at Belfast.

Meanwhile, an entirely new company, Elder Dempster Lines Ltd, was formed on 15 August 1932 to take over all the assets of the previous company, and *Achimota* was offered for sale at a much reduced price.

It was just at this time that Huddart Parker Limited was considering placing an order for the construction of a new liner to replace *Ulimaroa* on their trans-Tasman service. On 5 April 1932, *Ulimaroa* had arrived in Sydney at the end of her

M.S. "ACHIMOTA."

This view of *Achimota* on sea trials was published in The Motor Ship.

final voyage from New Zealand, and was laid up. Her place on the Tasman route was taken by the slightly larger *Zealandia*, but as she dated from 1910, this was only a temporary arrangement until a new ship could be obtained.

On 1 September 1932, the following article appeared in the *Sydney Morning Herald*:

> It is reported that Huddart, Parker, Ltd is contemplating the purchase of a new motor vessel for its service between Sydney and New Zealand. Although the company will neither confirm nor deny the report, it is understood that their superintendent engineer will leave Melbourne early this month for England, where he will inspect a vessel for which the company is stated to have made an offer.
>
> The vessel concerned is the 10,000 ton British motorship *Achimota*, an up-to-date and well-fitted steel, twin-screw passenger ship, which was completed last year by Harland & Wolff for the British and African Steam Navigation Co Ltd (Elder Dempster and Co. Ltd, managers). The vessel has never been commissioned, and it is stated that the shipping company has not taken delivery from the builders. The British and African Company was one of the Royal Mail Packet group recently acquired by a new company.
>
> If Huddart, Parker, Ltd acquires the *Achimota*, it will have a vessel ideally suited to meet the competition of the new United States-owned Matson liners, *Mariposa* and *Monterey*, which are now engaged in the New Zealand-Australia service, and recently included Melbourne as a port of call in their itinerary. It is not yet known whether the Australian company which now operates the *Zealandia* in the intercolonial service, will also run from Melbourne as well as Sydney, but, if it did so, it would have the advantage of being able to carry passengers between Melbourne and Sydney.

After inspecting *Achimota*, Huddart Parker decided the vessel would fill their requirements admirably, and in September 1932 they purchased the ship. It was an excellent deal for the Australian company, for a ship which cost £520,000 to build was sold for just £345,376.

The November issue of *The Motor Ship* carried a very interesting story, indicating Huddart Parker's early thinking on the name the ship they had just bought would carry. The story carried the headline:

The Sale of the 10,000-ton MS 'Campaspe' ex 'Achimota'

The liner 'Achimota', built for the African Steamship Co's service to West Africa, was purchased last month by Huddart, Parker Ltd, for the Australian coastal trade. Since her trial trip she has been laid up at Harland and Wolff's yard, so that she is a new ship. It will be remembered that Harland and Wolff built a large motor vessel, the 'Westralia', a few years ago, for Huddart, Parker, Ltd. The 'Achimota', which is a luxury liner of 10,000 tons gross, the length being 460 ft, the beam 63 ft. 6 ins., has accommodation for several hundred passengers. She will now be named the 'Campaspe' after an Australian river, and after a brief trial in the middle of November will leave for Australia at the end of the month. No modifications will be made, except that all the berths for the crew, which were originally 6 ft. in length, are to be 6 ft. 6 ins. long, to comply with Australian shipping regulations.

The mention of the ship being renamed *Campaspe* is intriguing, as this is the only time such a comment seems to have appeared in print. The Campaspe River is a tributary that joins the Murray River at Echuca, in northern Victoria, but maybe Huddart Parker decided the name was not suitable, or too difficult, and changed it to *Wanganella*, which is the name of a tiny town in southern New South Wales, near Deniliquin.

Very few alterations were required to suit the vessel for its new employment. As completed, *Achimota* had been fitted out with accommodation for 236 first class, 64 second class and 30 third class passengers, with provision for carrying deck passengers on short sectors along the African coast. This arrangement was altered to cater for 304 first class and 104 second class. First class accommodation, which included two suites and 81 single-berth cabins, was located amidships on the bridge and upper decks. Second class quarters, which included 28 two-berth cabins, were on the main deck aft. Every cabin in both classes featured hot and cold running water, but none had private facilities. The large increase in passenger capacity would not create a problem, as the ship would only be at sea for two days on most voyages, rather than the two-week trip from Liverpool to West Africa for which it had been designed.

The crew quarters, which were of very basic design for the native crews employed by Elder Dempster, had to be considerably upgraded to meet Australian standards. Officers' quarters were retained, with deck officers' cabins located below the bridge, while engineers had their cabins on the boat deck abreast the engine room casing.

When these alterations were completed, the vessel was renamed *Wanganella*, and painted in Huddart Parker colours, black hull with a white line at upper deck level, and dark yellow funnels. Although the

Stern view of *Achimota*.

Achimota laid up in Belfast. The vessel on the left being built is *Georgic* of the White Star Line.

liner would be operating across the Tasman Sea primarily out of Sydney, her port of registry was Melbourne, which was where Huddart Parker had their headquarters.

The public rooms were not altered, as they had been fitted out to a very high standard already. On the promenade deck, first class passengers were provided with a smoking lounge forward which featured a glass dome, also a reading room and oak-panelled smoke room, both fitted with open fireplaces. Second class passengers had a smoke room and lounge located in the deckhouse at the foot of the mainmast. The two dining saloons were on the main deck, first class forward and second class abaft beneath the aft funnel.

The machinery installed in the vessel was of particular interest at the time the ship was built. One description of this appeared in the book *Famous Liners of the Eastern Oceans*, by G. W. P. McLachlan, published in the late 1930s:

> Mechanically-minded travellers may be interested to learn that when she was delivered in 1932 she was considered one of the finest examples afloat of a motorship driven by four-stroke engines fitted with supercharge. Moreover, she possesses what was then regarded to be one of the most complete electrical installations ever provided in a passenger ship of her size.
>
> The generating sets, driven by Harland B & W engines, are at the forward end of the main engine room. There are three 250 kw units supplying the current for lighting, heating and power throughout the ship, and there is also an emergency 50 kw diesel-driven generator housed well above the waterline. The lighting consists of the equivalent of over 3,500 thirty-watt lamps, and special high-candle power lamps are installed to give light for the night working of cargo. The electric heating of the passenger accommodation alone absorbs the equivalent of 300 hp, and every bit of auxiliary machinery, both above and below decks, is electrically operated. In the kitchens electricity drives a dough mixer, potato peeler, ice cream machine, milk machine, baker's oven, toaster griddle, water boilers, fish fryers, range blowers, cold cupboards and beer coolers.

On 29 November 1932, *Wanganella* ran acceptance trials in Belfast Lough, which were completed successfully. A comprehensive report on the *Wanganella* appeared in the December 1932 issue of *The Motor Ship*, and is included in full over the next ten pages.

THE 10,000-TON MOTOR LINER "WANGANELLA" AT BELFAST.

THE PASSENGER LINER "WANGANELLA"

Huddart, Parker's Second Motor Ship, Originally the "Achimota." Twin-screw Pressure-charged 8,500 b.h.p. Harland and Wolff B. and W.-type Machinery

ALTHOUGH the motor passenger liner "Wanganella" was not built expressly for her present owners, Huddart, Parker, Ltd., neither was she intended for the service in which she will be placed, she appears singularly well adapted to the requirements which she is about to fulfil. The vessel was constructed recently for Elder Dempster and Co. and originally was named "Achimota"; in her intended capacity she would have been on the West African run with Liverpool as her home port. Due to matters concerned with reorganization, the delivery of the ship was not effected, and negotiations were brought to a successful conclusion by the present owners to acquire this fine vessel, which will be engaged in service between Australia and New Zealand, her port of registry being Melbourne. A map showing her route is published on page 314.

That the "Wanganella" is an exceptional ship will be readily acknowledged, we imagine, by all who travel in her. She is a liner of what is usually termed the intermediate type, with a gross register approaching 10,000 tons and pressure-charged machinery of approximately 8,500 b.h.p., giving her a maximum speed of probably 17 knots. Apart from the question of size, the accommodation has been planned on the most tasteful and comfortable scale. With a single exception, on account of a small matter of rearrangement, each cabin, first and second class (the total accommodation is for more than 400 passengers), has a portlight—no simple problem in a ship of the "Wanganella's" dimensions. With no exception whatever, every cabin is provided with hot and cold running water, and the same provision is made for the officers' and crew's accommodation.

What there is in the "Wanganella" failing to reach an up-to-date standard of equipment we have not discovered after a close inspection of the ship at Belfast, before she left on her maiden voyage. We stated in a note published recently in this journal that the only alterations effected were to provide longer berths for the crew. Actually, the modifications have been more extensive than we were at first led to understand. It was, no doubt, difficult to improve the passenger accommodation on a scale worth mentioning, for it was finished to serve an excellent purpose. On the other hand, the owners decided to examine what could be done to enhance the value of minor points. Chromium-plated bath fittings take the place of bronze parts; special furniture is provided in the officers' quarters; the engineers will enjoy a lounge; one thing after another places the vessel in a category of its own, and we left the "Wanganella" with a feeling that the owners, together with their superintendent engineer, Mr. C. S. Waugh, were leaving nothing undone to set an example of efficiency notable for its thoroughness.

The leading particulars of the ship are given in a table on the next page. She is the second motor vessel in the owners' fleet, and, in some respects at least, will not be regarded as wholly dissimilar. The first ship was the "Westralia" (built and engined, like the "Wanganella," by Harland and Wolff), but whereas the "Westralia" has the standard type of four-stroke single-acting Burmeister and Wain engine with atmospheric induction, the "Wanganella" is fitted with machinery having the Büchi system of pressure charging. The number of cylinders is the same in both ships and the bore corresponds, also the stroke.

This gives a good indication of the standardization of motor ship machinery, when a big motor liner can be built for one owner, taken over by another, used on a different service, and yet found to have machinery with the same number of cylinders and identical bores and strokes. Yet, so well does the Diesel engine adapt itself to the inclusion of special devices, the respective outputs are by no means the same. The "Wanganella" is somewhat larger than the "Westralia" and of nearly 2,000 tons greater gross register. The former vessel needs, therefore, higher power, and, incidentally, is designed for a higher speed. In one case we find machinery of 6,600 b.h.p., and in the other there is an output of probably 2,000 b.h.p. more.

When we allow that the "Wanganella" has machinery capable of developing 8,500 b.h.p. or so, we are basing our calculations on the corresponding engines of the Union Castle liner

One of the six-cylinder auxiliary Diesel-engined dynamos.

Length	460 ft.
Breadth	63 ft. 8 ins.
Depth	34 ft. 7 ins.
Draught	24 ft.
Freeboard amidships	10 ft. 11½ ins.
Gross register (approx.)	10,000 tons.
Machinery output	8,500 b.h.p.
Corresponding revolutions	105-110 per min.
Maximum speed	17 knots.
No. of cylinders, each engine	8
Cylinder diameter	740 mm. (29¼ ins.).
Piston stroke	1,500 mm. (59 1/16 ins.).
Auxiliary dynamos	800 kw.
Fuel capacity in double bottoms	1,090 tons.
Fresh-water capacity (approx.)	820 tons.
No. of passengers, first class	304.
No. of passengers, second class	104.

"Llangibby Castle," also Büchi pressure charged and described in our December, 1929, issue. The engines are, we believe, duplicates of those in the "Wanganella." Certainly, they have the same number of cylinders with an identical diameter and the same stroke. They are designed to run at 108 r.p.m., giving the ship a speed of 15¼ knots or thereabouts loaded, the speed when the vessel is light having been ascertained to be 16.9 knots. The "Llangibby Castle" is of 11,950 tons gross register (about 2,000 tons greater than the "Wanganella") and of correspondingly larger dimensions, so that if we assume the "Wanganella" to be capable of 17 knots when less than fully loaded, we are scarcely overstating the possibilities of the ship.

Main Particulars of the Vessel.

It has become customary to consider, for more or less rough measurements, that when the Büchi system of pressure charging is employed an output is attained of approximately 40 per cent. over and above that of an unsupercharged engine of the same size. In practice, however, far bigger excess powers have been obtained, but for marine work, where conservative figures are the rule rather than the exception, and where the shaft sizes are subject to Lloyd's regulations, the limits are restricted.

The engines of the "Westralia" are rated at 6,600 b.h.p. for a speed of 115 r.p.m. If we increase this output by 40 per cent. and adhere to the same revolutions we find that the machinery of the "Wanganella" is capable of delivering 9,200 b.h.p. As we have assumed the service power to be 8,500 b.h.p. we may be also justified in taking the corresponding revolutions as 106 per minute, bringing us back, as it were, within measurable distance of the "Llangibby Castle" and, further, making out a case for 17 knots. We have included certain of these assumed figures in the table referring to the main details.

Those of our readers who are acquainted with the principles of the various pressure charging systems—they have been dealt with very fully in these columns—are aware that the object is to obtain an increase in the mean effective pressure without substantially increasing the maximum combustion pressure. The Büchi system, which is applied to the "Wanganella's" engines, works according to such conditions and comprises an exhaust-gas turbine driving a blower which supplies air on the induction stroke. One set is fitted to each engine.

Basing the figures on 8,500 b.h.p. for the "Wanganella" and taking an arbitrary rate of 106 r.p.m., it can be calculated that the brake mean effective pressure would be about 102 lb. per sq. in. as against, say, 70 lb. or 75 lb. per sq. in. for an engine with atmospheric induction. In the Büchi system

The two Sharples purifiers for lubricating oil.

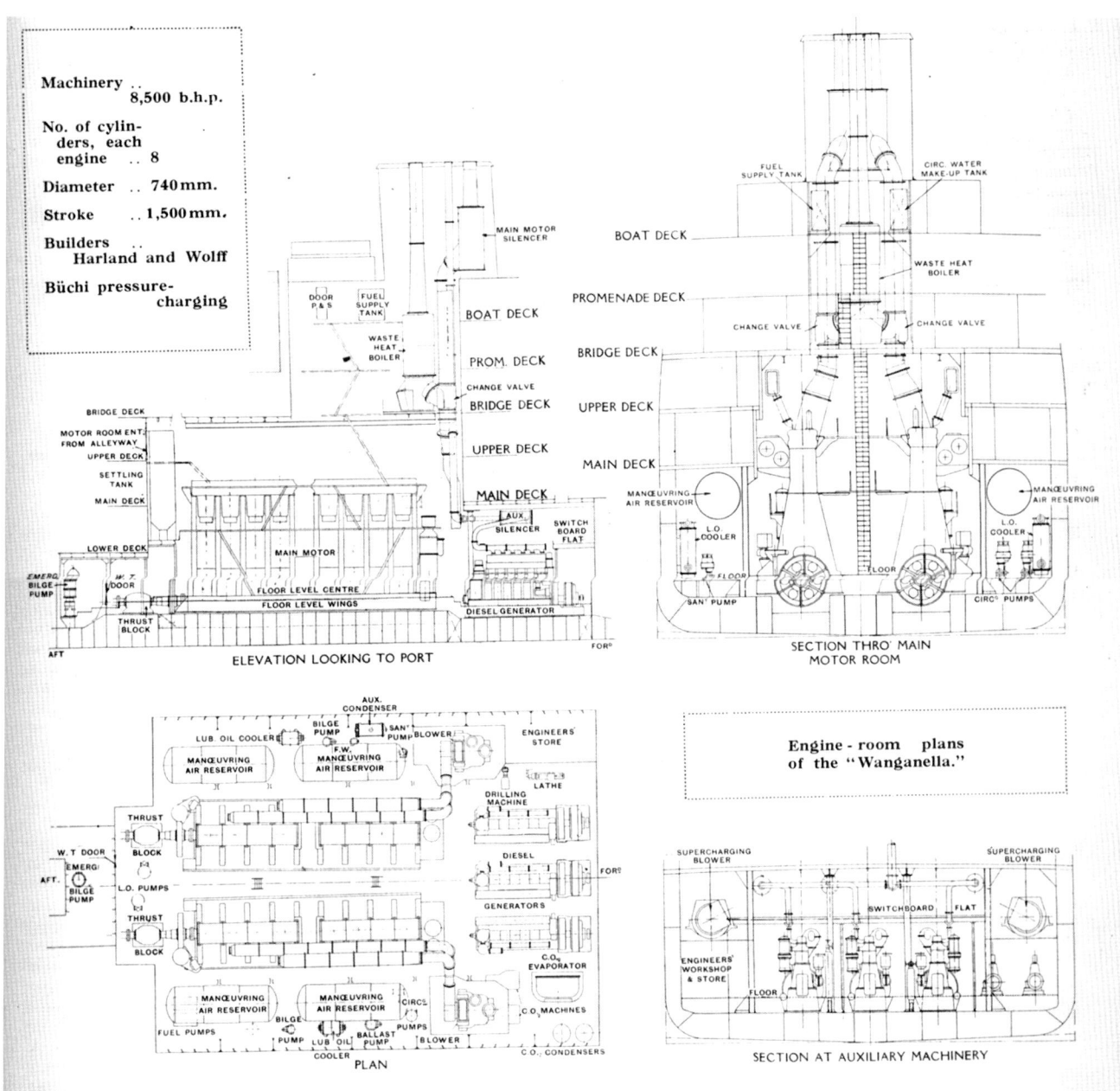

Machinery	8,500 b.h.p.
No. of cylinders, each engine	8
Diameter	740 mm.
Stroke	1,500 mm.
Builders	Harland and Wolff
Büchi pressure-charging	

ELEVATION LOOKING TO PORT

SECTION THRO' MAIN MOTOR ROOM

PLAN

Engine-room plans of the "Wanganella."

SECTION AT AUXILIARY MACHINERY

the inlet and exhaust valves have a considerable overlap in their timing—both remaining open together while the air under a slight pressure passes through the combustion space, cooling the exhaust valves and giving a thorough scavenging effect.

Meanwhile, it may be stated that the main engines in the "Wanganella" are of the standard Harland and Wolff-B. and W. single-acting four-stroke design (apart from the necessary modifications due to the application of pressure charging) with eight cylinders apiece, the dimensions having been given in the table. Square cylinder covers are provided and through bolts are fitted. The camshaft is chain-driven; this applies also to the auxiliary engines driving the dynamos. The main engines are secured direct to the tank top and are of the air-injection type with a single three-stage compressor located at the forward end, driven by the main crankshaft. It is of importance to note that the air supply for the first stage suction is taken from the turbo-blower.

Single-lever control is adopted for starting and speed regulation, whilst the fuel valve lift is variable to allow economy in the use of blast air when the engines are operating at reduced speeds. There is the usual reversing lever which actuates a servo motor, moving the camshaft in a fore-and-aft direction, also turning a cranked layshaft. This layshaft is provided with links which pull the cam rollers (on the lower ends of the vertical push rods) clear of the cams, while the camshaft takes up its correct position for ahead or astern operation of the engine. We may remark that the same general arrangement has been adopted with Burmeister and Wain engines for 20 years. It has proved demonstrably efficient, easily understood and mechanically sound in its conception.

The Turbo Blowers.

At each side of the engine-room is a platform for the exhaust gas turbo blowers. Their precise location will be noted from the plans above. The blowers are designed for a continuous pressure charge and are Brown, Boveri machines. They have an intake volume of 428 cubic metres per minute, a suction pressure (absolute) of 1.03 kg. per sq. cm.—this is a test figure—and an air delivery pressure of 1.31 kg. per sq. cm. when running at 3,200 r.p.m. The mean exhaust gas pressure before the turbine is 1.3 kg. per sq. cm., and that after the turbine is 1.05 kg. per sq. cm. The temperature of the exhaust gas

PLANS OF THE MOTOR PASSENGER LINER "WANGANELLA"

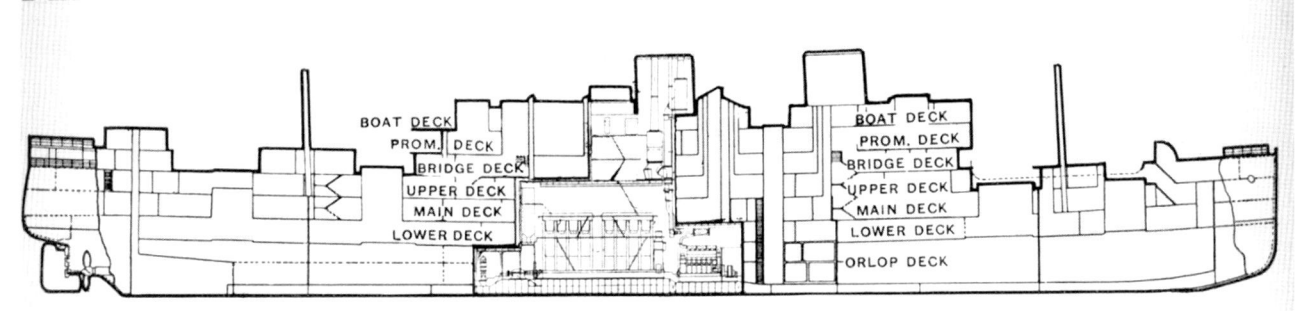

Owners .. Huddart, Parker, Ltd.

Shipbuilders .. Harland and Wolff, Belfast

Engine builders .. Harland and Wolff, Glasgow

Gross register .. (approx.) 10,000 tons

No. of passengers in first-class accommodation .. 304

Second-class passengers 104

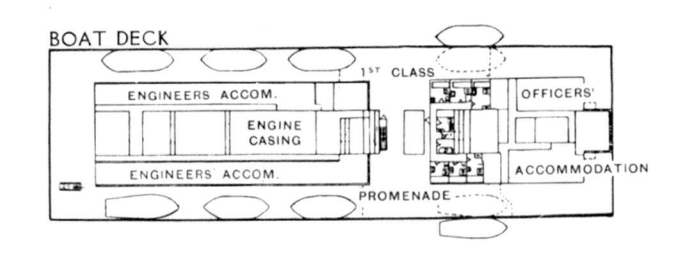

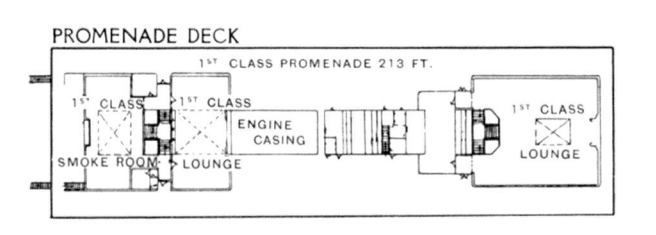

Length .. 460 ft.

Breadth .. 63 ft. 8 ins.

Depth .. 34 ft. 7 ins.

Freeboard amidships .. 10 ft. 11½ ins.

Corresponding draught 24 ft. 0¼ in.

Max. speed .. 17 knots

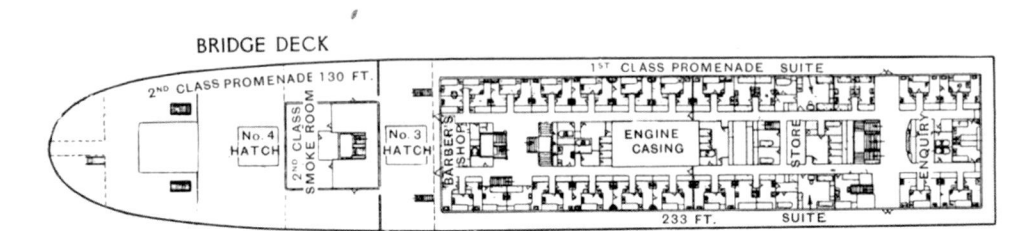

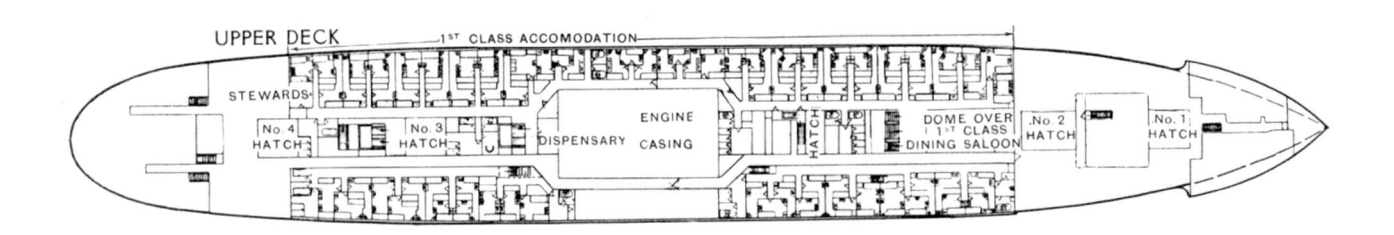

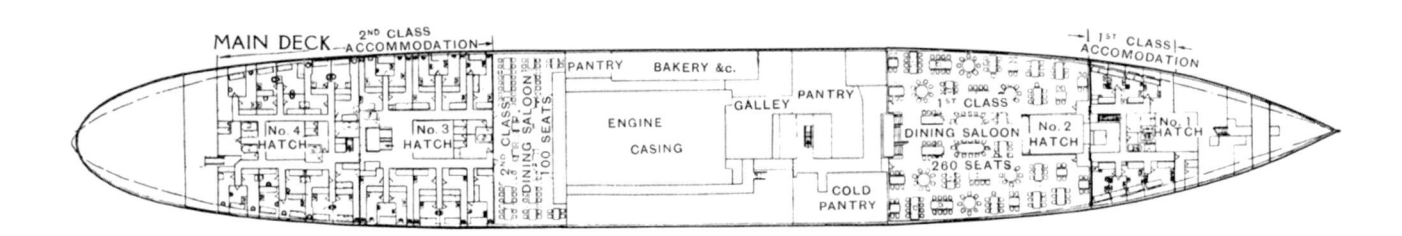

before the turbine is assumed to be 450 degrees C.

After the exhaust gases have left the turbo blowers they perform further useful work in a Clarkson thimble-tube boiler, of which the design is illustrated below. This boiler generates 4,000 lb. of steam per hour, at a pressure of 100 lb. per sq. inch, and further acts as a silencer, although there is an additional main silencer of small dimensions, as the whole of the exhaust gas supply is not required, a portion being by-passed. For use in port there are two Clyde oil fuel burners to produce the same volume of steam hourly. The boiler is 11 ft. 9 ins. high and 6 ft in diameter, the combustion chamber being 6 ft. 4 ins. high and the diameter 6 ft. The boiler weighs 11.75 tons empty, and the water contents weigh 2½ tons.

On the starboard side of the engine-room, located forward, are two Hall's refrigerating machines. These are of the CO_2 type and are electrically driven, the arrangement being in accordance with the usual practice and the design entirely standard. Aft on the port side are two Sharples centrifugal purifiers. Both of these machines are installed to deal with the lubricating oil and none is provided for the fuel, filters being employed for the purpose in question. The capacity of each separator is 300 gallons hourly.

A special feature of the system on the "Wanganella" is that the Sharples machines are able to take oil direct from the piston cooling circuit. By this means purification can take place with the oil at a temperature of, say, 140 degrees F. to 150 degrees F., and there is thus no necessity for previous heating. On the same side of the engine-room as the purifiers is a lubricating oil renovating tank, with a capacity of 100 gallons.

Cooling System.

Fresh water is used for cooling the main engine cylinder jackets and covers, the pistons being cooled by means of lubricating oil, while salt water is used for cooling the air compressors, also the auxiliary engines. Referring particularly to the lubricating oil supply, it may be mentioned that there are two Drysdale Centrex electrically driven pumps arranged aft. One of these pumps supplies every requirement, i.e., piston cooling, bearing oil supply throughout the main engines, thrust block lubrication, and the same for the bearings of the exhaust gas pressure-charging turbo blowers. There is no difference in the pressure used for any particular service, the supply being maintained at approximately 1 kg. per sq. cm., or roughly 14 lb. per sq. inch. These pumps, which are located between the thrust blocks, have a capacity of 140 tons hourly in each case.

Coolers are naturally required for both the lubricating oil and fresh water circuits. There are two fresh water coolers, one on the port side and one to starboard, each having an area of 1,720 sq. ft. Similarly arranged and located forward are two for the lubricating oil, in this instance the area being 1,650 sq. ft. Two sea-water circulating pumps are provided. Both are located on the starboard side of the engine-room and each has a capacity of 320 tons per hour. These pumps, which are of the Drysdale type, have, we believe, by far the largest capacity of any pumps in the ship. Located above the fresh water coolers on the port and starboard sides, respectively, are the two fresh water circulating pumps, also Drysdale units, supplying 130 tons per hour.

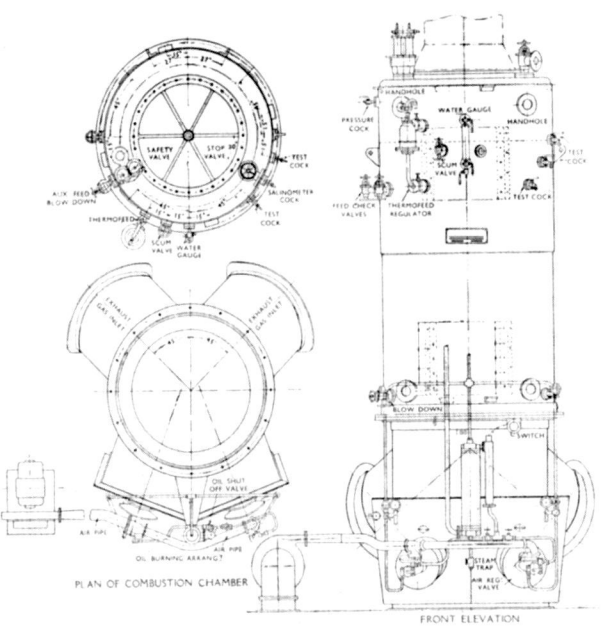

Clarkson exhaust gas boiler in the "Wanganella."

Auxiliary Diesel Engines.

It will have been noted from the table giving the leading details of the "Wanganella" that the electric load is comparatively heavy, namely 800 kw. This figure includes the current supplied by the emergency three-cylinder Diesel-engined dynamo. The machines for normal service are located side by side at the forward end of the engine room, the arrangement being shown in the plans. They form an installation of considerable importance, comprising three six-cylinder Harland and Wolff B. and W. type four-stroke single-acting air-injection engines.

These auxiliary engines, being fitted with oversize compressors with the customary receiver regulating device, make it unnecessary to provide an auxiliary compressor for charging the manoeuvring air containers. As with the main engines, blast injection of fuel is employed. The cylinder diameter is 330 mm., corresponding to practically 13 ins., while the piston stroke is 600 mm., which is approximately 23⅝ ins. With this appreciably large stroke-bore ratio the revolutions are moderate and the dynamos, each of which has a capacity of 250 kw., run at 225 r.p.m.

Manœuvring Air.

Whilst we have remarked that there is no separate auxiliary air compressor, it will be understood that a small machine is fitted, as usual, for emergency purposes. It is driven by a steam engine, and is arranged on the port side of the engine room forward. Four manoeuvring air reservoirs are fitted, two to port and a second pair to starboard. Each container has a capacity of 725 cubic ft. and is charged up to a pressure of 25 kg. per sq. cm., or approximately 355 lb. per sq. inch. The steam machinery other than the emergency air compressor comprises two boiler feed pumps of the Weir type, each capable of dealing with 4,000 lb. of water an hour. They are located forward on the port side and on the same side of the engine-room is a Liverpool Engineering and Condenser Co.'s evaporator, with a capacity of 3,000 gallons per hour. A Hocking distiller with the same capacity is fitted on the top platform of the machinery space.

Ship's Pumps.

Certain pumps particularly associated with the operation of the main engines have already been dealt with, and the remainder will receive a brief reference. There is a Drysdale sanitary pump on the port side, the capacity being 70 tons per hour, aft of this being a fresh water pump for ship's service, capable of supplying 20 tons per hour. Two Drysdale bilge pumps are provided farther aft on the same side of the engine-room, the capacity of each being 100 tons per hour. On the starboard side is a ballast pump of the same manufacture, the capacity varying between 70 tons and 180 tons per hour. In the shaft tunnel there is a Drysdale emergency bilge pump, capable of dealing with between 70 tons and 100 tons of water hourly. Aft on the starboard side is located a pair of oil fuel transfer pumps for supplying the service tanks.

For the main engines there are two sets of fuel filters. This oil will most probably be Palik Papan fuel with a specific gravity of about 0.92 at 60 degrees F. It has been found in the case of the "Westralia" that the fuel and exhaust valves run for four months with such fuel, no grinding being required in the meantime.

There is an Allen pump for the supply of hot salt water. Monitor alarms are fitted in the lubricating oil and circulating water piping.

VIEWS IN THE "WANGANELLA'S" ENGINE-ROOM

The intermediate platform is seen in the right-hand illustration, showing the camshafts, cranked layshafts and lower ends of the pushrods.

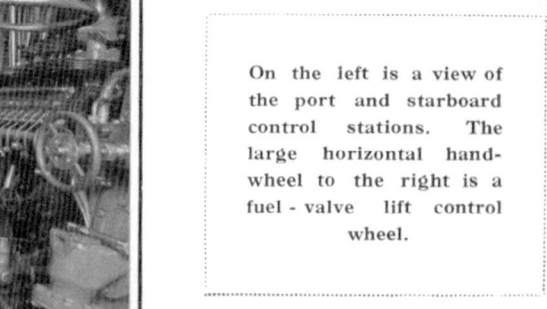

On the left is a view of the port and starboard control stations. The large horizontal handwheel to the right is a fuel-valve lift control wheel.

The platform at the level of the cylinder heads is shown on the right. Note may be taken of the method of stowing spare valves accessibly in a central position.

PUBLIC ROOMS IN THE MOTOR LINER "WANGANELLA"

A view showing part of the first-class dining saloon is on the left.

On the right is a general view of the first-class smoking lounge.

In addition to the first-class smoking lounge there is a smoke room, part of which is seen in the left-hand view.

ACCOMMODATION VIEWS IN THE MOTOR LINER "WANGANELLA"

The first-class reading room is shown on the left. There are two large book-cases let into the walls.

On the right are seen the fireplace and part of the dome, unusual in its design, in the first-class smoking lounge.

One of the suite rooms in the first-class accommodation is shown on the left. Each room has a private bath.

Deck Machinery.

In addition to ten Laurence, Scott electrically driven winches installed on the "Wanganella" there is a large warping winch on the poop, with an extended athwartships shaft having port and starboard drums. The capacity is 6 tons at a speed of 60 ft. per minute, or 3 tons at twice this speed, while the speed, light, is 200 ft. per minute. A 140-ampere motor drives the winch, current being provided at 220 volts.

Two 3-ton winches are arranged to serve No. 1 cargo hatch. These are capable of lifting their rated load at 80 ft. per minute, or 1 ton at 240 ft. per minute, the light hook speed being 350 ft. per minute. At No. 2 hatch there are two larger machines, each with a capacity of 5 tons at 70 ft. per minute, or 1½ tons at 235 ft. per minute, the light hook speed being the same as with the 3-ton winches. For No. 3 hatch there are two winches which correspond with those placed at No. 1, similar in size, capacity and speed, while the same particulars apply to the winches at No. 4 hatch.

The fifth pair of winches serves the store hatch. These are the smallest in the equipment and each is capable of lifting 1½ tons at a speed of 150 ft. per minute, or ½ ton at 400 ft. per minute. They have a light hook speed of 450 ft. per minute. Forward is installed a Clarke-Chapman electrically operated anchor windlass, driven by a 50 h.p. 220-volt motor which has a speed varying between 450 r.p.m. and 1,060 r.p.m. The motor is located on deck, but the electric controller gear is arranged in a special compartment below. The system employed may be described as a booster control with contactor reversers.

The steering gear, of the electro-hydraulic type, is of Harland and Wolff's manufacture, comprising Hele-Shaw Martineau apparatus. There are four rams arranged in a fore-and-aft direction. The pumps are driven by two Laurence, Scott electric motors and switchgear is fitted for an output of 36 h.p. A Diesel-engine-driven emergency dynamo is installed. This is a 227-ampere machine and the engine is a three-cylinder unit designed to run at 400 r.p.m. In the boat equipment is included a Parsons petrol-paraffin-engined lifeboat. A new provision in the ship is that of a printing press.

The Galley.

A most extensive galley and pantry arrangement is a distinctive feature of the "Wanganella." There is a large Wilson oil-fired installation, consisting of a double-sided galley with four oil burners. In addition, a charcoal-burning grill is fitted, together with an electric oven having three compartments, the loading capacity being 136 amperes. A Hobart mixing machine is provided, the drive being taken from a ¾ h.p. electric motor running at 1,750 r.p.m.

Another piece of machinery in the galley is a Wilson chain-driven electric potato peeler. In the bakery is an electric dough mixer and a steam prover. The ice cream machine is in two parts, power being provided by a shunt wound motor of 25 h.p. running at 500 r.p.m. This high power is an indication of its capacity. Apart from the galley equip-

Fireplace in the first-class lounge.

ment already mentioned are a steam-heated oven and a clean steam producer, the whole being an important and interesting installation. It is complete with a dairy, involving the provision of Chadburn milk-making machinery.

On the port side of the promenade deck is the gramophone repeating control room, various repeaters being placed in suitable positions in the public rooms. At the forward end of this deck is a glass-enclosed space, the general layout being spacious and attractive. To port are fitted special lights for illuminating this part of the deck when dancing takes place. The original wireless room forms part of some new accommodation which embraces seven single-berth cabins for cadets and passengers. The present wireless room contains an Australian-built 1½ kw. transmitting set for 600-800 metres wave-length, also for 15-50 metres short wave transmission.

The chief engineer has reserved accommodation with two entrances, one giving access from the boat deck and the other from a corridor. It comprises a sleeping cabin, together with a roomy office and separate bathroom, and the customary lavatory provision. There are altogether cabins for nine engineers and three electricians. The captain has a suite with a bathroom. The bridge has been altered in such a manner that the wheelhouse extends appreciably more forward than was originally the case, giving much additional enclosure.

Public Rooms.

Prominent among the first-class cabins are two suites de luxe, with the most tasteful decorative effects and furnishings on approved lines, each suite being differently treated. These apartments include their own bathrooms and lavatories, complete with a comparatively large space for the private stowage of trunks. It may be mentioned at this juncture that all the decoration and furnishing of the first-class public rooms and entrances are to the design of Messrs. Heaton, Tabb and Co.

These entrances, also the staircases, are novel in their conception and give a good general effect of space. Richly figured woods are employed and the handrails have been given a graceful sweeping appearance. The inquiry office is totally relieved of any suspicion of dulness and is surrounded by marble, on each side being arranged showcases. The design is such as to compel attention, as we noted whilst inspecting the ship.

There is a simplicity about the dining saloon, which is located on the main or C deck forward. The tables largely accommodate six persons, but some provide for a greater number. Trellis glazing is used for the windows and in the centre is a vaulted dome, whilst the lighting is concealed. An idea of the effective manner in which the work has been carried out will be gained from one of the accompanying illustrations of the accommodation.

The first-class lounge and reading room are at the forward end of the promenade deck. Modern Spanish decoration is used, grey veneered woods being relieved with bands of a quiet colour. The lighting is indirect. The reading room would perhaps better be termed a library, with two fine book-cases at the forward and after sides respectively, ample in size, we may suggest, for the purpose and an attraction of their own.

Not only is there a smoke-room, aft on the promenade deck, but adjoining is what is termed a smoking lounge, treated in a Spanish style with an octagonal vaulted ceiling. The walls are vellum-tinted and the round-headed windows are lattice-glazed. Tones of blue and ivory have been chosen for the furniture and the architraves of the doors are carved and treated in a similar manner.

Designed in the Italian manner and following the principles of the work of a well-known English decorator, Alfred Stevens, the smoke-room proper—as distinct from the smoking lounge—is quite an outstanding apartment, dignified in the treatment of its decoration and provided with a dome which is lighted by concealed lamps. Oak panelling is used for the walls and there is a fireplace with a marble mantelpiece, around being Spanish leather as a background, giving an unusual yet most harmonious effect.

Second-class Accommodation.

The accommodation for the second-class passengers is aft. There is a dining saloon on the main deck extending the whole width of the ship, having seats for 100 persons. A notable feature of this saloon is the excellent provision for ventilation. Aft of this saloon are the second-class cabins, of which 52 berths are additional to the number originally arranged. Those of the second-class cabins which we inspected appeared to be very little inferior to the cabins in the first-class quarters.

Promenade space for second-class travellers is available on the bridge deck for a length of 130 ft. Forward of this, first-class promenade space extends for another 233 ft., and the promenade deck above affords 213 ft. of additional space for exercise, while there is yet more on the boat deck. It will be seen, therefore, that the facilities are ample. Added to the accommodation, moreover, is a children's playroom, which is an extra item as compared with the original plans when the vessel was designed for service to West Africa.

Before the "Wanganella" left for Australia she underwent trials in Belfast Lough. This was on November 29, and it was arranged that she should proceed on her voyage immediately after the run in question. She had, however, previously undergone certain trials which took place when the vessel was completed, so that last month's run was supplementary and on behalf of her new owners, who, it may be added, are to be congratulated on acquiring a most outstanding ship.

The illustrations in this article are reproduced from photographs by Stewart Bale.

9

The 1930s

On 30 November 1932 *Wanganella* left Belfast on its delivery voyage to Australia, under the command of Captain G. B. Bates, who had transferred from *Westralia* and would remain with the ship for the next six years.

Very little information about the ship was released to the local press, although on 2 December a brief item appeared stating that *Wanganella* was to be fitted with an 'echometer', manufactured by local company AWA, when it arrived in Sydney. The echometer was described as 'a device by which 53 automatic depth soundings are taken, virtually giving a constant indication of the depth of water. It is fitted below the waterline, and ascertains depth by supersonic vibrations, which it transmits to the chart room, where it is shown on an indicator and recorded on a graph'.

On 6 December, the following item appeared in the *Sydney Morning Herald*:

> According to advices received in Sydney yesterday, the new Huddart, Parker motor liner *Wanganella* will arrive in time to commence service in the Australia-New Zealand service on January 12, when she will sail for Wellington.
>
> Arrangements have been made for the ship to make a special excursion to Milford Sound before returning to Sydney. She will then commence her regular service, making alternate trips to Auckland and Wellington, and probably extending to Melbourne, as a complement to the service now operated by the Union Company's steamer *Monowai*.
>
> A full description of the new vessel is now to hand. It reveals that she is of 9560 tons gross, with a length overall of 479 feet, a beam of 63 feet 6 inches, and a moulded depth of 34 feet 6 inches. She is equipped with two sets of single-acting, eight-cylinder Harland-Burmeister and Wain Diesel engines, with pressure induction, has a cruiser stern and two squat funnels. Eight watertight compartments are provided by seven bulkheads. The vessel has accommodation for 304 first-class passengers in single and three-berth cabins, and 104 second-class passengers, in two and three berth cabins.

Voyaging by way of the Mediterranean and Suez Canal, and making the trip in a record 31 days, the liner arrived in Sydney on 31 December, berthing at 2 Darling Harbour at 3 pm. The arrival of the new liner did not rate much mention in the local papers although an unusual coincidence was reported. For the delivery voyage, Mr L. S. Brew had been sent along by Harland & Wolff as the guarantee engineer, and the pilot who boarded *Wanganella* to bring it into Sydney Harbour turned out to be his brother, Captain A. Brew, whom he had not seen for twenty years.

For almost two weeks *Wanganella* remained in port, being prepared for entering service, and open for public inspections.

On Thursday, 12 January 1933, *Wanganella* departed 3 Darling Harbour at 4 pm on her first voyage across the Tasman Sea, with a full passenger list, berthing three days later in Wellington. From there the liner made a short cruise to Milford Sound before commencing the return voyage from Wellington back to Sydney. On Friday, 27 January, *Wanganella* left Sydney on her first voyage to Auckland, arriving there on 30 January.

Wanganella departed Sydney on 10 February for her second voyage to Wellington, returning to Sydney on the morning of 20 February. That same afternoon *Wanganella* departed on what was advertised as a 'special voyage' to Melbourne, being in that port for several hours on 22 February, and returning to Sydney on the morning of 24 February. The same afternoon, *Wanganella* left on her second voyage to Auckland.

The liner settled into a regular pattern of two round trips a month from Sydney, one to Wellington and the other to Auckland. From time to time the liner also made a quick round trip to Melbourne and back between New Zealand trips. The departure from Sydney on 6 April was advertised as an Easter Holiday Cruise, going first to Wellington, then Milford Sound and back to Sydney.

The arrival of *Wanganella* marked the end of the career of *Ulimaroa*, which had been laid up in Sydney through the winter of 1932, but was reactivated to operate the summer Hobart trade, her final arrival in Sydney being on Monday, 9 January 1933. Replaced on the Hobart service by *Zealandia*, *Ulimaroa* remained laid up in Sydney Harbour for over a year, until being sold to Japanese shipbreakers, leaving Sydney on 28 May 1934 and arriving in Osaka on 22 July.

Huddart Parker Limited now had a well-balanced fleet of passenger ships, with *Wanganella* on the Tasman Sea trade, *Zealandia* maintaining the service between Sydney and Hobart, and *Westralia* running from Sydney to Fremantle.

For many years Huddart Parker had operated their trans-Tasman service in conjunction with vessels operated by the Union Steam Ship Company of New Zealand Ltd. Since November 1932, the Union Line representative had been *Monowai*, a vessel of slightly greater size than *Wanganella*, but with a somewhat similar background. Throughout most of the next thirty years, the career of *Wanganella* would be intertwined with that of *Monowai*, another liner that had endured an unfortunate introduction to service.

Monowai had been built as *Razmak* for the P&O Line, and designed to operate a fast passenger and mail feeder service between Aden and Bombay. In an unusual arrangement, the hull had been built by the Greenock shipyard of Harland & Wolff, being launched on 16 October 1924, then towed to Belfast, where the quadruple-expansion machinery, boilers and superstructure were added, and the internal fitting out completed.

Razmak was handed over to P&O on 26 February 1925, and at that time provided accommodation for 142 first class and 142 second class passengers. The vessel measured 10 602 gross tons, had twin propellers, and a service speed of 18 knots. On 13 March *Razmak* left London on a one-way positioning voyage to Aden, then entered service in the Indian Ocean.

In 1926, P&O abandoned the Indian Ocean feeder service, and *Razmak* was placed on a new route from Marseilles to Bombay. This service was also abandoned, in 1929, and *Razmak* was laid up in England, as P&O had no real use for the ship. Then fate took a hand when the Union Line lost one of their trans-Pacific passenger ships, *Tahiti*, which sank on 17 August 1930 after the propeller shaft broke and tore a huge hole in the hull of the ship when it was in the middle of the Pacific. This left the company one ship short on their service from Sydney to San Francisco. *Razmak* was seen as an ideal replacement, and as the Union Line was a member of the P&O Group, the ship was quickly transferred to the New Zealand company, being renamed *Monowai*.

After being refitted to carry 280 first class and 203 second class passengers, *Monowai* steamed to Sydney, from where she departed for the first time on 27 November 1930 on the long route across the Pacific via Wellington and Tahiti to San Francisco. On her second departure from Sydney, on Thursday, 22 January 1931, Captain A. T. Toten had been

Razmak was built for the P&O Line.

Monowai in the 1930s (Dallas Hogan collection)

instructed to make a fast trip to Wellington, providing weather conditions were favourable, in order to test the Bauer-Wach exhaust turbines which had been fitted to the machinery before *Monowai* left Britain.

Departing Sydney Heads at 5.04 pm, *Monowai* quickly worked up to full speed, though using only five of her six boilers. On the first day at sea the vessel ran into northerly winds, creating a heavy swell and westerly set, while in Cook Strait there was a strong ebb tide which delayed arrival at Wellington Heads by at least half an hour, to 1.47 pm, but this was still early enough to break the previous record, set by the Matson liner *Malolo* in November 1930, by one hour and eight minutes, the new time being two days 18 hours 43 minutes.

Unfortunately, the entry of *Monowai* into service coincided with a world trade recession, and the Union Line decided the ship was too large to remain on the San Francisco route all year. On 28 May 1931, *Monowai* departed Sydney on a voyage to Vancouver while one of the regular vessels was undergoing overhaul. Returning to Sydney on 17 July, *Monowai* was temporarily placed on the shorter trans-Tasman trade. On 3 September 1931, *Monowai* returned to the San Francisco route, but from February 1932 had to compete with the brand-new Matson liners *Mariposa* and *Monterey*. They were larger and faster than *Monowai*, and also heavily subsidised by the United States Government, so the Union Line ship just could not compete. On 26 October 1932, *Monowai* departed San Francisco for the last time, and the Union Line abandoned the route altogether.

Monowai was transferred back to the trans-Tasman trade, and Captain Arthur H Davey assumed command in Sydney on 24 November 1932 having come from the *Maunganui*. Next day, *Monowai* left Sydney on a voyage to Auckland, completing the voyage in a new record time of 71½ hours. At that time the Matson Line was including a call at Melbourne in the schedules of *Mariposa* and *Monterey*, so the Union Line decided that the route for *Monowai* would be extended to include a call at Melbourne on a regular basis. It had been intended that the *Monowai* would proceed up the Yarra River and berth in Victoria Dock, but Captain Davey and the local harbour master concluded that the ship was too long and deep to do this safely. Thus *Monowai* always berthed at Station Pier.

Monowai arrived in Melbourne for the first time in December 1932, after a particularly uncomfortable voyage down the coast from Sydney into a south-westerly gale. Despite this, Captain Davey managed to berth his ship exactly on the scheduled time, and without the aid of tugs. On the ship's second arrival in Melbourne, on 14 January 1933, a large sunfish became impaled on the bow as *Monowai* was coming up Port Phillip Bay. Captain Davey had to bring his command to a full stop, and then go into reverse before the sunfish was dislodged, later to wash up on the beach next to Station Pier.

When *Wanganella* entered the Tasman service in January 1933, she and *Monowai* settled down to a period of friendly rivalry on the joint operation. *Wanganella* also made monthly round trips from Sydney to Melbourne between Tasman voyages, the first leaving Sydney on 20 March, arriving in Melbourne two days later, the ship's first visit to the southern city.

On these voyages, *Wanganella*, being an Australian-registered vessel, was allowed to carry passengers between the two ports, but *Monowai*, being a New Zealand ship, could only carry passengers coming from or going to New Zealand.

It soon became apparent to the Union Line that

sending *Monowai* to Melbourne was not a paying proposition, and the call was dropped after the visit on 26 April 1933. However, *Wanganella* continued to make a monthly round trip to Melbourne for several more months, the last visit at that time being on 6 September. Subsequently both *Wanganella* and *Monowai* operated from Sydney to either Auckland or Wellington on a regular schedule.

Monowai was by far the faster of the two, and in March 1933 set a new record between Sydney and Wellington, two days 15 hours and 35 minutes, over three hours better than the previous record, at an average speed of 19.48 knots. In May 1933 *Monowai* was temporarily taken off the Tasman to make several trips to Vancouver while the regular ships were drydocked, being replaced on the Tasman by the veteran *Marama* until *Monowai* returned in October.

From time to time *Wanganella* would be taken off the trans-Tasman trade to operate a special voyage, or a cruise. On 26 December 1933, *Wanganella* departed Sydney on a cruise to Hobart and Melbourne, though passengers were also able to disembark or join in Hobart. The same itinerary was repeated from Sydney on 20 February 1934, returning on 26 February. For both these cruises the fares ranged from £9 in first class and £7-10-0 second class.

Between these trips *Wanganella* made regular voyages to New Zealand, but two of these voyages had extra attractions and were advertised as cruises. On 26 January 1934, *Wanganella* left Sydney for Auckland, then cruised to Whangaroa, and Russell in the Bay of Islands where it was advertised, 'Passengers will be landed to participate in sports', and Great Barrier Island. After calling again at Auckland, *Wanganella* returned to Sydney. On 8 February, *Wanganella* left Sydney for Wellington, from where it made a short cruise to Milford Sound and George Sound, going back to Wellington then making the voyage to Sydney. At Easter in 1934, *Wanganella* made a short cruise to Lord Howe Island, departing Sydney on 31 March, returning on 4 April.

Extolling these cruises, the Huddart Parker advertisement promised: 'Deck games of every description provided, music broadcast throughout the ship for dancing, also a full programme of talking pictures, and swimming pool'. The swimming pool was a temporary canvas structure erected on an open deck.

Monowai also made occasional cruises, usually in the summer months from December to March. Some of these cruises departed Auckland and visited the Northland coast and Bay of Islands, while from Wellington the ship would make a circumnavigation of South Island, with a call at Dunedin and visits to various natural wonders, including Milford Sound.

Wanganella on her first visit to Melbourne (WSS Victoria).

These cruises were also advertised in Australia, with the added bonus of a return trip across the Tasman.

In January 1934, *Monowai* made a special cruise that started in Sydney, going first to Melbourne, then across the Tasman to Milford Sound and other popular inlets, then Port Chalmers and Wellington, returning directly to Sydney.

The cruises were enjoyable breaks in an otherwise regular routine of Tasman crossings for both *Wanganella* and *Monowai*, though sometimes the voyages were anything but routine. In February 1934, the New South Wales coast was being lashed by some of the worst weather experienced in several decades. *Monowai* was in Sydney, and the departure time was delayed to avoid running straight into the full fury of the storm.

Even then, the ship met a heavy swell and force 8 winds blowing from the south-east as it passed through Sydney Heads, bound for Wellington. The rough weather continued for the next 24 hours, and one huge wave smashed two windows in cabins on A Deck as well as three windows in the first-class smoking room. Once through the storm, the rest of the voyage was in very mild conditions, demonstrating the vagaries that can be experienced in the Tasman Sea.

Wanganella also began making an annual nine-night winter cruise to Noumea and Norfolk Island, the first being scheduled to depart Sydney on Saturday, 23 June 1934, returning on 2 July. Only first class passengers would be carried, the fare being from £12-10-0. Advertisements for the cruise promised: 'An opportunity for a delightful holiday at a reasonable cost. The vessel is replete with every up-to-date facility for the entertainment of passengers.'

In order to fit this cruise into the timetable, *Wanganella* was due to arrive in Sydney from New Zealand and depart on the cruise the same day, instead of having the usual four-day layover. Unfortunately all did not go to plan, as bad weather affected the crossing, and on 23 June the *Sydney Morning Herald* reported:

> As the Huddart Parker intercolonial liner, *Wanganella*, is not expected to arrive at Sydney from Auckland until 3 o'clock this afternoon, the departure of the Orient R.M.S. *Otranto*, for London, has been postponed until 4 o'clock. The *Otranto* was to have sailed at noon, but, owing to the fact that some of the passengers on the *Wanganella* are booked to leave by the *Otranto*, it was decided by the Orient Company to put back the liner's sailing time for four hours.
>
> The *Wanganella* is now scheduled to sail at 9 pm for a cruise to Noumea and Norfolk Island, and not at 4 pm.

Returning to Sydney on Monday, 2 July, *Wanganella* did not immediately resume the Tasman service, but remained in port for a week, leaving on 10 July for a round trip to Melbourne, and on 14 July departing Sydney for Auckland.

With *Zealandia* taken off the service between Sydney and Hobart for overhaul, *Wanganella* then made a special relief voyage on the route. Departing Sydney on 23 July, *Wanganella* arrived in Hobart on the morning of 25 July, leaving the next evening to return to Sydney on the afternoon of 28 July, and two days later departed on a voyage to Wellington.

During October 1934 the Melbourne centenary celebrations attracted a large number of interstate visitors to the southern city, and *Wanganella* was scheduled to make three trips from Sydney during the month, departing on 2, 15 and 29 October. These were scheduled between regular Tasman trips, keeping the ship busy throughout the month.

Going into the summer of 1934/35, *Wanganella* was again scheduled for some special trips that were advertised as cruises. The liner made two round trips from Sydney to Hobart and Melbourne, departing on 24 December 1934 and 19 February 1935. In between these trips the liner made two cruises in conjunction with regular voyages to New Zealand. Departing Sydney on 25 January for Auckland, *Wanganella* made a cruise to the Bay of Islands before returning to Sydney on 5 February.

Leaving on 7 February, *Wanganella* went to Wellington, then made a cruise to Milford Sound. On 18 February *Wanganella* left Sydney on another voyage to Wellington, also followed by a cruise to Milford Sound.

Monowai made several short cruises during the summer months, but then the two liners resumed their regular service across the Tasman until the spring. On 18 April, *Wanganella* departed Sydney on a special Easter cruise to Lord Howe Island, returning to Sydney on 23 April.

Wanganella also made another nine-night winter cruise, departing Sydney on 20 July 1935 for Noumea and Norfolk Island, the fare being the same as the previous year. The liner returned to Sydney on the morning of 29 July, and the same afternoon departed for Wellington.

It was also in July 1935 that *Monowai* made its first cruise to the islands, from Auckland, lasting two weeks. The first port of call was Nuku'alofa, where Queen Salote joined the ship for the rest of the cruise. After a visit to Vavau, *Monowai* went on to make a quick entry into the harbour at Pago Pago, but did not stay there, then went past Tin Can Island en route to Levuka, and finally Suva.

Wanganella in Milford Sound (Dallas Hogan collection).

The end of July saw the retirement of one of the longest serving masters on the trans-Tasman trade, Captain Wylie. On 31 July the *Sydney Morning Herald* reported:

> When the *Zealandia* returns from Newcastle this evening, Captain W. J. Wylie, one of the best known shipmasters on the Australian and New Zealand coasts, will relinquish command, and retire after 45 years service in the one company. He was in command of the *Ulimaroa* for more than 24 years.
>
> With the retirement of Captain Wylie, Mosman residents will no longer observe the strange signals from the ship that have probably mystified them for many years. Invariably when the *Zealandia* was going up or down the harbour, and passing Bradley's Head, he would wave a white handkerchief from the bridge, and as invariably a white sheet would be waved in response from a balcony window in a Mosman home. Captain Wylie was either greeting or waving a farewell to his wife. At night time a light would flash from the bridge and another light would twinkle an answer from the balcony. It was a ritual that was observed throughout the captain's career.
>
> Captain Wylie was never in a wreck. His commands included *Elingamite*, *Burrumbeet*, *Wimmera*, *Riverina* and *Wanganella*. A few months after he was transferred to the old *Zealandia* from the *Elingamite*, in 1902, the latter vessel was lost on the Three Kings, New Zealand. The *Zealandia* steamed to the aid of the *Elingamite* and saved 91 persons.
>
> During the war Captain Wylie was in command of the *Ulimaroa*, engaged in transport work, and for four years carried Australian and New Zealand troops to England and Egypt. On several occasions the *Ulimaroa* narrowly escaped being torpedoed.

In September 1935, *Monowai* was again required to operate one round trip to Vancouver, and *Marama* was brought back onto the Tasman trade until *Monowai* returned late in October.

Wanganella made two further cruises to Tasmania in the summer of 1935/36, the first departing Sydney on 21 December 1935, going first to Melbourne and then Hobart, returning to Sydney on 28 December. The second cruise left Sydney on 18 February 1936, visiting Hobart first and then Melbourne, returning to Sydney on 24 February.

For the summer of 1935/36 *Monowai* operated three New Zealand cruises which passengers could join from Sydney, the first departing on 20 December, going to Auckland, then the Bay of Islands and back to Auckland, returning to Sydney on 2 January. The next day *Monowai* departed Sydney on a special trip that went first to Milford Sound, then Wellington and Auckland before returning to Sydney. The third cruise, departing on 31 January 1936, went first to Wellington, then down the west coast of South Island to Milford Sound, back to Wellington, and returned to Sydney on 13 February.

Apart from occasional cruises such as these, *Wanganella* and *Monowai* maintained a regular pattern of trans-Tasman voyages from Sydney, with *Wanganella* also making an extension to Melbourne once a month.

During 1936 *Wanganella* made several more cruises, including the Easter trip to Lord Howe Island and the nine-night winter cruise to Noumea and Norfolk Island, departing Sydney on 18 July. However, this was the last time this cruise would be operated in the 1930s.

One of the passengers to join that cruise was Norman Lapin, and sixty years later he recorded his memories of that trip:

It was a Wednesday afternoon in July 1936 in Bathurst, Central West N.S.W. that I was sitting in a barber's chair having a haircut and reading the Shipping Advertisements in the *Sydney Morning Herald* that I noticed that T.S.M.V. *Wanganella* was leaving on the following Saturday evening at 7:00 pm bound for a 9 day cruise to Norfolk Island and Noumea in French New Caledonia. Halfway through the haircut I determined that I was going to be on that ship 3 days later, my reason being that I wanted to meet 'Jug' Adams and his wife 'Aunty Bet' Adams with whom my late Father and brother had stayed in their home on Norfolk Island in February 1932 for a month, and with whom my family was in regular contact. The Adams' were direct descendents of John Adams, a mutineer on the H.M.S. *Bounty* under Captain Bligh.

Three days passed after I had made the phone bookings and payments of £14 ($28) for a first class ticket for a voyage into the periphery of the romantic and adventurous South Seas of Fabled Legend.

I had never been to sea before in my life and had never been on a passenger boat before despite my being 23 years old at the time. So it was the Huddart Parker Ltd Twin Screw Motor Vessel named *Wanganella* that was to change forever my concept of life itself and my attitude and outlook on travel, adventure and knowledge and friends that were permanently made as a result of the trip.

Wanganella left No. 3 Wharf Darling Harbour at about 8.30 pm with a most colourful departure, paper ribbons by the ton. For my fare I was bedded down in a second class cabin with four bunks, but the voyage was billed as a first class ticket with every first class amenity available for every passenger. The cabin was quite spacious and suited the needs of the occupants.

It was known quite well at the time that Huddart Parker had made a good buy of this ship and that they had not overpaid in the least for the ship, the price being some £300,000 ($600,000). Today such a ship could not be bought for many millions of dollars, considering the quality of the fittings and accommodation. The ship was not built to suit the weather between Sydney and New Zealand, but was built for a much colder climate.

Whatever may be, *Wanganella* was a good ship to travel on and was very modern for her days at sea. All the reasonable amenities were available, and being in the middle of the Great Depression, a trip aboard her was a very commendable consideration in terms of travel comfort, quality of catering and the general run of items that make up a trip to be memorable and to be of the utmost comfort in every respect.

For this trip *Wanganella* sailed from Sydney with a full load of passengers, as under the economic circumstances of the time, the Great Depression was in its middle and it was really the beginning of cruising as such for the mass of the people. People from all walks of life were able to mingle with one another in every way, as being a first class travel adventure the ugly spectre of second and third class passengers did not exist.

After several days, *Wanganella* reached its first port of call, Norfolk Island, where she anchored about 400–500 metres from the shoreline, as there was no shore anchorage being available, on account of the topography of the island.

The passengers were let off the boat by heavy wicker baskets holding from eight to twelve people onto a barge or small rowing boat which took them ashore. Once on land the passengers were then free to meet and mingle with the inhabitants of Norfolk Island in a most informal manner, and they were received ever so well by the island folk. As regards myself I let it be known to the first people I met that I was anxious to meet up with 'Jug' Adams and 'Aunty Bet' Adams. By bush telegraphy they received the message at the other side of the island and came down to meet me. They were most friendly and more than pleased that a strong contact had been made. After a complete days adventure of meeting up with the Quintal Family, also direct descendants of a Bounty mutineer, it was time to go back to the shoreline and be placed in a rowboat and taken to the landing stage where we would be hauled up to the main deck.

All aboard, and the engines started up to take us on our way to Noumea in French New Caledonia where we would arrive in several days. On arrival at Noumea we were taken on a tour of the town and the environs, as Noumea at that time was at the end of the world and quite primitive compared to today. But the people were most friendly and hospitable and helped to make the stay more memorable by staging a 'Grande Balle' in honour of the passengers of the *Wanganella* at the Town Hall of Noumea, which was a most brilliant affair, and still is in my memory after sixty-six years have passed. The music was absolutely superb as was the affair itself, lively and full of vigour that is not seen today. Incidentally the entrance to the 'Grande Balle' was only 9 francs which in those days was about 9 cents of our money, the proceeds going to a French Charity.

Next morning at about 6 am the anchor of *Wanganella* was raised and the journey back to Sydney and everyday reality commenced to the chagrin of the passengers, who had really enjoyed themselves in this out of the way place.

Amongst the notable passengers was a Mr Jackson, a former Lord Mayor of Sydney, accompanied by his secretary, Miss Lucy Gray, Mr Goyda Henry, who was a well-known commercial aviator in his time, and his brother who was a Member of the NSW State Parliament, and a Mr Frank Muller who was a bon viveur and who lived at The Astor in Macquarie Street at the time. The passengers were very well mixed in every way, and it was really a most important trip that gave me open sesame to further travel.

Being a reasonably fluent speaker in French, which I had learned in high school over a period of 4 years study, I was able to speak to the people in Noumea, who I found most hospitable and most friendly. Without the knowledge of French in this circumstance so much could not have made such a difference to my life in the future, when I returned to Noumea four more times to keep up the friendships that had started in 1936, and where the people had been really marvellous to me personally.

Wanganella returned to Sydney on the morning of Monday, 27 July, and departed the same afternoon on a Tasman voyage to Wellington, once again as a two-class liner.

The Union Line had for many years operated several services across the Tasman, apart from the main route between Auckland or Wellington and Sydney. At one time they had needed several ships for their famous horseshoe service from Sydney to Auckland, Wellington, Lyttelton, Hobart and Melbourne. This route had been abandoned by the time *Wanganella* entered service, but the Union Line were still operating *Maheno* and *Marama* on a shorter version of that route, from Wellington and Lyttelton to Melbourne only.

In 1935 the Union Line had taken *Maheno* out of service, with *Marama* due to be withdrawn in 1936, and in a bold move, considering the world was gripped by a major depression, the Union Line ordered the construction of a new liner, which would be the finest they ever operated.

Launched at the Vickers-Armstrong shipyard at Barrow-in-Furness on 25 February 1936, the new liner was named *Awatea*. On speed trials, and using only four of her six boilers, the new vessel attained 22 knots. Larger than both *Wanganella* and *Monowai* at 13 482 gross tons, *Awatea* offered exceptional comfort to her passengers, being capable of carrying 377 in first class, 151 in second class and 38 steerage class. There was also 164 000 cubic feet/4646 m^3 of general cargo space, with an additional 23 500 cubic feet/666 m^3 for refrigerated cargo. In general outline *Awatea* resembled a larger version of the inter-island ferry *Rangatira*, and although fitted with two funnels the after one was a dummy.

On her delivery voyage *Awatea* departed the Clyde River in Scotland on 5 August, voyaging by way of the Panama Canal to Wellington. Despite using only three of her six boilers, and travelling at her most economical speed, *Awatea* averaged 17.08 knots, setting a new record for the passage of 28 days 6 hours 33 minutes, beating the previous record by eighteen hours, arriving in Wellington on the morning of 3 September.

Awatea was a truly outstanding liner, and on 3 September *The Dominion* newspaper published an extensive article describing the ship and its features, which included the following:

A masterpiece of British shipbuilding science and art, the Union Steam Ship Company's new trans-Tasman express liner *Awatea* ... has been described by Vickers-Armstrong Ltd who built her at Barrow-in-Furness as the finest ship they have ever turned out, and by Sir Charles Craven, chairman of that firm, as the fastest and most luxurious liner of her tonnage in the world.

The first class dining saloon on B Deck, measuring 80 ft in length by 70 ft breadth, and accommodating 264 persons at a sitting, is superbly appointed. Panelled in bleached Nigerian cherrywood and sapele mahogany bandings, the general effect of which [is to] give the room an extremely comfortable appearance.

A gallery for the orchestra is at one end and a bow-fronted balcony extends across the other, its handsome front being in a special aluminium alloy. Beautifully decorated glass in sliding grilles which are fitted to each window, and skilfully arranged mirrors, add to the appearance of this great apartment, the fittings and appointments of which add to its magnificence. A children's dining room and playroom adjoins the dining saloon.

The great lounge is a magnificent room panelled in straight-grained ash and black bean with Macassar ebony in narrow strips as relief ... Large couches in green and comfortable armchairs in pink and beige are grouped around low tables of pale gold polished wood. Gorgeous carpets and rugs tone in with the appointments of this room, which is said to be one of the most beautiful apartments ever fitted in a ship. A permanent cinema screen is skilfully concealed at the after end of the lounge.

Club rooms are a novel feature of the *Awatea*. That reserved to the use of the ladies is a delightful apartment in rose and ivory furnishings and fittings with gilt enrichments on natural coloured satinwood panelling. The men's club room is a comfortable apartment in which English brown oak is used in contrasting squares relieved with long panels of rich red leather studded with Staybrite steel bosses.

Accommodation is provided in the *Awatea* for 337 first-class passengers in 164 one, two or three-berth staterooms on the Boat Deck and A, B and C decks. The staterooms represent the very latest ideas in seagoing comfort and luxury and are fitted with telephones and hot and cold running water. There are 25 special staterooms, each with its private bathroom. Fourteen have two berths and 11 single berths. These cabins are panelled by master craftsmen in beautiful woods. The furniture and other fittings in each cabin match the walls ... and there are tall mirrors and capacious wardrobes. All these cabins have bedsteads; over each bed is a cleverly screened reading lamp and every cabin has its telephone finished in ivory.

On B and C decks accommodation is provided for 151 tourist-class passengers in 42 beautifully furnished and fitted cabins. Comfortable accommodation for 38 steerage passengers is provided on C Deck aft.

The tourist-class dining saloon on B Deck is a handsome apartment with seating accommodation or 123 persons. A bar and bar lounge is arranged at the fore-end.

The tourist lounge and smoking room are on A Deck and there is a cinema-projection room at the after end of the lounge. A promenade and swimming-bath for tourist-class passengers are arranged at the after end of the Promenade Deck.

After being open for public inspection on 13 and 14 September, when thousands of people swarmed aboard to admire the new liner, *Awatea* departed Wellington on 15 September 1936 for Auckland, arriving on the morning of 17 September, having made the fastest ever passage between the two ports. At 5 pm on Friday, 18 September, *Awatea* departed Auckland on her maiden crossing of the Tasman Sea to Sydney. The vessel was under the command of Captain Arthur H. Davey, whose name would always be associated with the ship.

Using only four boilers, *Awatea* completed the voyage in 2 days 13 hours 40 minutes. Instead of going to the Union Line wharf at No. 5 Darling Harbour, she berthed at Circular Quay on Monday, 21 September. Leaving again on 25 September, *Awatea* made the return trip to Auckland in a slightly quicker time, carrying 409 passengers. This was achieved despite running into some very bad weather, and also having to reduce speed to 17 knots so the ship would not arrive before the scheduled time of 8.30 am on 29 September.

Despite being restricted by having to maintain a regular schedule of arrival and departure times, *Awatea* soon had broken all records for the Tasman routes. Departing Sydney on 9 October 1936, *Awatea* averaged 20.45 knots on a voyage to Wellington, setting a new record time of 2 days 12 hours and 33

Awatea arriving in Auckland.

minutes. This time was bettered in early November and again in late December, but on the voyage that departed Sydney on 1 January 1937, *Awatea* reduced the time to 2 days 9 hours and 15 minutes, at an average speed of 21.62 knots.

Awatea also set a new record for the return voyage from Wellington to Sydney, two days 12 hours and 26 minutes. This was further eclipsed when the vessel arrived in Sydney on 10 March 1938, having completed the voyage from Wellington in 2 days 11 hours and 11 minutes.

On the route between Sydney and Wellington *Awatea* faced no serious competition for these records, as neither *Wanganella* nor *Monowai* was capable of similar speeds. On the Auckland service the situation was quite different, as *Awatea* was up against the two modern Matson Line vessels, *Mariposa* and *Monterey*. In July 1932, *Mariposa* had beaten the record between Sydney and Auckland previously set by *Maheno* in 1907, and in January 1936 *Monterey* set a new time for the voyage from Auckland to Sydney, of 2 days, 10 hours and 12 minutes. In October 1936, *Awatea* was able to set a new record for the voyage between Sydney and Auckland, 2 days 11 hours and 36 minutes, but the record for the trip from Auckland to Sydney remained with the Americans.

Awatea was set a more stringent timetable that *Wanganella*, often spending no more than nine hours in port between voyages. The only time *Awatea* was off the Tasman trade was in January 1937, when the liner made a four-day cruise from Auckland to Whangaroa, the Bay of Islands and Port Fitzroy, departing on 19 January, the only cruise it ever made.

In May 1937, *Awatea* entered the Cockatoo Island Dockyard in Sydney Harbour for a major overhaul, lasting over two months. It was during this overhaul that the ship's funnels were heightened by 9 feet/2.7 m, to stop soot falling on the after decks when the liner was at sea. While this change solved the soot problem, it radically altered the streamlined appearance of the ship.

Also during the overhaul, severe damage to the main propulsion reduction gearing was discovered. Repair work involved stripping down the gearing cases so the old gearing could be removed and replaced with new gearing of a different design, which had been manufactured in Britain and shipped to Australia. The turbines were also closely inspected but found to be in good order.

On 27 July 1937, *Awatea* conducted sea trials off the New South Wales coast, and for the first time all six boilers were fired up. It was reported in the press that the ship achieved a maximum speed in excess of 26 knots, although the official announcement put the top speed at just over 23 knots.

Awatea returned to the Tasman trade at the end of July, with a voyage from Sydney to Auckland, from where it was due to sail again on Friday, 6 August 1937. One of the Matson liners, *Monterey*, was also due to depart Auckland for Sydney the same day, the first time *Awatea* had been able to directly compete with one of the American liners. *Awatea* left first, followed four hours later by *Monterey*, but the two liners did not sight each other during the crossing. At the same time, *Wanganella* was on a voyage from Wellington to Sydney.

On the morning of Monday, 9 August 1937, the three liners passed through Sydney Heads, *Awatea* leading the way at 7.30, followed by *Wanganella* at 9.32, then *Monterey* at 10.18. This meant that *Monterey* had made the crossing one hour and 15 minutes faster than *Awatea*, but had not beaten its own record, as both ships had been forced to reduce speed for almost a day when they encountered heavy weather.

Captain Davey was determined that *Awatea* would take the record from the Americans, but needed the right conditions and situation to do it. The opportunity arose on Friday, 3 September, when both *Awatea* and *Mariposa* were scheduled to depart Auckland for Sydney. Heavy rain during the day delayed the loading of cargo, so *Awatea* was almost six hours late in departing, while *Mariposa* did not get away until the next day.

Encountering favourable weather in the Tasman on Saturday, Captain Davey ordered that a fifth boiler be brought into service, and speed increased to over 24 knots, but on Sunday the weather deteriorated, and speed had to be reduced. Despite this, *Awatea* arrived off Sydney Heads just before 7 am on the Monday morning, having completed the voyage in 2 days, 9 hours and 31 minutes, cutting 41 minutes off the time set by *Monterey*.

On its next voyage from Auckland, weather conditions were ideal for *Awatea* to make a concerted effort to create an even better time. Departing Auckland on 1 October 1937, a special speed trial was run over a 24-hour period during which *Awatea* maintained an average speed of 23.35 knots, covering 576 nautical miles. Even then the ship was not utilising its maximum power, but the average speed for the entire trip was 23.1 knots, and the previous record was eclipsed by 2 hours and 4 minutes. The new time of 2 days 7 hours 28 minutes would not be beaten for 24 years, until June 1961, when the *Oriana* made the trip from Sydney to Auckland in 47½ hours, at an average speed of 27 knots.

On 25 October 1937, *Awatea* arrived in Auckland

to complete another record-breaking voyage, having taken 2 days 10 hours and 52 minutes on the crossing from Sydney, beating the record set exactly a year earlier by 44 minutes.

Awatea now held the record time for all the major routes across the Tasman Sea in both directions. To celebrate this, the Union Line commissioned Cockatoo Dock to construct a stainless steel greyhound, which was mounted proudly on the fore truck on *Awatea* to symbolise its title of 'Queen of the Tasman Sea'. When Captain Johanson of the *Monterey* saw the emblem, he sent a message to Captain Davey asking why he had a kangaroo at his masthead!

The arrival of *Awatea* meant *Monowai* was sometimes used on other routes, leaving the Tasman trade to *Wanganella* and the new liner. While *Awatea* regularly made news with record-breaking voyages, *Wanganella* continued to maintain a regular service across the Tasman without attracting too much attention.

In a preview of things to come, on 27 December 1937 *Centaurus*, an Empire-class flying-boat operated by Imperial Airways, had taken off from Rose Bay in Sydney Harbour on the first exploratory flight to New Zealand, landing on Waitemata Harbour in Auckland. The next day *Samoan Clipper* became the first Pan American Airways flying-boat to arrive in Auckland, on a flight from San Francisco, Hawaii and Pago Pago, on its way to Sydney.

Although neither of these flights immediately resulted in the establishment of a regular air service across the Tasman, it was clearly only a matter of time before travellers would have the choice of making the journey by a ship taking over three days or an aircraft, which at that time took about eight hours.

On the same day that *Centaurus* took off from Sydney, *Wanganella* arrived there in the morning from Wellington, and the same afternoon departed for Melbourne.

At 1.40 am on 28 December 1937, when off the south coast of New South Wales, *Wanganella* and the 271 gross ton Red Funnel Line trawler *Durraween* were involved in a collision about 18 miles/30 km off Montague Island. The bow of the trawler was badly buckled, and two members of the crew injured, while *Wanganella* suffered some damaged plates on the starboard side, immediately below the forward funnel. Shortly after the collision, *Wanganella* turned around and headed back to Sydney, as did the *Durraween*.

According to the report of the incident in the *Sydney Morning Herald* next day:

> Both ships were able to return to Sydney. The *Wanganella* arrived in the afternoon, and the *Durraween* berthed at Woolloomooloo last night. No one on the *Wanganella* was injured, but two men on the *Durraween* were thrown violently against parts of the ship when the collision occurred and received injuries for which they were treated on their return to port.
>
> The *Durraween* steamed slowly up the harbour and took up a berth at Woolloomooloo. Entrance to the wharf was strictly forbidden, and those seamen who left the ship observed a strict reticence. They told Press representatives that they had been forbidden to divulge any details of the collision. Two members of the

Wanganella in the late 1930s.

trawler's crew stated that there was a slight mist at the time of the collision.

However, a reporter was later able to interview one of the injured men, Peter Stanhope, after he had been treated in hospital and allowed to go home.

Stanhope, who was on watch at the time of the accident, was interviewed by a *Herald* representative at his residence in Victoria Street, Darlinghurst. He had already retired to bed. He said that at the moment of the impact he was flung against the wall, and remembered very little of what happened afterwards. 'I was knocked unconscious,' he said, 'and I have been in a daze ever since. I am sorry I cannot tell you anything.'

Most of the 13 members of the crew were asleep when the accident occurred, and they were flung from their bunks. Evidence of the great force of the impact was apparent by the *Durraween*'s bows. For about six feet they were buckled and twisted into a hundred shapes and indentations. It is stated that her bows had been reinforced, otherwise it seemed that the *Durraween*'s plight would have been even more serious.

The bow of the *Durraween* struck the *Wanganella* a glancing blow on the starboard side, near the first class dining room. The force of the impact threw six stewards from their bunks in the 'glory hole' immediately abaft the point of collision, but none of them was injured. Rudely awakened by the shock, passengers rushed on deck in their night attire, but there was no panic. Officers and crew praised the coolness of the women.

'The most thrilling experience of my life,' was the way one woman passenger from New Zealand described the collision. 'My cabin was down on the starboard side astern, and I got the full effect of the crash,' she said. 'I was awake in an instant before the noise had died down. I thought at first the ship had blown up; I could not have wasted much time in getting up on deck, as I seemed to be the first there.

'Everybody seemed to take it all very calmly, and I took my cue from the others. We could see the trawler near the ship's side, but it was some time before we connected her with what had happened. Word was passed around quickly that there was no danger, and many of the passengers started to drift off to bed. By the time that the ship's head was turned around in the direction of Sydney, there were very few left on deck, and it must have come as a surprise to most in the morning to find that we were bound north instead of making for Melbourne.'

The actual point of impact was at the outer end of a transverse watertight bulkhead at the after end of the first class dining saloon. Two strakes above the waterline and two below were started by the buckling of the bulkhead, about nine or ten plates being affected.

After inspection of the damage by the Chief Engineer (Mr Wylie), who was lowered over the ship's side, repairs were made by bolting two plates along the upper damaged strake. Water was shipped through the plates below the waterline, but it was kept well in hand by pumping.

The *Wanganella* arrived at Sydney from New Zealand on Monday, and left Sydney the same afternoon for Melbourne carrying 108 passengers. On her return yesterday, 44 passengers were transferred to the *Orungal*, whose departure for Melbourne was delayed to receive them. An inspection of the ship on berthing revealed a heavy dent on the starboard side reaching a maximum depth of about nine or ten inches above the waterline. The plating had been reinforced by two heavy plates bolted outside the top damaged strake.

In the dining saloon were signs of a slight buckling of the bulkhead, giving evidence of the force of the collision. The asbestos panelling of the saloon was cracked, and a wireless loudspeaker had been smashed.

The most serious damage noticed to the stewards' quarters was to a porthole, of which the brass frame was bent and the glass shattered. The manager of Huddart Parker Ltd (Mr T. J. Parker), who boarded the ship with other officials of the company immediately she berthed, said that the damage was 'negligible'.

Wanganella went into drydock at Cockatoo Island so the hull below the waterline could be inspected. This showed that the damage to the ship was only slight, and could be quickly repaired.

Wanganella had been scheduled to depart Sydney for Auckland on 31 December, but this was delayed to Monday, 3 January 1938. Ten days later *Wanganella* departed on a voyage to Wellington, then on 24 January left Sydney for Melbourne.

While *Awatea* proudly held all the trans-Tasman records, the Matson liners *Mariposa* and *Monterey* were not far behind, and striving to reclaim the records between Sydney and Auckland. The Union Line was adamant that *Awatea* was not to become involved in any races with the American liners, and their schedules did not coincide for a lengthy period. This changed on 10 June 1938, when both *Awatea* and *Mariposa* were due to depart Auckland for Sydney. *Awatea* left on time at 5 pm, but *Mariposa* was an hour late when it pulled away from the dock at 11 pm.

As they approached Sydney Heads *Awatea* and *Mariposa* were almost together, while coming from a more southerly direction was *Wanganella*, on a voyage from Wellington, though it had left a full day earlier than the other two. *Awatea* passed through Sydney Heads at 5.05 pm, followed at 5.10 by *Wanganella* and *Mariposa* at 5.15.

Quizzed later by newspaper reporters, both

Captain Davey and Captain William Meyer of the *Mariposa* denied they had been engaged in a race. Asked for his comment, Captain Bates of the *Wanganella* replied, 'It was just like three horses racing abreast down the straight. It was a wonderful sight. It will probably never happen again.' Sadly, these last words would prove to be only too true.

Later in 1938 Captain Bates retired from command of *Wanganella*, being replaced by Captain Robert Darroch, who would remain with the ship for the next decade.

Wanganella continued to ply her way back and forth across the Tasman, carrying passengers and cargo, and animals as well. Mostly these were horses and cows, but sometimes a more unusual selection of animals would be carried, and they did not always enjoy their seagoing experience, as described in the following story published in the *Sydney Morning Herald* on 5 April 1938:

SEASICK ELEPHANTS
Rough Passage from N.Z.
CIRCUS COMES TO SYDNEY

Nine elephants gazed dismally over the side of the *Wanganella* as the vessel berthed yesterday after a rough passage from New Zealand. They had stood in practically the same position since the vessel left New Zealand and for hours were under a continual shower of salt spray as the seas came over the vessel's bows.

Forming part of Wirth's Circus, the elephants were accompanied by lions, tigers, leopards, monkeys, wombats, dogs, horses, and bears.

Mollie, a sprightly young elephant of 72, was the worst sailor. With tears in her eyes she was 'seedy' for most of the trip. Princess Alice, 151 years old, thought nothing of the buffeting. She has made 18 Tasman crossings and has been round the world twice.

On the trip one of the elephants, in a 'don't care' mood, poked his trunk into the nearby cabin of the chief steward, knocked over the lamp, and picking up the bedspread drew it through the porthole and consigned it to the deep.

Harold, the orang-outang, was the worst sailor of the circus. As soon as he felt the slightest motion, he clapped his hands to his head, closed his eyes, and was ill. The sight of food or drink made him shudder. His reactions were exactly those of a human being.

In mid-November 1938 *Wanganella* was taken off the Tasman trade to undergo maintenance, being replaced for two round trips by *Westralia*. The first motorship to be built for Huddart Parker Limited, *Westralia* was delivered to the company in 1929, and was placed on the major inter-state service from Sydney and Melbourne to Adelaide and Fremantle, with a departure from either terminal port every four weeks. By 1938 the route had been extended to include a call at Brisbane as well.

On 5 November 1938 *Wanganella* departed Sydney for Auckland, being due to commence the return trip on Friday, 11 November, but this was prevented by a waterside strike. It was not until Wednesday, 16 November, that *Wanganella* was able to depart Auckland, arriving back in Sydney on 20 November.

Meanwhile, *Westralia* had departed 3 Darling Harbour at 2.30 pm on Saturday, 19 November, on its first voyage across the Tasman Sea, bound for Wellington. This was followed on 2 December by a departure from Sydney for Wellington. On returning to Sydney, *Westralia* underwent a brief refit before resuming its place on the Fremantle trade with a sailing from Sydney on 24 December.

Wanganella returned to service with a departure from Sydney on 16 December for Wellington, followed by a 31 December voyage to Auckland.

Going into 1939 *Wanganella* maintained its regular schedule across the Tasman Sea. World War II started on 3 September 1939 when *Wanganella* was in Sydney, and departed for Melbourne on 4 September..

Westralia in the 1930s.

10

World War II

The outbreak of war in Europe in September 1939 did not have any immediate impact on the liners involved in the trans-Tasman trade, with both *Wanganella* and *Awatea* maintaining their regular schedule into 1940. However, *Monowai* was requisitioned by the New Zealand Government on 21 October 1939, and converted for war service as an armed merchant cruiser. The war had caused a huge reduction in the number of passengers travelling across the Tasman, so the vessel's removal did not cause any major problems.

It was not until the middle of 1940 that the war really impacted on the trans-Tasman trade. On 19 June 1940, *Wanganella* was approaching Auckland on a voyage from Sydney when a distress message was picked up from the Canadian-Australasian Line passenger liner *Niagara*. It had left Auckland the previous day bound for Suva, Honolulu and Vancouver, but early the following morning struck a mine, and quickly began to sink. Less than two hours after the explosion *Niagara* had sunk, leaving survivors in lifeboats until *Wanganella* arrived on the scene.

Despite the danger of also hitting a mine, *Wanganella* rescued 340 of the people in lifeboats, being assisted by the small New Zealand coaster *Kapiti*, then continued her voyage to Auckland. The minefield had been laid just four days earlier by the German commerce raider *Orion*.

Two months later, *Wanganella* was lucky to avoid a closer encounter with *Orion*. On 20 August 1940, *Wanganella* was again en route from Sydney to Auckland when, at 5 pm, *Orion* came across the New Zealand Shipping Company vessel *Turakina*, en route from Wellington to Sydney. Although his vessel was armed only with a single gun at the stern, Captain J. B. Laird fought the raider for over two hours until his ship was reduced to a blazing hulk. *Orion* then sank *Turakina* with two torpedoes, and 35 persons, including Captain Laird, lost their lives; *Orion* took on board 73 survivors. *Wanganella* was only about 100 miles/160 km north of the scene of this battle, and the raider had cut across her course, missing the liner by only a few hours.

In July 1940, *Awatea* was taken off the Tasman trade, and replaced by *Maunganui*. *Awatea* made a quick trip to Manila to collect women and children who had been evacuated from Hong Kong, and carry them to Sydney. With the loss of the *Niagara*, *Awatea* was then needed for two round trips from Sydney and Auckland to Vancouver, which kept her busy until the end of year.

In December 1940, *Awatea* was called upon to carry 700 New Zealand troops to the Middle East in convoy US8. The ship was still painted in Union Line colours, and her luxurious accommodation was not converted in any way, so the troops had a very comfortable voyage. Departing Wellington on 20 December, accompanied by *Dominion Monarch*, the pair arrived in Sydney on 23 December.

Five days later *Awatea* and *Dominion Monarch* departed Sydney, along with *Queen Mary* and *Aquitania*, while in Bass Strait *Mauretania* also joined the convoy from Melbourne. After a stop in Fremantle, the convoy went on to Ceylon, where the troops were transferred to other vessels to complete their trip to the Middle East. On returning to Australia, *Awatea* made several more voyages to Vancouver during 1941. In September 1941 *Awatea* was requisitioned by the British Government while at Vancouver, and converted into a troop transport.

Wanganella and *Maunganui* continued to operate the Tasman trade until January 1941, when *Maunganui* was requisitioned. This left *Wanganella* to carry on the trade alone, but on 19 May 1941 the ship was requisitioned by the Australian Government for conversion into a hospital ship. This brought the regular trans-Tasman passenger service to a halt, leaving many New Zealanders stranded in Australia. On 26 September 1941 the Union Line inter-island ferry *Rangatira* left Wellington at 7.30 pm for Sydney, making a fast passage to arrive at 3 pm on the 29th. With every cabin full and extra mattresses placed in public rooms, *Rangatira* left Sydney at 11 pm on the 29th, arriving back in Wellington at 5.15 pm on 2 October.

Wanganella was converted into a hospital ship at Port Melbourne. Walls between cabins were removed to make large wards, with permanent cots for about 400 patients, using a standard pattern that had been found satisfactory in earlier hospital ships. When required, an additional 150 canvas cots could be erected in an emergency.

There were some swinging cots, which were used in special fracture cases, but mostly fixed cots were fitted, both single and double-tiered, with 3 feet/1 m of space round each cot where possible. Special wards were provided for orthopaedic cases, infectious diseases, and mental afflictions. The Tudor Lounge became a fully-equipped operating theatre, including a plaster room and X-ray department, and was fitted with air-conditioning. A dental surgery was fitted on the shelter deck.

The hull was repainted white with a wide green band, broken by three red crosses which could be illuminated at night, while her official number, 45, was painted near the bow. The funnels were painted a lighter shade of yellow, with a red cross on the forward one. The ship was officially designated His Majesty's 2/2nd Australian Hospital Ship *Wanganella*.

Most of the merchant navy officers and crew remained with the ship in its new role, while the Navy was responsible for maintenance and the movements of the vessel. The medical staff was drawn from the Australian Army Medical Corps, the senior medical officer administering the unit as an army general hospital of from 300 to 600 beds.

The medical staff embarked at Port Melbourne on 28 July 1941, and *Wanganella* departed on 31 July for Sydney, berthing there on 2 August. The ship remained in Sydney four weeks, then embarked the 2/13th Australian General Hospital unit.

Leaving Sydney on 30 August, *Wanganella* stopped overnight in Melbourne, then continued to Fremantle for another overnight stopover. Arriving in Singapore on 15 September, the members of the 2/13th AGH disembarked. Less than six months later they would all be either prisoners of war, or dead.

Having embarked 142 patients suffering from various illnesses, and 216 other passengers, *Wanganella* departed Singapore on 17 September, stopping at Fremantle before arriving in Melbourne on 29 September, and Sydney on 2 October.

Wanganella as a hospital ship (WSS Victoria).

On 7 October *Wanganella* left Sydney on a much longer voyage, to Port Tewfik at the southern end of the Suez Canal. On the outward voyage the ship carried the 2/12th Australian General Hospital to Colombo, then went on to Egypt to collect casualties, arriving in Port Tewfik on 2 November. As the hospital ship moved into the port, it passed the hulk of the former British liner *Georgic*, which had been built by Harland & Wolff at the same time as *Wanganella*. *Georgic* was set on fire during a German bombing raid on the port on the night of 14 July 1941, and run aground to prevent it sinking.

One night when *Wanganella* was berthed in Port Tewfik, the Germans launched a bombing raid. Captain Darroch, no doubt mindful of the fate that had befallen *Georgic*, wanted to move his ship into the bay and illuminate it to show it was a hospital ship, but British Naval authorities refused him permission, and ordered the lights be kept off. Despite having a British corvette alongside firing at the German aircraft, *Wanganella* was not damaged in the attack.

The fourth engineer, Doug Taylor, recalled an amusing incident that happened while *Wanganella* was in Port Tewfik on this trip.

The Clarkson Exhaust Gas Thimble Tube boiler was very popular in motor ships 50 years ago. They consisted of a vertical outer cylindrical shell with an inner vertical flue with a multitude of thimbles expanded into it protruding into the gas flow. This resulted in giving the water/steam a pulsating effect. They operated at sea on exhaust gas and in port with an oil burner. The whole outer shell could be lifted vertically at survey time.

We had one such boiler in the top of the engine room in HMAHS *Wanganella*. I recall arriving in Port Tewfik and seeing TSMV *Georgic* burnt out and on the sand bank. Our orders were for a quick turn around as it was not a healthy place to be in.

All engineers were below, hot, sweaty and oily, changing head compressor valves, crank case inspection etc. when the telephone rang. I answered it and the voice, who I thought was the bosun, said 'there are sparks coming out of the funnel'. I cheekily replied 'what do you expect snow flakes' and hung up.

I dispatched a junior to clean the oil burner and the next thing the Chief Engineer arrived on the plates enquiring who had answered the phone. On owning up he gave me a roasting as it had been the Captain who had phoned down.

Wanganella berthing at Station Pier, Melbourne.

Departing Port Tewfik on 5 November, carrying 349 patients and 173 passengers, mostly troops returning home, *Wanganella* stopped briefly at Colombo on 15 November, and arrived in Fremantle on 24 November. Leaving the next day, the vessel was in Adelaide on 29 November, and Melbourne on 1 December, arriving back in Sydney on 3 December, and Brisbane on 6 December. Having discharged all patients and passengers, *Wanganella* returned to Sydney on 8 December 1941, the day Australia declared war on Japan.

Zealandia, which had operated across the Tasman for a year before *Wanganella* entered service, was also taken up for military service in June 1940, and converted into a troopship by Cockatoo Dockyard in Sydney. Designated as Hired Transport, Number KZ6, *Zealandia* departed Sydney on her first trooping voyage on 30 June, carrying 890 troops and their supplies to Darwin. This was the first of several trips to Darwin, then during 1941 *Zealandia* was used to transport troops to Papua New Guinea until being designated for a voyage to Singapore with 754 troops of the 8th Division. *Zealandia* then resumed her voyages to Papua New Guinea.

On 24 January 1942, *Zealandia* left Sydney with troops on board, and arrived in Darwin on 6 February. The wharves were all fully utilised, so *Zealandia* had to anchor out in the harbour, with disembarkation for the troops a slow process into barges. *Zealandia* was still at anchor in Darwin Harbour, having unloaded only half her cargo, when Japanese aircraft attacked on 19 February. A bomb exploded in No 3 hatch, just behind the engine room, setting *Zealandia* on fire. The blaze spread rapidly, and *Zealandia* later sank, leaving her two tall masts showing above the water. Amazingly, of the 145 men on board at the time of the attack, only three were killed.

Wanganella made another two trips to Egypt, which departed Sydney on 13 December 1941 and 13 March 1942. Doug Taylor recalled:

During one of the trips on the HMAHS *Wanganella* to the Middle East one of our refrigerated meat rooms 'went off' and the contents had to be dumped over the side. As a result of this, as well being the senior watchkeeper, I was suddenly put in charge of the refrigeration, which consisted of two CO_2 compressors, two brine pumps, one brine tank and one condenser all in the engine room while the refrigerated chambers were in No. 3 hold.

CO_2 plants are not at their best with the high sea temperatures in the Red Sea and to add to the problem a brine circuit had been taken off the original system to an air-conditioning plant in the operating theatre for use when an operation was in progress. I was having trouble holding the temperatures down in the refrigerating chambers and on testing the brine density with a Twaddell hydrometer (what a strange name) I found it to be too low resulting in a tendency for icing in the coils in the brine tank.

The Chief Engineer, John Wylie, asked me what the problem was so I told him I would have to empty our small stock of Calcium Chloride into the tank. He showed me a letter from the Admiralty stating that Calcium Chloride was in short supply and had to be conserved. Being an old navy man from WWI he would not allow me to add our small stock to the tank, and 'to find something else wrong'. Well I did find that one of the two brine centrifugal pumps was wired wrongly and thus running in the wrong direction (although it still pumped it was at reduced efficiency).

I battled on to Sydney where we tied up at our berth, No. 3 Darling Harbour. On the first night in I was Duty Engineer when the 2nd Electrician, who had been

Zealandia on fire in Darwin Harbour (Dallas Hogan collection).

down on the wharf, rushed aboard to tell me that the previous ship at the berth had discharged drums of Calcium Chloride which were still there. He hooked a drum on, I drove the winch and we hauled a drum aboard, cut it open and put its contents into the brine tank, later dumping the empty drum overboard to destroy the evidence. The next trip the refrigerator was working 100%. When the Chief asked how I achieved this I replied 'a bit of this and a bit of that' and the Chief stated 'I told you it was not a lack of Calcium Chloride'. 'Yes Chief,' I answered. After all these years I apologise to the consignee.

Wanganella made her first voyage to New Guinea with a departure from Sydney on 28 May 1942, arriving in Port Moresby on 3 June. This was followed by another two voyages to Egypt, then 1943 started with a second visit to Port Moresby, and on to Milne Bay. *Wanganella* spent the rest of 1943 and early 1944 making four voyages to Egypt and two trips to New Guinea.

On 24 March 1944, *Wanganella* departed Sydney on trip number 13 as a hospital ship, the destination being Taranto in Italy. No doubt there would have been some superstitious persons on board who wondered if this trip would be unlucky, but things seemed to be going well as the ship made its usual stop at Fremantle, then headed across the Indian Ocean, arriving in Bombay on 14 April, and anchoring out in the harbour.

The Bombay docks were filled with ships of all types and sizes, working a variety of cargoes. Just after 4 pm, the entire area was rocked by two huge explosions on a cargo ship, the *Fort Stikine*, berthed in the port, and a huge column of black smoke rose high into the sky. The concussion from the blast caused *Wanganella*, anchored 2 miles/3.2 km away, to shudder violently, and it soon became apparent that a terrible disaster had occurred.

Built in 1942 by the Prince Rupert Dry Dock & Shipyard Co., at Prince Rupert in British Columbia, Canada, and now managed by the Port Line for the Ministry of War Transport, *Fort Stikine* had left Birkenhead on 24 February 1944 carrying a cargo of aeroplanes and their stores, explosives and ammunition bound for Karachi, and a further consignment of explosives and stores for Bombay. Having arrived at Karachi on 30 March, and discharged the cargo destined for that port, the holds were filled with more cargo for Bombay, including cotton, timber, lubricating oil, resin and sulphur. On arrival in Bombay, *Fort Stikine* berthed in Victoria Dock, where explosives were not usually unloaded.

On 14 April, a fire broke out in No. 2 hold on *Fort Stikine*, where some of the cotton was loaded, along with other flammable goods. As water was played on the blaze, burning cotton began to float about, and some ended up under the magazine where some of the explosives were stored. At 4 pm a large explosion occurred, and the fire spread rapidly to other parts of the ship, including No. 4 hold, where more explosives were contained. At about 4.30 pm a second explosion occurred, much larger than the first, and *Fort Stikine* completely disintegrated.

The second explosion caused a 'tidal wave' to sweep through the packed dock. Seventeen ships were totally destroyed either by the explosion or the massive wave, and five more were badly damaged. The 3935 gross ton *Jalapadma* was lifted bodily by the wave and washed onto a wharf shed, ending up with a broken back. An area of 100 acres/40 ha around the explosion scene was devastated, and casualties included 336 people killed and over 2000 injured. It was the worst maritime disaster of the war years not caused by enemy action.

Wanganella was the right ship in the right spot at the right time. As the full extent of the calamity became apparent, local hospitals were soon filled to capacity with injured, and the medical staff of *Wanganella* were asked to assist as a Casualty Clearing Station. By 6 pm boats were arriving laden with injured people, and the operating theatre was in constant use for 36 hours straight. For four days the ship's wards were filled, and medical staff worked around the clock until spaces could be found for the injured in hospitals ashore.

An eye-witness account of this incident was written some years later by a former crew member, J. Bratton:

> Arriving shortly after 11 am, the ship was anchored in the harbour, out about three-quarters of a mile from the dock area. As I recall, the explosions took place about 4 pm. Both explosions rocked the ship and threw many on board out of their bunks.
>
> Shortly after the second explosion, Captain Darroch was ordered to bring the ship in as close as possible. As the hospitals ashore were over-loaded, the *Wanganella* was used as a hospital.
>
> Lt.-Col. Brown-Craig, in charge of Army personnel, had his team of doctors and nurses operating round the clock for eight days, desperately trying to save the lives of hundreds brought out to the ship.
>
> Members of the crew, including myself, ran a shuttle service with lifeboats from ship to shore, picking up survivors where possible. A report was received the ship had been sunk, of course this was untrue, but my hat goes off to the magnificent work done by the medical staff on board.

The hospital ship *Wanganella* (Dallas Hogan collection).

Another former crew member, Con Gall, later recalled:

I was 'bucko' on the *Wanganella* at the time. The purpose of being in Bombay was to transport British wounded from the Burma campaign to Port Said for transfer to the *Oranje* for repatriation to the UK. We arrived and anchored in Bombay Roads, about a mile off the docks. I was in the shower when an almighty explosion occurred and the ship felt as if it had been lifted out of the water and shaken. My immediate thought was a midget submarine had torpedoed the adjacent tanker. On running to the forecastle there was a tremendous pall of smoke and flames everywhere in the docks. We could see flames leaping up high over the warehouses and sheds. Some 30–45 minutes after the explosion a second erupted, debris was scattered and set fire to everything in the area. This must have been in the ammunition dock as for some hours there were more explosions and it looked like oil tanks were erupting.

About half an hour later we started to receive injured dock workers and seamen. They arrived in ship's boats, launches, canoes, anything that would float. We rigged the derricks on No. 4 hold where a lifting device for stretchers was stowed. For walking casualties we lowered the gangway where the deck crew and medical orderlies assisted them aboard.

The operating theatre, which was the old Promenade Lounge on the saloon deck, commenced work and was in use for 36 hours non-stop. During the night a ship of about 5,000 tons glowed red hot, in the morning it was a crumpled black shell. The following day we were still receiving casualties from the ships and docks. Dozens of bodies were floating with debris around the anchored ships, my recollection of this was the natives in canoes robbing the bodies.

As 'bucko' messenger on the bridge, I saw an interesting side of our Master (Captain Robert Darroch). After a couple of days we needed watering and despite repeated calling by Aldis [signal lamp] the signal station would not answer. Captain Darroch called to me to take him the International Signal Book. He asked me to make the signal 'Am coming in. Urgently need water.' Within ten minutes the Port Authorities called us up and told us to stay where we were. A couple of hours later a water lighter came alongside. We took this opportunity to off-load the 8 or 9 bodies we had stored in the lazaret. These were patients who did not survive.

Another few days elapsed before we could go alongside to discharge our Bombay casualties and embark our British patients for transit to Port Said.

From this horrific disaster the *Wanganella* emerged with honour and dignity. On our return to Bombay some three months later, we received a great reception from all in port as we proceeded to anchor. My part in all this was very small and humble, but I am proud to have been a part of Australian maritime history.

Then it was time for *Wanganella* to fulfil the role that had brought it to Bombay, embarking British military patients who were being sent home. Leaving Bombay on 20 April, *Wanganella* went on to Egypt, where the British patients were transferred to another hospital ship, *Oranje*, for the final stage of their voyage home.

Wanganella passed through the Suez Canal, and crossed the Mediterranean Sea to the Italian port of Taranto, where just over 1000 wounded New Zealand troops were embarked.

On the voyage back, *Wanganella* called at Colombo on 22 May, leaving a short time before Japanese bombers attacked the port, sinking the cruiser that *Wanganella* had been moored alongside. After a brief stopover at Fremantle, *Wanganella* went directly to Wellington, arriving on 10 June, and Lyttelton two days later.

Returning to Sydney on 16 June, *Wanganella* spent two weeks in port, then left again for Egypt and Taranto to collect more New Zealand casualties, returning them to Wellington and Lyttelton in late September.

Arriving back in Sydney once more on 29 September, *Wanganella* remained there until 22 November, and finished 1944 with a short trip from Sydney to Darwin and back. Reaching Sydney on 8 December 1944, *Wanganella* underwent an extensive overhaul over the next four months. This was probably the result of engine problems that had developed on a voyage home from Egypt.

In his excellent book *Hospital Ships*, Rupert Goodman reproduced the following account provided by Fourth Engineer Doug Taylor, concerning a major incident that occurred on the ship:

> When the hospital ship HMAHS *Wanganella* was returning from one of her numerous trips to the Middle East during World War II with a full load of wounded, she suffered a cracked piston in the port main engine. The weather was bad at the time and the ship was rolling heavily. Now a cracked piston was not an unknown occurrence in this type of engine and it had been evidenced by puffs of smoke coming from the particular piston cooling-oil return observation hopper.
>
> Owing to the motion of the ship it was decided to 'hang the unit up' rather than dismantle and fit a new piston, until such time as the weather moderated, as heavy weights were involved and all the lifting gear was hand operated and cumbersome.
>
> Thus the engine ran for a time on seven cylinders, resulting in extra vibration as the engine was no longer in balance. Unfortunately, this extra vibration affected those patients with limbs in plaster. After discussions with the Chief Medical Officer it was decided to stop the engine and fit a new piston, even though this was a hazardous task with the ship rolling so much.
>
> Under the direction of the Chief Engineer, John Wylie, the job was completed successfully and without incident.

Wanganella did not depart Sydney again until 7 April 1945, going north to Torokina, Lae and Jacquinot Bay, returning to Sydney on 23 April.

On its next voyage, due to depart Sydney on 17 May 1945, *Wanganella* was due to embark the entire 2/9th Australian General Hospital on the day prior to departure, but this was thwarted when the Sydney wharf labourers went on strike, a common occurrence at that time. Despite the fact that *Wanganella* was due to leave on a mission of mercy, the wharf labourers refused to allow any passengers or cargo to be loaded.

An alternative was quickly organised, and *Wanganella* left Sydney on 17 May, and went the short distance to Newcastle, where there was no strike, berthing at Lee Wharf. This was the only time *Wanganella* went to Newcastle, and the only visit by a hospital ship to that port during the war years. In September 1997, a plaque commemorating the visit was unveiled on an outside wall of the Queens Wharf Brewery building.

While *Wanganella* was on its way to Newcastle, the Army requisitioned a train to carry the medical personnel to the port, where they arrived in the evening, and were taken straight to the ship. In addition to the 2/9th AGH, nurses from the 2/4th AGH as well as the 2/1st and 2/3rd Casualty Clearing Stations joined the ship, to be taken to Moratai.

Wanganella departed Newcastle on 19 May, making an overnight visit to Brisbane before heading north to the islands. In a voyage lasting 82 days, *Wanganella* went first to Hollandia, Morotai and Tarakan, then back to Morotai, remaining there for a week.

Leaving Morotai on 2 July, *Wanganella* went to Labuan Island and Tarakan again, returning to Morotai on 10 July carrying 1040 patients as well as 456 other personnel. After another week in Morotai, *Wanganella* went to Balik Papan, returning to Morotai on 22 July. With a full complement of patients on board, *Wanganella* left Morotai for the last time on 28 July, making a brief stop at Lae before returning to Sydney on 8 August, ending what was destined to be her final wartime voyage as a hospital ship. On 15 August Japan surrendered.

The end of the war in the Pacific did not mean a quick return to commercial service for *Wanganella*, though, as her staff and facilities were now needed by released prisoners of war who had been held in terrible conditions by Japan.

Ten days after the Japanese surrender, *Wanganella* left Sydney, going first to Morotai on 6 September, then to Labuan, embarking extra medical personnel at each place. The vessel was ordered to go to Kuching in Sarawak, arriving there on 12 September, and boats were sent away to locate former prisoners of war. What happened next was described by Sister Wrexford, who was waiting for the first patients to be brought to *Wanganella*, as recorded in the book *Hospital Ships*:

> The following day our shockingly emaciated patients arrived in small boats. Their faded remnants of uniforms literally hanging on them, they made a brave attempt to mount the gangway unaided … a demonstration of

Wanganella with red crosses painted out after the war ended (Jan Edwards collection).

the indomitable spirit that had kept them alive for three and a half years and a moving experience for the whole ship's company. At first they protested at being treated like patients. Soon they fingered the white sheets on the bunks, giggled as they donned pyjamas, drained their china cups and looked at them in wonder. Then they asked questions. The hideous ulcers, sores and swellings seemed to fade as we talked.

Len Morris had been in the Batu Lintang prison camp at Kuching for over three years, and when the war ended he weighed a mere 73 pounds /33 kg. He later recalled:

My first real sight of the hospital ship occurred at a range of well over a mile ... Distances and sizes of things at sea can be very deceptive ... I realised she was far bigger in all respects than I had imagined. *Wanganella*, for such was her magic name, rode quietly at anchor unperturbed by wind or tide, unreal, dazzling white, clinically neat, a heavenly ship waiting patiently as a lover to receive us ... I swayed with the motion of the MTB. My liberator Massey laughed at my weakness but enthused, 'This is one hell of a good ship. You'll be alright now cobber!' It seemed a contradiction in terms to call *Wanganella* 'a hell of a ship'; to me she appeared as a vessel from another world, but I understood his concern to reassure me that indeed there was now hope of a future for us all.

The port side of the ship towered high above us. I viewed with dismay the formidable rank of steps leading from the launch to the main deck ... The slow energy sapping climb began. Each patient, for that was what we had become, was escorted by male Australian nurses. They were taking good care, that even as we had been snatched from under the Japanese heel, we should not fall now, and be claimed by the sea ... After an eternity of endeavour, advancing one step at a time, one by one we reached the deck. Behind me a voice avowed 'I would not like to have to do that all over again.' It was Slim Landers. I was not sure whether he meant the climb up the gangway or the three and a half years at Batu Lintang.

Wanganella then returned to Labuan, where British patients and Australians needing more intensive care were transferred to hospitals ashore, their places on the ship being taken by other released prisoners of war. *Wanganella* went on to Balik Papan to collect more patients, and was due to head for Sydney but was diverted to Hollandia, where an outbreak of meningitis needed treating. After returning briefly to Morotai to refuel and take on fresh water, *Wanganella* voyaged back to Sydney, arriving in early October.

On 27 October, *Wanganella* left Sydney on what was destined to be its final voyage as a hospital ship. At Labuan on 10 November patients and medical personnel due to return home were embarked. The vessel made a slow voyage back to Sydney, arriving on 23 November 1945.

Late in 1945, *Wanganella* was released from government service, and handed back to Huddart Parker Limited, but it would take almost a year to refit the liner for commercial service again. During her war service, *Wanganella* travelled over 251 611 miles/402 578 km, and carried 13 385 passengers, mostly sick and injured troops.

On 4 June 2003 at the Devonport Maritime Museum, in Tasmania, a new stained-glass window was dedicated to those who served in *Wanganella* as a hospital ship in World War II.

Prior to the war, *Wanganella* had operated across the Tasman Sea in conjunction with *Monowai* and *Awatea*, owned by the Union Steam Ship Company of New Zealand. *Monowai* had been taken over for military duty within months of the war starting, but *Awatea* was not requisitioned until September 1941, though prior to that date the liner had been engaged in various military voyages.

Awatea was converted into a troopship in Canada, and saw extensive service over the following year, usually travelling in convoys. On 22 August 1942, *Awatea* collided with an escorting destroyer, USS *Buck*, which was cut in two and sank. *Awatea* limped back to Halifax for repairs, and when these were completed the vessel crossed the Atlantic to Glasgow, to be prepared for participation in 'Operation Torch', the planned landings in North Africa.

On 8 November 1942, *Awatea* landed her troops at Algiers, and was scheduled to withdraw from the area. Instead, *Awatea* boarded troops rescued from another vessel that had been disabled, and took them to Jijelli to capture an airfield, but high seas prevented their being landed. *Awatea* was ordered to take these troops to Bougie, where they disembarked on 11 November.

Awatea then set course for Gibraltar, but the same afternoon the vessel was subjected to an intense attack by German bombers. Although several aircraft were shot down, *Awatea* was hit by several bombs, and set on fire. The captain made a gallant attempt to beach his ship, but the flames were spreading too quickly. *Awatea* was abandoned, and after burning for several more hours, the liner sank during the night of 11 November.

Monowai was requisitioned by the New Zealand Government on 21 October 1939, and work began on converting the vessel into an armed merchant cruiser at the Devonport Dockyard in Auckland. On 11 February 1940 the work was halted, but resumed on 23 June.

The vessel was commissioned into the Royal New Zealand Navy on 30 August 1940 as the Armed Merchant Cruiser HMS *Monowai*, fitted with eight 6 inch guns, two 3 inch anti-aircraft guns and six 20 mm guns, machine guns and depth charges. Captain Morgan and most of the engineering officers remained with the ship throughout the war.

Monowai served initially in the South Pacific, steaming over 140 000 miles/224 000 km during the next two and a half years, mainly escorting freighters, tankers and liners between Australia, New Zealand and Fiji. There were also a number of voyages taking troops from New Zealand to Fiji, Noumea, Tonga and Norfolk Island.

From 1 October 1941, after the Royal New Zealand Navy was established as a separate entity, the vessel became HMNZS *Monowai*.

On 16 January 1942, *Monowai* was escorting *Taroona* from Fiji back to Auckland when they were attacked by gunfire from the Japanese submarine *I-20*. *Monowai* fired her port-side guns in reply, the rounds just finding the range as the submarine

Monowai as an armed merchant cruiser (Bob McDougall collection).

crash-dived. *Monowai* and *Taroona* steamed at top speed through poorly charted waters to avoid possible torpedoes, and reached Auckland safely. Japanese records later revealed that *I-20* had fired four torpedoes at *Monowai*, but all missed.

On 24 April 1943, *Monowai* left Auckland bound for Great Britain, to be handed over to the British Ministry of War Transport and converted into an assault-landing ship on the Clyde. The work entailed considerable structural alterations, and the installation of twenty landing barges capable of landing 800 troops. Commissioned into the Royal Navy in February 1944, *Monowai* carried troops from Glasgow to Suez, then went to Taranto and Sicily before returning to Britain.

In April 1944, *Monowai* arrived in the Solent to carry out invasion exercises, then boarded 1800 British and Canadian troops on 3 June. On the evening of 5 June, *Monowai* slipped out of the Solent, being the largest vessel in the armada heading for the beaches of Normandy. As D Day dawned next morning her troops began disembarking into landing barges, to be sent ashore on 'Gold Beach'. Fourteen of the landing barges were destroyed by mines or underwater obstacles as they approached the beach.

Over the next five months, *Monowai* made twenty round trips to the beaches, carrying 30 000 troops. Between November 1944 and March 1945, *Monowai* carried a further 43 000 troops on 25 trips between Southampton and Le Havre. Apart from two brief occasions during boiler cleaning, steam was maintained on the main engines continuously for twelve months, and altogether *Monowai* made 45 crossings to France.

Following an overhaul, *Monowai* was sent to Odessa with released Russian prisoners of war, departing Plymouth on 22 April. Over the succeeding months, the vessel made numerous trooping voyages, then was sent to Colombo to prepare for the planned Allied landings in Malaya. When Japan surrendered in August 1945, *Monowai* was sent as a 'mercy ship' to Singapore, arriving on 8 September 1945.

Having embarked 650 service personnel and 199 civilians who had been prisoners of war in the notorious Changi Prison, on 13 September *Monowai* departed Singapore, and on 8 October arrived at Liverpool. The next five months were occupied with trooping voyages from Taranto and Suez to Karachi and Cochin, from Suez to Lagos, and from Suez to Bombay. After that *Monowai* spent a further five months in the Indian Ocean, visiting Colombo, Cocos Island, Madras, Calcutta, Port Swettenham, Vizagapatam and Rangoon.

By now *Monowai* was in a very run-down condition. The vessel returned to Sydney on 29 August 1946, and a few days later was released from military duty and handed back to her owners.

It is interesting to note that throughout the war a model of the historical Maori canoe *Tainui* and a Maori ceremonial cloak presented by Princess Te Puea Herangi were carried on the bridge of *Monowai*. These were tokens that, according to Maori tradition, afforded protection from an enemy, and Captain Morgan, in a defiant gesture linking him with the Maori members of his crew, wore the cloak whenever his ship was in danger of attack. After the war Captain Morgan sent the model canoe and cloak to the Auckland Naval Base where they are now on display.

At first the Union Line was far from enthusiastic about restoring *Monowai* for commercial service, as the ship was in very poor condition, especially the engines. However, the company was anxious to resume the trans-Tasman passenger service as soon as possible, so they decided to go ahead. As the Union Line workshop in Sydney was fully committed on the restoration of *Aorangi*, *Monowai* was placed in the hands of the Mort's Dock & Engineering Company, and it was hoped the liner would resume its place on the trans-Tasman service by the middle of 1947.

However, work on the ship stopped after just three weeks, due to a crane drivers' dispute. For seventeen weeks *Monowai* lay untended, until on 17 February 1947 work started again.

11

Post-War Problems

By the beginning of 1946 the thousands of New Zealand residents who had been stranded in Australia for the duration of the war were becoming anxious to return home. In an attempt to assist them, the Australian Government announced on 7 January 1946 that it would make the veteran coastal liner *Katoomba*, still serving as a troopship, available for a return trip from Sydney to Wellington, departing later that month. The vessel would then resume its trooping duty with another voyage to the islands to bring more Australian troops home.

The announcement of the special voyage to New Zealand had included a warning that the vessel would still be in troopship configuration, and provide only 'austerity' quarters for the passengers, though the number to be carried would be limited to 600 to provide some comfort. Despite this, the Sydney office of the Union Steam Ship Company of New Zealand, who had been appointed agents for the voyage, was rushed with applicants. Within days the ship was fully booked, and scheduled to depart Sydney at noon on Friday, 18 January 1946.

Katoomba had been built in 1913 for McIlwraith, McEacharn Limited, to operate on the major coastal route from Sydney and Melbourne to Adelaide and Fremantle. At 9424 gross tons, it had originally provided accommodation for 209 first class, 192 second class and 156 third class passengers.

Katoomba differed from the other coastal liners of the period in having three propellers, the outer shafts being driven by two coal-fired 8-cylinder triple-expansion reciprocating engines while the centre shaft was powered by a low-pressure turbine, a most unusual arrangement, but one which at one time made *Katoomba* the fastest liner on the coastal trades, with a service speed of 16 knots.

Katoomba saw service as a troopship in foreign waters during the final years of World War I, then resumed her place on the Australian coastal trade, and in the 1930s was also used for cruises to the Pacific Islands and New Guinea. *Katoomba* would probably have been sold for scrap in the early 1940s had not another war intervened.

With the more modern liners taken up for war duties, *Katoomba* had remained on the coastal trades, but also made several special voyages carrying troops to Darwin and New Guinea. When *Katoomba* arrived in Sydney on 13 August 1942, it was taken over for war service and extensively refitted to carry 1200 personnel. *Katoomba* subsequently saw service carrying both Australian and American troops during the various campaigns to oust the Japanese from the islands north of Australia. With the end of the war in 1945, *Katoomba* was used to bring Australian troops home from the islands.

On 3 January 1946, *Katoomba* arrived back in Sydney from Torokina carrying 1479 troops, berthing at 4 Darling Harbour. The vessel, which was still a coal burner, was then prepared for the special voyage to New Zealand. During the morning of 18 January the 600 passengers arrived at the Darling Harbour wharf and boarded, but behind the scenes trouble had been brewing on the previous day over the size of the crew signed on for the voyage. As the *Sydney Morning Herald* reported on 18 January:

Nearly 600 passengers for New Zealand who have been stranded in Sydney for some time may be further delayed by the tactics of an extremist element in the Communist-controlled Seamen's Union.

The announced sailing time of the liner *Katoomba* has been put back from noon today to 5 pm because of a dispute over the size of her crew.

The *Katoomba*, which is under charter to the Commonwealth Government, was taken off her troopship run to take back to New Zealand as many as possible of the 2,000 persons who are stranded in Sydney.

Under an agreement between the Seamen's Union and the Maritime Industry Commission, three men fewer

Katoomba.

are carried in the crew on this run to New Zealand than on the tropical run.

The Maritime Industry Commission has already ruled that the vessel should sail with the smaller crew than is carried in the tropics, but it is stated that officials of the Seamen's Union have made no serious attempt to ensure that the vessel is manned and gets away on time.

Most non-Communist members of the *Katoomba*'s crew are willing to take the liner to sea, but they have been overruled by the extremist elements in the union.

If the dispute is not settled today the 600 passengers will be seriously inconvenienced. They had been warned when the Commonwealth Government first announced that the *Katoomba* would make the passage that they would travel under 'austerity' conditions because it had not been possible completely to reconvert the troopship accommodation to normal passenger line standards. This announcement, however, did not stop a rush to secure accommodation on the liner.

Despite intensive negotiations on the afternoon of 18 January, the dispute was not resolved, and *Katoomba* remained alongside the dock overnight. While the majority of the crew went about their business as usual, the stokers refused to work, and called a meeting for 8 am on 19 January to decide whether to agree to operate the ship with three less men than were required for tropical voyages. The *Sydney Morning Herald* reported on 19 January:

The 'austerity' liner *Katoomba*, with nearly 600 New Zealand passengers already on board, may be delayed indefinitely if the stokehold section of the crew at a meeting in the ship at 8 am today decide not to man the ship.

The *Katoomba* was to have sailed for Wellington yesterday. Most of the passengers had given up their land accommodation in Sydney, and last night they were accommodated in the ship. The crew was at work with the exception of the stokehold complement, and passengers were provided with meals.

It is known that nearly all the firemen, in addition to all other members of the crew of the *Katoomba*, are quite willing to take her to sea, but there are one or two militants who are standing out, with the support of union officials.

The departure of the ship has now been fixed tentatively for 10 am today from No. 4 Wharf Darling Harbour, but whether she will sail will depend upon the decision of the firemen.

If the dispute becomes long drawn out the Commonwealth Government, which is anxious to allow the 2,000 New Zealanders stranded in Sydney to get home, will have to consider alternative transport. To do this at the present time would seriously affect other phases of the shipping industry.

Three members of the Gladys Moncrieff Company were dissatisfied with the accommodation in the *Katoomba*, which till lately has been a troopship, and told the general manager of J. C. Williamson Ltd. they would refuse to sail. They had their dinner on board last night, and later changed their minds, agreeing to make the voyage. The remainder of the company will leave Melbourne for New Zealand next week.

The outcome of the meeting of the 21 men of the *Katoomba*'s stokehold complement held aboard the liner that morning was another refusal to allow the ship to depart unless an extra three men were added to the stokehold crew. The response to this decision was to pay off the 21 men, and try to recruit a new stokehold crew that would allow the ship to sail on the afternoon of Monday, 21 January. Meanwhile, on the Sunday passengers waiting on board the ship decided to take matters into their own hands, as reported in the *Sydney Morning Herald* on Monday, 21 January.

> Impatient passengers on the liner *Katoomba* yesterday organised a 'three bob a head' fund to pay the wages of three additional firemen.
>
> The 600 passengers hoped to raise £60 for the firemen's wages by subscription, but they were told the dispute was between the Federal Government and the union on a matter of principle and not of finance.

On the Monday morning the Director of Shipping, Mr R. A. Hetherington, held another meeting with the Seamen's Union, but they remained adamant that a crew would not be supplied for the stokehold unless three additional men were employed. As a result, the ship could not depart on Monday afternoon, and late in the day Mr Hetherington announced that the voyage to New Zealand had been cancelled. On Tuesday, 22 January, the *Sydney Morning Herald* reported:

> Cancellation of the *Katoomba*'s voyage to New Zealand yesterday annoyed many of the 600 intending passengers, some of whom have furniture stored in the holds, and cannot easily find new accommodation in Sydney.
>
> The Union Company requested only passengers without shore accommodation to remain on the ship after the cancellation of the voyage was announced, but most passengers stayed on board last night.
>
> A passengers' protest committee ... sent a cable message to the Acting Prime Minister of New Zealand, Mr Walter Nash, asking him to take action on their behalf.
>
> The *Katoomba*'s stewards held a meeting and decided to continue to look after the passengers until transport was provided for them. Last night many people brought their beds out on deck to avoid the heat.
>
> It was thought that the *Wanganella*, now a hospital ship, might have been able to make the trip to New Zealand, but, as she is committed to bring troops from the Wewak area, the Government decided not to interfere with her schedule. No other ship is expected to be available for at least a week.
>
> Arrangements have been made for passengers who have no other accommodation to remain on board the *Katoomba* until a relief ship can be obtained. The passengers include women and young children. Some of the women are travelling without their husbands. Many families on board have all their household furniture stored in the *Katoomba*'s hold. Dozens have no homes in Sydney, and say they have no coupons and very little money.
>
> The *Katoomba* has 2,000 tons of cargo for New Zealand. Discharge of this will begin this morning. The cargo will go to New Zealand by the first available cargo ship.

At first it appeared that this was the end of the plan to send *Katoomba* to New Zealand, but the plight of the passengers stranded on board was a source of major concern. With accommodation ashore almost impossible to find, and the passengers no longer entitled to receive ration coupons so they could obtain essential food and other items, the Commonwealth Government agreed to cover their costs while they stayed on board the ship, and some crew members remained on board to look after them, though most of the crew was signed off.

At the same time further talks were initiated between the warring parties in the hope that a settlement could be reached. It took almost a week, but on Monday, 28 January, there seemed to have been a breakthrough, as reported in the *Sydney Morning Herald* on 29 January:

> The liner *Katoomba*, which has been held up in Sydney since January 18, is expected to sail for New Zealand with 550 passengers late on Thursday afternoon. A dispute over the number of firemen to be carried has caused the delay.
>
> The Director of Shipping said last night that it had been arranged for the *Katoomba* to sail for Wellington. From that port she would go to Torokina (Solomons), and Rabaul (New Britain), to bring Australian troops back to the mainland. Mr Hetherington said that it was proposed to carry 24 firemen, the number required under tropical articles.
>
> The Seaman's Union, he said, would hold a stop-work meeting this morning, and a call for crew to man the vessel would be made this afternoon. It was expected that it would take until Thursday afternoon for the ship to load coal bunkers and stores.

The decision to have *Katoomba* steam directly from Wellington to the islands, instead of returning first to Sydney, was a face-saving tactic for both parties to the dispute. As the ship would be going into tropical waters on the voyage, crew would be signed on tropical articles that included the provision of 24 firemen for the entire voyage, which had been the cause of the dispute.

Unfortunately, things did not go exactly to plan. On the Tuesday a question was raised regarding the ship being able to load sufficient bunkers in Sydney for the entire round trip, and while this was sorted out the call for a crew was postponed, and the departure put back a day, to Friday.

On 30 January a new crew was signed on, including 24 firemen, and work began on re-loading the cargo removed when the trip was cancelled, but it was going to take longer than anticipated, so the departure was delayed again, to 11 am on Saturday, 2 February, at which time the vessel managed to depart, the passengers having now been on board for over two weeks. As the *Sydney Morning Herald* reported on Monday, 4 February:

> The 560 passengers on the liner *Katoomba* cheered and sang as the vessel, which had been held up since January 18 by a dispute with the firemen, moved out of Darling Harbour on Saturday morning on its voyage to New Zealand.
>
> The departure, watched by a large crowd on the wharf, had something of the picturesqueness of a pre-war sailing. Passengers had no streamers, but found an obvious substitute.
>
> Most of the passengers had been living on the ship for more than two weeks while the dispute was being settled. They had urgent priorities for New Zealand.
>
> More than 1,500 people are still seeking passages to New Zealand.

Katoomba was well past her best by the time this voyage to New Zealand took place, and the vessel spent three days at sea before arriving in Wellington on Wednesday, 6 February. It was no doubt a great relief to the passengers to disembark and finally be home again.

Once the cargo had been unloaded, *Katoomba* left Wellington for the islands, picking up troops as planned at Totokina and Rabaul, arriving back in Sydney on 23 March. This was destined to be the last voyage *Katoomba* would make under the Australian flag. Too old and worn out to be worth reconditioning for the Australian coastal trades, the liner was laid up in Sydney until being sold a few months later to a Greek company, for which she served twelve years before being broken up.

There were still many New Zealanders stranded in Sydney and longing to return home, so in mid-1946, prior to being released from military service, the coastal liner *Manunda* was scheduled to make two trips from Sydney to New Zealand and back, carrying both military personnel and civilians. Fortunately neither of these voyages was disrupted in a similar way to that of the *Katoomba*.

The first of the *Manunda* voyages departed Sydney on 30 July 1946, going to Wellington, returning to Sydney on 10 August. Two days later, *Manunda* departed on a second voyage to Wellington, arriving back in Sydney on 21 August.

Manunda then loaded 950 tons of general cargo to be carried to Melbourne, departing Sydney on 31 August, and arriving in Melbourne two days later, to be refitted for a return to the coastal trades.

Although there were still hundreds of New Zealanders in Australia who wished to return home, no plans were brought forward for further trips across the Tasman by Australian vessels, and they would have to wait until *Wanganella* was available to take up a regular service again.

Manunda.

12

On the Rocks

Through 1946, work on refitting *Wanganella* for a return to commercial service had continued, but was not completed until October 1946. A couple of external alterations were made at this time, the original after deckhouse being joined to the main superstructure, and a new deckhouse added at the stern.

In her post-war guise, *Wanganella* carried 316 passengers in first class and 108 in second class, with a crew numbering 160. First class accommodation, which included two suites with private facilities, was amidships on the bridge and upper decks, while the second class cabins were located aft on the main deck. First class public rooms, which were mostly located on the promenade deck, included a main lounge which featured an overhead glass dome, a reading room and a smoking room. Second class had a separate lounge and smoking room aft on the same deck. The two dining saloons were on the main deck.

Instead of immediately resuming her place on the trans-Tasman trade, *Wanganella* was dispatched on a round voyage to Vancouver, on behalf of Canadian-Australasian Line. Of the two liners this company had operated before the war, *Niagara* had been sunk, while *Aorangi* had survived but was still undergoing a refit, a job that eventually took two years.

So, on Thursday, 31 October 1946 *Wanganella* departed Sydney on the voyage across the Pacific, the longest commercial trip the liner would make in her career. The first port of call was Auckland, then on to Suva, Honolulu and Vancouver. Leaving Vancouver on 27 November, *Wanganella* returned to Sydney on Saturday, 28 December.

The post-war Tasman trade would be rather different to that of the 1930s. As seemed to happen

Post-war appearance of *Wanganella* (David Cooper photo).

too often in the war, the newest liner on the route, *Awatea*, had been sunk, while the older vessels survived. On 17 February 1947, work resumed on refitting *Monowai*, but as the liner had been extensively altered for war service the job of restoring her to her pre-war status was lengthy, and it would be two years before the vessel was ready to resume service. Until then, the entire trans-Tasman service would have to be carried by *Wanganella* alone.

On Thursday, 16 January 1947, *Wanganella* departed Sydney on her first post-war trans-Tasman voyage, which took her to Wellington for the first time in almost six years. The ship was fully booked for the voyage, and departures from both Sydney and New Zealand were booked out for several months ahead. On returning to Sydney, *Wanganella* was scheduled to depart on 30 January for Auckland, then 13 February for Wellington, thus providing a fortnightly service with voyages to alternate ports. Huddart Parker had been very pleased to get the ship back into service so soon after the war ended, and looked forward to a profitable period, but their joy was to be very short-lived.

On the evening of 19 January, *Wanganella* entered Cook Strait, then turned to port to pass through the entrance to Wellington Harbour. This could be quite a tricky passage, especially in bad weather, but on this night the sky was clear and the seas calm. Despite this, at 11.43 pm *Wanganella* ran hard aground on Barrett Reef, a dangerous rocky outcrop in the centre of the entrance to Wellington Harbour. It later was discovered that a mistake had been made by officers on the bridge when interpreting the various buoys that marked the safe channel.

Immediately the ship went aground frantic attempts at refloating began by putting the engines full astern, but to no avail. Eventually it was realised that the liner was caught firmly by the rocks, and would require extra help to be refloated. As there appeared to be no immediate danger of the ship sinking, the passengers remained on board for the rest of the night, being ferried ashore next morning along with 60 non-essential crew. Three of the Wellington Harbour tugs, *Toia*, *Kahanui* and *Terawhiti*, joined forces to try and pull the liner free at high tide, but their attempts were unsuccessful.

On 21 January 1947 the Wellington newspaper,

Wanganella on the rocks (R. W. Brookes collection).

This map of the location where *Wanganella* ran aground was published in the Wellington newspaper, *The Dominion*, on 21 January 1947 (R. W. Brookes collection).

The Dominion, reported:

Today, the fate of the Huddart Parker liner *Wanganella* hangs in the balance. Disaster overtook the ship at 11.43 o'clock last night when, in fair weather, she ran on to Barrett's Reef at the entrance to Wellington Harbour.

Life-jackets were issued to the passengers, numbering nearly 400, among whom there was no panic. In the early hours of this morning, rescue measures were brought smoothly into action.

Small vessels from the port took off the passengers in relays, and they were brought safely to Queen's Wharf, where the ordinary Customs inspection was made. The only thing to suggest that there was an emergency was the distribution of refreshments at the wharf to passengers, who landed with bare necessities as their only luggage.

This circumstance, so casual as the passengers came ashore in brilliant sunshine, much in the manner of people returning from a harbour excursion, typified the whole catastrophe.

For the tragedy was that a liner which is familiar to many thousands of New Zealanders on the Tasman service, which gave valiant performance during the war

Front page of *The Weekly Times* published in Auckland on 29 January 1947 (R. W. Brookes collection).

Aerial view of *Wanganella* on Barrett Reef (R W Brookes collection).

as a hospital ship, and which was on the first voyage to resume the passenger service from Sydney, should have come to grief in clear weather.

The disaster happened quietly, and with the same sense of unreality as this morning's spectacle of unworried passengers disembarking from 5.10 o'clock onwards from several small vessels. There had been an excellent crossing of the Tasman, apparently a happy augury of the *Wanganella*'s resumption of her civilian life.

The night was dark but mild. The sea was smooth. Many of the passengers had retired, but others were about the decks enjoying at a late hour their final night aboard ship and the serene conditions.

A bump was felt by nearly all on board, but it was not sufficient to cause alarm or to disturb some sleepers. There are conflicting stories about its severity, but most agree that the shock was slight, and rather gradual. Certain it is that the passengers did not generally realize that the *Wanganella* had struck Barrett's Reef and was in a position which would have been perilous in unfavourable weather.

Within a few minutes, the report spread throughout the ship that the *Wanganella* was on the reef. To the passengers who assembled on deck, wearing life-jackets at the instructions promptly given by members of the crew, it seemed incredible that a disaster had occurred. The peace of the night in no way suggested the reality.

The reactions of the passengers were well described this morning by a visitor from Brisbane, Miss E. L. Dickson 'I had just retired, and had put out the light,' she said. 'There was a shock, but it really did not seem to be alarming. Indeed, I thought that the anchor had been dropped, and I remarked to another woman in the cabin: "Haven't we arrived in port early?"

'Then a steward came around and said we must put on our life-jackets. I asked him, "Is this official?" and he said it assuredly was. We could not believe that anything serious had happened.

'We all went up on deck. There was not the slightest sign of panic. Everybody was calm and good-humoured, and there was hot tea for all within five minutes, it seemed.

'It was quite a harmless sort of shipwreck, and I went down to the cabin after a while to complete my packing. The worst thing is that everybody had a sleepless night.'

The passengers included several distinguished visitors. Admiral of the Fleet Lord Tovey, Lieutenant-General Sir Noel Beresford-Peirse, Lord Nuffield and Archbishop

Wanganella on the rocks, showing how close the liner came to a real disaster (R. W. Brookes collection).

The twisted bow is clearly visible (Nick Tolerton collection).

This view from the stern quarter shows the lifeboats swung out, and a slight list to starboard (R. W. Brookes collection).

John Panico all reached Queen's Wharf in the harbour ferry, the *Cobar*, about 9.30 am. This was the first trip on which any appreciable number of male passengers were brought from the *Wanganella*. The earlier relays from the liner brought women and children first.

The sound as the liner struck the southern end of the reef did not awaken many residents of Breaker Bay, about a mile from the scene of the disaster. The first indication which most of them had that anything was amiss was the steady flow of cars, beginning in the early hours today, along a road which is usually deserted at night.

A woman resident said she was to have left for Sydney in the *Wanganella* this week. Her husband, who was awake, heard the crash as the ship struck. The sea was perfectly calm, and the liner, ablaze with lights against the velvety black of the night, made an unforgettable picture.

Usually, the persistent sound of the whistling buoy at Barrett's Reef could be heard throughout the night on a calm evening or when a southerly wind blew, the resident said. The buoy could not be heard from the shore last night or early this morning, presumably because of the light northerly wind, which would have carried the sound out to sea.

With the coming of daylight, sightseers arrived in crowds at Breaker Bay. They came on motor-cycles, bicycles and foot, and scrambled for vantage points. Traffic notices to the effect that no parking was allowed in the Pass of Branda were ignored at first, but a traffic officer quickly restored order.

The ship struck at 11.43 pm New Zealand time, one passenger said. The ship's clocks, which had not been adjusted to New Zealand time, showed 10.55 pm when the liner stranded. It had been intended to adjust the ship's time at midnight.

A woman passenger stated that a dance was being held on deck when the liner struck. She felt a shudder pass through the ship, but she thought that the anchor had probably been dropped at the entrance of the Heads. The dancing continued, and that fact reflected the unconcern of the passengers. All of them were quiet and orderly, and patiently waited their turn before transferring to the vessels which brought them into port.

Until the ship was approached quite closely from the direction of Wellington, she appeared to be simply another liner making port in the normal way. The list to starboard was almost imperceptible.

But within half a mile of the *Wanganella* it was possible to see that the dark brown patch right against the bow was a rock and the rock was part of a submerged reef on to which the liner had slid evenly. The bow was lifted slightly – about four or five feet – above normal.

Getting alongside in the *Cobar* about 10.10 am to take off the cabin luggage was tricky with a small southerly swell and rising northerly wind. On her previous trip the *Cobar*'s top deck had been slightly damaged when a swell lifted her against one of the *Wanganella*'s lifeboats, which had been slung outboard after the liner stranded.

The business of getting luggage from the liner to the *Cobar* was tedious in the absence of cargo nets. The 46 packages taken aboard the *Cobar* were all lowered by light line from A Deck. The handles of one or two bags being lowered broke and both dropped into the sea, but were rescued by the *Cobar*'s crew with a boathook.

The *Cobar* had earlier taken off a considerable number of passengers. The first were, however, brought ashore in the Harbour Board's pilot launch, *Arohina*. Other vessels on the scene earliest today were the tugs, *Terawhiti*, *Toia*, and *Natone*.

An examination of the *Wanganella*'s bows and port side, as seen from a launch, revealed that the foot of her straight stem had been torn and buckled for a distance of about five feet. Below the buckle, so far as could be seen, the receding portion of the hull, which is of a semi-arc-form design, had not been damaged, but further aft there appeared to be a rupture of her plating below the water line. The white line separating her black hull paint from the underwater red suggested that the decks and side had suffered at this point.

On the starboard side of her bow, and hard against it, is the outermost rock of the reef, projecting about 16 feet from the water at low tide. Another rock, just visible above low water, is hard against the vessel's side at a point immediately below the bridge. The *Wanganella* appears to be lodged in a cleft between the two rocks.

She is not noticeably down by the stern; her uneven appearance at noon today appears to be due to the fact that the falling tide has left her bow slightly raised on the reef, while the after part is afloat.

At 11.10 am the *Toia* put a steel hawser aboard the *Wanganella* on the starboard quarter and the *Cobar* cast off for the return to Wellington without having had a chance to take the mails aboard, or more than the few suitcases and packages of cabin luggage.

But all of that seems paltry when lined up against a handsome liner in distress. As the *Cobar* came alongside there was none of the usual happy exchange of small talk between the ship and 'shore' and the banter of crew to

Tugs attempting to pull *Wanganella* free (R W Brookes collection).

crew. The *Wanganella*'s crew were solemn men, along with those officers who were on deck.

As soon as the *Cobar* left the *Wanganella*'s side with luggage, the Harbour Board tug *Toia*, which had been standing by, came up astern of the stranded ship and passed a line up to her quarter. She then took the strain and at 11.40 am was pulling hard. Shortly after this the *Wanganella* began to run her engines astern as well in an apparent endeavour to free herself. About a quarter of an hour later the Union Company tug *Terawhiti* arrived as extra assistance.

These initial attempts to pull *Wanganella* free of the rocks proved unsuccessful, and it quickly became clear that a major salvage operation would have to be mounted to refloat the liner.

Inspection of the damaged area of the ship revealed that the hull had been punctured by rocks on both sides of the bow. Most damage was on the port side, which had been ripped open as far back as the bridge, causing the forward holds to flood. A major threat was posed by the weather, because a storm sweeping in from the south at that time could have proved fatal to the liner.

The grounding of the *Wanganella* made headline news in Australia, and on Wednesday, 23 January the *Sydney Morning Herald* carried the following report written the previous day:

> Further all-out attempts to shift the Tasman liner *Wanganella* have failed. When preparations were well advanced to get the ship off this morning a long, rolling swell caused suspension of the operations. Three tugs had to stand by impotently.
>
> Although firmly lodged on the reef, the *Wanganella* was surging badly in the swell, and the effects of this were depressingly visible by late in the afternoon. Seeming almost to sag from a point under the bridge, the bows of the liner had settled by at least three feet; and her stern had been raised higher out of the water.
>
> Even at high water glimpses of her rudder were seen, and her list had increased to at least 10 degrees. Tonight the liner is being pounded by a heavy and direct southerly swell. Salvage efforts will be continued tomorrow.
>
> The shelf of rock under her bow extends as far aft as the bridge. Jagged holes have been torn in her two forward holds, and she is also making water in No 3 hold.
>
> Immediate prospects of salvaging the liner are not regarded optimistically. When the tide was at flood this afternoon there was 20 feet of water in Nos 1 and 2 holds.
>
> The cause of the grounding of the *Wanganella* is unknown. There was no pilot on board the liner when she went aground. The master, Captain R Darroch, held a special exemption certificate permitting him to enter port without one.
>
> Many solutions to ease the *Wanganella*'s plight are being considered. One suggestion is to release the liner by cutting off her bows, a salvage practice found successful during the war.
>
> Another suggestion – made by the Minister of Marine, Mr O'Brien – is to blast the rock beneath the *Wanganella*'s bow, and thus release the ship.

For seventeen days *Wanganella* remained firmly aground on Barrett Reef, and throughout this entire period the stormy weather Wellington was famous

A dramatic picture of *Wanganella* on Barrett Reef, with the tug *Toia* off the stern (R. W. Brookes collection)

for stayed away. In fact, since that time long, mild conditions in Wellington have been referred to as 'Wanganella weather'.

Another attempt to refloat Wanganella on 26 January was also unsuccessful, and it was decided to send a diver down to inspect the hull, and the rocks on which the liner was sitting. The following report, filed from Wellington on 28 January, appeared in the Sydney Morning Herald the next morning:

> A new attempt to refloat the Wanganella is likely on Thursday, when sealing of the liner's flooded holds is expected to be finished.
>
> A vivid salvage drama has been enacted in the past two days, giving experts more optimism than they have shown since the liner went aground nine days ago.
>
> The central figure was the Australian diver, Mr. John E. Johnstone, who earned fame in the war-time salvage of the Niagara's gold. He has made a complete survey of the damage to the ship and also the contours of the rocks which have been holding her fast.
>
> Working underwater in a fast-running tide and a six-foot swell, he examined every foot of the reef with a courage and efficiency described as 'almost beyond words'.
>
> The examination has shown that three ledges of rock grip the hull firmly, but Mr. Johnstone has found parts of the reef crumbling under the liner's weight. This weakness may prove a decisive factor when buoyancy is added in the liner's forepart.
>
> Forty welders and boilermakers have toiled night and day to make Nos 1 and 2 holds airtight. By tomorrow it is hoped to be able to force out the water in these holds. All bulkheads are holding firmly.
>
> The trouble over the tug crews' wages has been settled and they have returned to duty.

The next attempt to pull Wanganella free of the rocks was made on Saturday, 1 February. It was not successful, and arrangements were made for another attempt a few days later. On the night of 6 February Wanganella was finally hauled free of the rocks, and towed stern first into Wellington, with the bow very deep in the water, only being kept afloat by pumps.

An eye-witness account of what happened during these days, written by John Leslie, the mate on Toia, one of the tugs involved in the salvage, was published in Sea Breezes magazine in May 1967, from which the following is extracted:

> All who saw the Wanganella from the shore, as she lay helpless although for all the world like a vessel still under way, felt a deep interest in this handsome twin-funnelled liner.
>
> Salvage gear and tugs were marshalled in an intensive effort to save her, while the unpredictable Cook Strait weather continued to smile benignly.
>
> Wellington's Harbour Master (Captain D. M. Todd) had a shipwreck at his door and a telephone in each hand when I called next morning. Capt. Todd appointed a few extras to his staff during the Wanganella salvage operation and in a 45-second interview – all the time he could spare – he appointed me mate of the tug Toia. At the time I was on leave.
>
> An hour later I reported to the Toia's master, Captain J. E. Hancox ... My previous tug service was nil, but I learned a lot from watching Jim Hancox during the salvage.
>
> Three tugs were employed. They were the Toia (formerly the St Boniface), a Royal Navy deep-sea rescue tug on loan to the Wellington Harbour Board with a 1200 hp engine, the Union Steam Ship Company's Terawhiti and, later, the Kahanui from Wanganui.
>
> Capt. Hancox got the best out of his small crew, and for a boatswain he had a gem in Leo Smith. I recall also the chief engineer, Mr. T. J. Weir, who was asked for a lot of power, and provided it. It was the Toia that did most of the towage.
>
> Hopes rose and fell as salvage work continued. Everything that could be attempted was tried, but the Wanganella budged little, if at all. Days passed with brilliant weather. She sometimes yawed a little and lifted imperceptibly to the low southerly swell from Cook Strait. That was all.
>
> About the Wanganella's deck, officers and men worked hard and long while a nearby fog-buoy moaned monotonously and mournfully.
>
> Her 400 passengers and mail had been landed by assorted and hastily summoned craft, and the squat, but handsome, buff-funnelled Wanganella remained a shadow of the bright carefree Tasman liner which she had been.
>
> Distinguished passengers who went ashore included Admiral of the Fleet Lord Tovey and his wife; Archbishop Panico, Apostolic Delegate to Australia and New Zealand; Lord Nuffield, and others. The Wanganella's trip had been smooth. The weather was fine and a dance was in progress even when she hit the reef.
>
> The tugs' efforts were reinforced by the use of mushroom anchors and hawsers from the Wanganella's stern. Even the combined towing, plus the winches' pull and the powerful sternward thrust of the Wanganella's twin screws were unavailing. Some hundred of tons of valuable fuel were pumped overboard to lighten her further, a most unorthodox procedure at a harbour entrance. It had little effect but sent a long brown streak as far as the eye could see over the strait, towards the mountains of Marlborough. Some oil slick returned the next day on the flood tide.
>
> During this period the Wanganella dominated our

whole lives, but the *Toia* was not always at the end of a towline. She had other tasks to do but she was never very far away, and it was the *Wanganella* that was always uppermost in the minds of her crew.

Craft of many sizes and types ferried mechanical technical equipment out to the *Wanganella*. This was, in turn, installed about her decks until she was one mass of humming auxiliaries. Powerful air compressors, supplied at the request of the Wellington Harbour Board, ran noisily and continuously, keeping down the water in the flooded forward holds. The ship was alive with contractors, technicians and labourers. Huddart Parker & Co. Ltd, her owners, engaged the noted Melbourne diver, John Johnstone, who had salved the *Niagara*'s gold.

This salvage operation aboard the *Wanganella* herself was a brilliant achievement for those who conceived it and for those who executed the plans. The days passed by in glorious '*Wanganella* weather', as it was called by holiday makers and thousands of others.

For 18 days the *Wanganella* lay helpless, and no response came to the efforts of the combined teams. Over the air, night and day, came voices from radio telephones previously installed by the Wellington Harbour Board under the direction of Capt. Todd.

With the utmost efficiency, authorities, pilots, craft, crews, technicians, employees and equipment were blended into a smooth, well-drilled team. On the hill-top, the signal station did yeoman service in relaying messages from wreck to tugs, to pilot vessels, to the city, and so on. Cook Strait continued to behave but received anxious glances.

Time was on the *Wanganella*'s side but not for long. The great day was February 6, 1947, when she swung or yawed just a little, yet noticeably, from the shore, and a long southerly swell showed increasing signs of making. That afternoon, greyish and still, she gave her first signs of hope to the patient *Toia*, fast on her quarter.

Special broadcast notice was given. This was D-day, or rather D-night. Cars raced from all over the capital city to give traffic officers the biggest problem in years. For days earlier, vehicles had lined the shore, with sun glinting on their brightwork. Hundreds of binoculars had been turned on the scene since the beginning, not only from shore but from passing ships. We could see them ourselves for we too had binoculars. Even by night, car headlights had remained switched on for hours, watching and waiting.

This night as the swell increased there was a sense of urgency. All but key men were removed from the restless liner for the *Wanganella* was showing signs of life.

With only the stalwart *Toia* attached, she rolled easily and lifted herself clear of her resting place. She swung slowly; she floated, at a precarious angle of buoyancy,

Wanganella being berthed in Wellington on the night of 6 February (Nick Tolerton collection).

Two views of *Wanganella* berthed in Wellington, with the bow resting on the bottom (R. W. Brookes collection).

Wanganella alongside the wharf in Wellington (R. W. Brookes collection)

but she floated. A miracle perhaps, but she was off. We promptly forgot all that we might have learned about ship stability for she defied every law. I don't recall anyone aboard the tug saying much at the time, but if they did, it would have been similar to the words which Hillary used when he conquered Everest.

Precariously, and at an amazing angle of trim, the *Wanganella* lined up for the harbour channel, meekly following the *Toia*'s manoeuvring. Stern-first and heavily down by the head, she rode. At this unseamanlike angle, and brilliantly lit as though for a first night performance, and it was a performance which thousands witnessed, she made painful progress up Wellington Harbour, whose shores were lit by the headlights of hundreds of cars. Capt. Hancox handled the *Toia* and her crazy tow superbly and silently, as usual.

In due course she was fast to her berth, but still in a state of emergency, and kept afloat by mechanical means and sweat.

Soon after berthing, *Wanganella* was further illuminated by flashes, as reporters and photographers did their job. Next morning I had a farewell look aboard. Her magnificent public rooms were a mass of muddy footprints, machinery and humming auxiliaries. Men were swarming over her like ants. She was filthy, but afloat.

Once *Wanganella* was alongside a wharf, the pumps that had been keeping the water level under control in the holds were stopped, and the bow of the liner allowed to sink to the bottom. Temporary repairs were carried out to make the forward holds watertight, then they were pumped dry to reduce the draught so *Wanganella* could enter the local drydock.

A report on the salvage of *Wanganella* appeared in the 1 March 1947 issue of *The Harbour*, under the headline '*Wanganella* Will Sail Again':

On February 6 the *Wanganella* was successfully salved from her precarious position on Barrett's Reef and towed to a berth in Wellington Harbour. There was widespread rejoicing as the news became known, and Messrs Huddart Parker Ltd, the owners, were the recipients of many congratulations.

Speaking after the ship had been berthed, Captain G. McDonald, Huddart Parker's marine surveyor, said that the liner's double bottom had been ripped out from the bow back to the bridge. 'The ship is too far down at the bow to be moved into the dock at present,' Captain McDonald said. 'The bow is drawing 36 feet, whereas the maximum depth of water over the keel blocks in the dock is only 25 feet. I am confident that with increased use of compressed air sufficient buoyancy can be obtained. The *Wanganella* jumped, heaved, and nearly threw us off our feet as she came off the rocks, but after that she settled down a bit.'

Diver E. Johnstone described the salvage as a miracle, but added, 'The miracle was brought about to a large extent by hard work, experience and ingenuity. Captain McDonald and Mr. John Dilworth, a salvage expert of London, devised a most ingenious salvage method – the only one which could have saved the ship. Her bottom was so badly torn it was hopeless to try to patch numbers one and two holds.

'There was a pinnacle of hard rock extending five feet into the two holds above the keel, also a ledge of rock underneath on which the ship was pivoting badly. We had to lift her off the rocks, and the only way was to gain buoyancy, so we sealed the forward holds, deck hatches, trunkways and ventilators. Air was forced in and water thereby forced out of the holds.

'The port side of No. 2 hold had a gaping hole 20 feet deep by 13 feet, but the position changed daily with the ship bumping on the reef. My first examination showed five holes in No. 1 hold, but in three days I lost count of the number. On my past experience, I say that this is an outstanding piece of salvage. The ship could easily have been lost. Yesterday we were afraid of the weather and swell, and it was only in desperation that we got at it last night. When I saw her moving I knew she was right.'

A Court of Inquiry which subsequently investigated the mishap found that it had been caused by default on the part of the master, 69-year-old Captain Darroch. The Court decided, with extreme regret, to suspend his certificate for three months. The presiding magistrate added: 'Captain Darroch is a master mariner of great repute, with more that half a century of seafaring life. His has been a long, and, up to now, blameless career. He has a long record in the past of good and efficient service as a master, both in peace and war, of which he may justly be proud. At the time of this unhappy disaster he had already passed the age at which many master mariners have retired.'

An official statement estimates that repairs would take at least three months.

This last comment was extremely optimistic. On 18 February it was decided that conditions were suitable to move *Wanganella* from the wharf to the drydock.

Just as the move was about to start, several members of the crew who had been signed on for the short trip from berth to drydock demanded extra payment. When this was refused the defiant men walked off the ship, but it was decided to go ahead with the move anyway, using a scratch crew. Despite the difficulties encountered, *Wanganella* was successfully moved from the wharf and placed in the drydock on the afternoon of 18 February.

Wanganella in the floating dock on 18 February 1947. The damage to the bow is clearly visible (R. W. Brookes collection).

This photo of *Wanganella* in the floating dock was taken in April 1947 (R. W. Brookes collection).

The repair work was constantly delayed by industrial disputes, and by the end of April only six days work had been done. Then two hundred men employed by the repairing firm, Wm Cable & Co., resigned. Work stopped altogether when claims by unions for extra money were refused, and the ship was declared 'black'. Eventually work resumed, and on 27 May sufficient temporary repairs had been completed to allow the liner to be refloated and removed from the drydock. *Wanganella* was towed to Clyde Quay to await the delivery of a prefabricated bow section that had been built by Harland & Wolff in Belfast, and was being shipped out to Wellington.

A court of inquiry convened to investigate the cause of the grounding came to the conclusion that Captain Darroch, who had remained in command of the liner throughout the war years and was now 69 years old, was to blame for allowing the ship to enter the harbour on the wrong side of the navigation lights that clearly marked Barrett Reef. Captain

Darroch had his master's ticket suspended for three months. He had been with Huddart Parker for forty years, but this incident effectively put an end to his seagoing career.

The sudden loss of *Wanganella* for an indefinite time was a major disaster for Huddart Parker, who had no suitable vessel available to call upon as a replacement. In fact, the only vessel that could be found to fill the breach on the trans-Tasman trade was the veteran steamer *Wahine*, owned by the Union Steam Ship Company of New Zealand. Built for the overnight ferry service between Wellington and Lyttelton, *Wahine* had recently been replaced on that route by the brand-new *Hinemoa*, and was lying at anchor in Wellington Harbour as a relief ship. Despite the fact that she only had very small cabins, and could at best carry a maximum of 300 passengers, *Wahine* was to be the emergency stopgap on the Tasman trade for almost two years.

Wahine had been built by Wm Denny & Bros at Dumbarton, in Scotland. Launched on 25 November 1912, and completed five months later, *Wahine* was 374 feet/114 m long, and 4436 gross tons. It was fitted with coal-fired geared turbines driving three propellers, and proved to be a very fast ship, achieving an impressive 21.33 knots on trials, well above the speed stipulated in the contract. The vessel made its first ferry trip from Lyttelton on the night of 19 July 1913 to Wellington. Cabin accommodation was provided for 404 first class passengers and 188 in second class.

In July 1915, the British Government requisitioned *Wahine*, and it arrived in Plymouth on 7 September, then went to London to be converted into a dispatch carrier, being based in the Mediterranean operating between Malta and Mudros, in Greece. The vessel created a huge amount of interest in Malta by its ability to steam at high speed in reverse through the ships thronging the harbour until there was enough space for it to turn around and proceed out to sea. This was facilitated by the bow rudder fitted to assist the ship when it was berthing at Lyttelton.

In May 1916, *Wahine* returned to Britain to be converted into a minelayer, and subsequently carried out 76 missions in the North Sea, laying 11 378 mines between July 1916 and April 1919. Released from military duty, the vessel was refitted at the Denny shipyard and returned to New Zealand, resuming its place on the overnight ferry service from Wellington on 17 February 1920.

The only major accident to befall *Wahine* occurred in 1936, on the morning of 5 June, as the vessel was approaching the dock in Wellington through thick fog. As it was swinging to berth stern-in, the bow became impaled on the Pipitea Wharf, where it remained stuck for several hours. The damage was so extensive *Wahine* was out of service undergoing repairs until 18 August.

Wahine remained on the ferry service after war broke out in 1939, but in November 1941 it was sent on a trooping voyage to Fiji, the first of several such trips over the next few years. In September 1942 *Wahine* was sent on a quick trip to Sydney, then

The inter-island ferry *Wahine* took over the Tasman trade.

over the next six months made voyages to the New Hebrides, New Caledonia, Norfolk Island and Fiji.

Between these voyages, *Wahine* operated on the overnight ferry service between Wellington and Lyttelton. The vessel was departing Wellington on the night of 19 September 1943 when it collided with the minesweeping trawler *South Sea* inside Wellington Harbour. The smaller vessel sank, but fortunately there was no loss of life.

In November and December 1943, *Wahine* made more voyages from Wellington to Sydney and back. On 1 March 1944, having been guaranteed safe passage by the enemy, the vessel left Auckland carrying Japanese nationals to Sydney, where they were exchanged for New Zealanders who had been under Japanese control. On returning to New Zealand, *Wahine* returned to the inter-island ferry service.

In 1946, *Wahine* was given an extensive refit, during which the accommodation was altered to 550 passengers in one class. When the new *Hinemoa* entered service on the inter-island ferry service on 10 February 1947, *Wahine* was withdrawn from that trade, and was to have been laid up as a reserve vessel.

Now, however, the vessel was immediately prepared to operate across the Tasman Sea to Sydney as a replacement for *Wanganella*. Because of the length of the voyage, the number of passengers was reduced to 300.

With a full complement of passengers who had been anticipating the comparative luxury of *Wanganella*, *Wahine* left Wellington on 14 February 1947 on her first voyage to Sydney, arriving there four days later, berthing at 13 Darling Harbour. The vessel left Sydney on 21 February on its voyage back to Wellington. On 28 February *Wahine* departed Wellington on its second voyage to Sydney, arriving on 4 March, and for the next three months operated a regular schedule.

Wahine remained on the Tasman trade until its departure from Sydney on 30 May. When the ship arrived in Wellington on 3 June, it was laid up for the rest of the winter, and there was no regular passenger service across the Tasman Sea. On 12 September 1947, *Wahine* left Wellington again bound for Sydney, arriving on 16 September, and leaving on the return trip three days later. *Wahine* continued to make regular trips on the route for the rest of the year. In all *Wahine* made sixteen return trips across the Tasman Sea in 1947.

Wahine continued to maintain the service across the Tasman Sea during the first months of 1948. In February the vessel was due for an overhaul, and after arriving in Sydney on Tuesday, went to Mort's Dock where the work was done. This included the fitting of a new outer casing to the forward funnel. On the Saturday, the ship was ready to return to service, and took its scheduled departure.

In the *Commercial Australian* on 17 March 1948 there was a small item stating it had been announced that *Wahine* would be taken off the Tasman trade on 18 May 1948, and be replaced by *Monowai*. The item also indicated that the refit of *Monowai* was not expected to be completed until the end of the year, and in the interim there would be no passenger service between Australia and New Zealand.

Wahine departed Sydney for the last time on 14 May 1948, arriving in Wellington on 18 May. For the rest of 1948 there was no passenger service provided by Huddart Parker or the Union Line across the Tasman. In all, *Wahine* made only ten round trips across the Tasman Sea in 1948.

Wahine was then required on the Lyttelton route again while one of the regular ships, *Rangatira*, underwent a refit. When its period on the Lyttelton trade ended, *Wahine* was laid up at anchor in Wellington Harbour as a relief ship for the inter-island ferry service. In July 1951 the vessel was chartered by the New Zealand Government to carry a contingent of troops to Korea.

Wahine departed Wellington on 2 August, carrying 570 troops and a crew of eighty. Following a call at Cairns, the vessel went on to Darwin, leaving there on 14 August. At 5.40 am on 15 August, *Wahine* ran hard aground on the Masella Reef, being held firm from the bow to the engine room. All aboard were rescued by the tanker *Stanvac Karachi*, and returned to Darwin. Unlike *Wanganella*, salvage attempts on *Wahine* were unsuccessful, and the vessel became a total loss.

It was not until 20 January 1948 that *Wanganella* was again placed in the drydock to have the damaged bow removed and the new bow fitted, and other hull repairs completed. This was quite a lengthy process, and the liner stayed in drydock until 28 October. Once *Wanganella* had been refloated, there was still a considerable amount of further work to be done before the vessel could return to service.

At the beginning of December 1948 there were positive indications that the trans-Tasman passenger service would be resuming early in the coming year. *Monowai* was nearly ready for sea trials after a lengthy refit, while repairs on *Wanganella* were almost completed, and the vessel was due to return to service by the end of the month.

It was later reported that the cost of salvaging *Wanganella* had come to about £60,000, with an additional £5,800 paid to the eighteen crew members who had remained on board the ship throughout the period it was aground. The cost of repairs and drydocking was reported to be in the vicinity of £300,000, so the overall cost of saving and repairing *Wanganella* was more than Huddart Parker had paid to acquire the ship in 1932.

After 21 months out of service, *Wanganella* finally returned to the Tasman Sea trade with a departure from Wellington on 9 December 1948. Under the command of Captain H. F. Norrie, and carrying a full complement of 358 passengers, the liner arrived back in Sydney on 13 December, having averaged 16 knots on the voyage, and berthing at 3 Darling Harbour.

The first four round trips from Sydney were all scheduled to go to Wellington, the first departing on Thursday, 16 December, then every second week. It was not until 10 February that *Wanganella* left Sydney bound for Auckland, but this was followed by two more voyages to Wellington before a departure on 24 March to Auckland, followed by another trip to Auckland leaving on 7 April.

A view of the repaired bow of *Wanganella* (Nick Tolerton collection).

Post-war deck plan of *Wanganella* (Paul Joyce collection).

Comfortable Seating Arrangements—Dining Room

Restful Atmosphere of the Lounge

Marble Fireplace—Promenade Deck Lounge

Purser's Office

A Corner of the Library

Artistically Furnished Smoking Lounge

Music Room

OCEAN TOURS
by the
HUDDART PARKER LINE

T.S.M.V. "WANGANELLA," 10,000 TONS.

New Zealand Services:

SYDNEY & AUCKLAND—SYDNEY & WELLINGTON

Australian Interstate Services:

T.S.M.V. "WESTRALIA."

BRISBANE and SYDNEY, MELBOURNE, ADELAIDE, FREMANTLE, also SYDNEY and HOBART

The vessels when reconditioned will be replete with every facility for the comfort and entertainment of passengers. All Services will be resumed as soon as practicable.

Full information will be supplied on application to:

HUDDART PARKER LIMITED

(Incorporated in Victoria)

Head Office:
464-466 Collins Street,
Melbourne.

10 BRIDGE STREET, SYDNEY.
Tel.: BW 1441.

Branches and Agencies
at all Ports.

13

A Slow Decline

Just over six weeks after *Wanganella* returned to service she was rejoined by *Monowai*, and the Tasman trade could once again operate as it had done in the pre-war years.

Work on refitting *Monowai* had proceeded throughout 1948 at Mort's Dock. A major consideration was the machinery, which had received very little attention during the war, so the engines were disassembled and given a complete overhaul. During the refit a number of changes were made which quite drastically altered the vessel's appearance. The mainmast was removed and replaced by a pair of Samson posts, while the funnels were altered from round to an elliptical shape. The forward well deck was filled in, to improve crew accommodation, and the forward section of the promenade deck was screened with windows. The wooden bridge front, which before the war had been painted white, was sanded back and varnished.

The interior of the ship was completely renewed, with accommodation being installed for 179 first class and 205 cabin class passengers. The public rooms were decorated in a contemporary character, except for the first class smoking room which was panelled with cedar in English Renaissance style. The former music room was enlarged to form a new first class lounge, with six staterooms being erected in the old lounge. All furnishings and fittings for the public rooms were new. The final cost of the reconditioning came to just over £1 million.

Monowai spent several weeks in the Woolwich Drydock during September, then final touches were completed over the next three months. *Monowai* left Sydney Harbour on 18 December 1948 for two days of sea trials, which were completed successfully, with a maximum speed of 17 knots attained. These trials created so much public interest that a Sydney radio station sent along a reporter who gave live

Post-war appearance of *Monowai*.

Monowai in Waitamata Harbour, Auckland.

descriptions of the trials, and had an interview with the master, Captain George Morgan.

On 24 January *Monowai* made her first post-war departure from Sydney, having finally completed her lengthy refit. With both liners back in service, a regular schedule of departures from Sydney to Auckland and Wellington was established once again. Soon *Wanganella* and *Monowai* were operating with full complements of passengers on most trips, providing between them a weekly service between Sydney and New Zealand.

The schedule arranged for *Wanganella* called for two successive round trips to each New Zealand port on a regular fortnightly sailing schedule. For example, *Wanganella* left Sydney on 24 February and 10 March for Wellington, then made two trips to Auckland, departing on 24 March and 7 April.

Through 1949 and 1950 *Wanganella* and *Monowai* maintained a regular service back and forth across the Tasman Sea. During this period the only event of note involving either of the ships came in November 1950, when Captain George Morgan retired and was replaced on the *Monowai* by Captain Frank Young, an Australian born in Neutral Bay, Sydney in 1902.

Although both *Wanganella* and *Monowai* were engaged in a relatively short service across the Tasman Sea, their captains had to be able to cope with some of the most extreme weather conditions found anywhere in the world, and conditions in the ports could also present major problems. Noted New Zealand maritime historian, the late Jack Churchouse, served in the *Monowai* as fourth mate under Captain Young, and later wrote this about a departure from Wellington:

> At 3 o'clock the voyage began and as always Captain Young piloted his vessel. He was a first rate ship handler, which was dramatically illustrated on one occasion when sailing from Wellington. At the time a strong northerly gale was blowing and no sooner had the *Monowai* cleared the end of Queen's Wharf as she went astern that the full force of the wind caught her. The vessel immediately began to drift to leeward towards Taranaki Street Wharf.
>
> To counteract this Captain Young dropped an anchor, going astern on the port engine and ahead on the starboard engine until the *Monowai* was heading towards Jervois Quay. He then went astern on both engines and by adjusting their revolutions brought his vessel stern first down harbour until off Aotea Quay, when she was turned. No doubt this was an occurrence not unfamiliar to Captain Young, but his cool precision and masterly handling of the *Monowai* was a pleasure to witness.

A major industrial dispute between employers and waterside workers in New Zealand started in late March 1951 when the watersiders refused to work overtime. The New Zealand Government, which supported the employers, was determined to smash the watersiders' union and introduced emergency regulations, under which the army was brought in to work the wharves.

New Zealand seamen then went on strike in support of the waterside workers. On 6 April *Monowai* was preparing to depart Wellington when a large number of seamen walked off the ship in sympathy with the striking waterside workers. The voyage was cancelled, and *Monowai* remained idle at Wellington. Eventually the entire New Zealand waterfront came to a stop.

At first *Wanganella* continued to operate across the Tasman, with crew members being used to smuggle money to New Zealand from various unions in Australia to support their New Zealand comrades. However, when *Wanganella* arrived in Sydney on 2 May the entire crew, in sympathy with their New Zealand counterparts, walked off and resigned, having declared New Zealand ports 'black'. *Wanganella* was laid up in Sydney, and yet again the trans-Tasman trade ground to a halt.

After two months of idleness, *Wanganella* was reactivated, and a new crew signed on, to enable the liner to make a special trip from Sydney to Tasmania and Melbourne while the regular Bass Strait ferry, *Taroona*, was undergoing a refit.

Wanganella departed Sydney for Hobart on 6 July, reviving, albeit briefly, a service Huddart Parker liners had operated regularly until 1940. *Wanganella* arrived in Hobart on 8 July, having 85 passengers on board, of whom 40 disembarked, while 70 joined the ship for the trip to Melbourne.

Wanganella left Hobart on 10 July, making an overnight trip around the coast to Burnie, berthing there for the day before making an overnight passage to Melbourne. Leaving Melbourne on the evening of 12 July, *Wanganella* made an overnight passage back to Burnie, then went on to Hobart, arriving there on 15 July. Embarking 128 passengers, the liner left Hobart on 17 July for Sydney, arriving there on 19 July.

By the time *Wanganella* completed her round trip to Tasmania, the strike in New Zealand had been settled, having lasted 151 days, and normal services could be resumed. *Monowai* made her first departure from Wellington for Sydney on 20 July, while on 26 July *Wanganella* left Sydney bound for Wellington once again. The two ships resumed their regular schedules for the rest of 1951 and into 1952.

Vessels often had to battle heavy seas on the trans-Tasman route, sometimes suffering damage and injuries to passengers. Most of these incidents did not rate a mention in the local press, but one particularly bad voyage that did make the news occurred in May 1952 – nine passengers were injured as *Wanganella* crashed through high waves when it encountered two cyclones in succession on its way from Auckland to Sydney, resulting in the arrival being delayed by several hours.

Wanganella arriving in Hobart on 8 July 1951 (David Cooper photo).

On Tuesday, 27 May 1952, the *Sydney Morning Herald* carried the following report:

Some passengers were slightly injured and equipment was damaged when the Tasman liner *Wanganella* was battered by cyclonic storms on Saturday night and Sunday.

The *Wanganella* arrived from Auckland at 3.45 pm yesterday – eight hours late. The ship's officers described the seas as 'mountainous'.

When the first blow struck, many passengers were in the lounge. People were unseated and furniture displaced.

Deck furniture was ripped from its mountings and an after gangway was smashed in two. One half dangled over the side of the liner and there was danger of it fouling the screws until officers and crew, with the aid of deck life lines, managed to cut it clear.

In the second-class section of the ship two five-eighth thick plate glass windows were broken.

Captain H. F. Norrie said: 'It was a heavy sea. The drop of from 30.1 to 29 in the barometer was steep. To make things worse we were just through the first blow when we were struck by the second cyclone. At times we were struck by gusts which I estimated at 60 knots.'

A stewardess said not more than 30 of the 302 passengers attended the dining saloon after Saturday night. An officer said the crew quarters in the stern of the ship received the full force of the storm. All the alleyways were flooded with water. 'At one stage we were hove to for three hours,' he said.

Mrs A. N. A. Jones, of Benalla, Victoria, said she was seated in a lounge chair when a heavy sea struck the ship on Saturday night. 'I was flung to the floor,' she said. 'Furniture was thrown about the lounge and I received bruises and abrasions.'

Mr. Harry Morris, of Adelaide, who went to Mrs. Jones's aid, was hurled across the lounge. He received abrasions. A stewardess who tried to help Mrs. Jones was struck by furniture. Because of the danger of moving furniture the captain ordered the lounge closed.

Passengers and officers all said the *Wanganella* behaved very well and was lucky to escape so lightly from the buffeting she received.

Despite the battering *Wanganella* received during the stormy voyage, no major damage was inflicted, and the vessel was able to leave again a few days later as scheduled.

On 7 July 1952, *Wanganella* arrived in Sydney from Wellington, and went to Cockatoo Dockyard for an extensive refit. On 29 July *Wanganella* entered the Sutherland Drydock, being refloated on 2 August, but remained at Cockatoo until 6 August. It was during this refit that the windows on the promenade deck were extended further aft.

Wanganella had been scheduled to depart on 7 August, but this was cancelled due to a crew dispute, which was only settled two days later when Huddart Parker called for a new crew, and the ship finally got away on 9 August at 11 am, with 350 passengers on board

During 1953, an officer from *Wanganella* was involved in an interesting court case. On 18 January the third officer, who was in charge of the watch, had allowed three female passengers to visit the bridge, and to take a turn at the wheel. Mr T. Parker, managing director of Huddart Parker Limited, witnessed this, reported the incident to Captain Norrie, and instructed the captain that the officer concerned be stood down. When the ship arrived in Sydney the third officer was offered the option of

Wanganella with extended Promenade Deck windows (Fred Roderick photo)

resigning or being dismissed. Instead, he complained to the Merchant Service Guild, who instituted a court case.

When the matter came to court, the third officer agreed that the women had been standing at the wheel, wearing his cap, but pointed out that the helmsman was holding the wheel at all times. Captain Norrie gave evidence that it was common practice to allow passengers on the bridge, and to steer the ship for short periods when conditions were good. When asked why he had stood down the third officer, Norrie said he had obeyed the instructions of the managing director.

In handing down his judgment, Mr Justice Foster said that, despite being managing director of the company that owned the ship, at the time of the incident Mr Parker was 'no more or no less than a passenger', and the master could have been offended by his presence on the bridge. In the circumstance, the third officer should be reinstated. By this ruling, the practice of allowing passengers on the bridge was able to continue.

On 2 August 1953, *Wanganella* encountered another major storm, during which ten passengers suffered injuries, one being taken to hospital when the ship berthed in Sydney.

During 1953 *Wanganella* and *Monowai* between them made 49 return crossings of the Tasman. The average berth utilisation for the full year was 75 per cent of capacity, but during the summer months both ships were fully booked on every voyage.

Over the next few years *Wanganella* continued to operate regular alternating voyages from Sydney every two weeks to either Wellington or Auckland, in conjunction with *Monowai*. In April 1955 *Monowai* was caught in a particularly severe storm, resulting in injuries being suffered by eight passengers.

The schedule followed by *Wanganella* in 1956 was similar to previous years, with alternating voyages from Sydney to Auckland and Wellington, and an annual period of maintenance, which usually involved the cancellation of one round trip.

Wanganella returned to Sydney from Auckland on the morning of Monday, 13 August 1956, berthing at 1A Darling Harbour. *Wanganella* later moved to 8 Glebe Island, where it remained for several days, then was moved to the Cockatoo Island Dockyard to undergo a major refit, and also be placed in the Sutherland Dock to undergo survey.

With *Wanganella* due to be out of service for a longer period than usual, Huddart Parker withdrew *Westralia* from the Australian coastal trade to maintain the trans-Tasman service. *Westralia* had arrived in Sydney on 3 August, then went to Morts Dock for a refit. On Thursday, 16 August, *Westralia*

Wanganella and *Monowai* berthed together in Darling Harbour, Sydney, with *Manunda* just viisible on the right (R. W. Brookes collection).

departed 6 Darling Harbour at noon on a voyage to Auckland, arriving there on 20 August, and the *Auckland Evening Star* reported:

> Outside appearances are often deceptive, as witness the Huddart Parker cargo-passenger ship, *Westralia*, now on her first visit to Auckland since 1938. The vessel has caused more than one Aucklander to classify her as an old-fashioned ship with not many more voyages left in her. They would not, of course, have been on board her, because when once inside, it becomes a difficult task to control superlatives.

Westralia returned to Sydney on 27 August, and subsequently maintained a two-week schedule of departures over the next two months, departing Sydney on 30 August for Wellington, and again on 13 September.

The departure of *Westralia* from Queen's Wharf, Wellington was on the afternoon of 20 September, and it was reported in *The Beacon* that, as the liner was turning and her stern swung into view, two women who had been animatedly waving to a departing friend suddenly saw on the stern the words:

WESTRALIA
MELBOURNE

One said excitedly to the other, 'Oh! Look! They've got the wrong name there – she's going to Sydney and they've put Melbourne!'

Westralia completed her stint on the Tasman trade with two more voyages to Auckland, departing Sydney on 27 September and 11 October, returning to Sydney on 22 October. *Westralia* resumed its place on the coastal trade to Fremantle with a departure from Sydney on 2 November.

During the period *Westralia* was operating across the Tasman, *Wanganella* was given an extensive overhaul, and several internal alterations were made as well. The vessel was berthed alongside 8 Glebe Island for a week while 1000 tons of steel plates, gravel and sand used as ballast was removed, so an examination could be made of the double-bottom tank tops, 'tween decks and internal hull.

The following item, written by Captain Norrie, appeared in the September 1956 issue of *The Beacon*:

> Nothing looks so dismal as a passenger ship under overhaul and walking around the decks of 'Wanganella' as she lay at Glebe discharging ballast was a depressing experience.
>
> From the holds emerged rusty steel plates which had

Westralia.

TIMETABLE—NEW ZEALAND-SYDNEY SERVICE
1956-1957

Vessel	Leave Sydney	Arrive Auckland	Arrive Wellington	Leave Wellington	Leave Auckland	Arrive Sydney	Vessel
Monowai	Oct. 5	—	Oct. 9	Oct. 12	—	Oct. 16	Monowai
*Westralia	Oct. 11	Oct. 15	—	—	Oct. 18	Oct. 22	*Westralia
Monowai	Oct. 19	—	Oct. 23	Oct. 26	—	Oct. 30	Monowai
*Wanganella	Oct. 25	—	Oct. 29	Nov. 1	—	Nov. 5	*Wanganella
Monowai	Nov. 1	Nov. 5	—	—	Nov. 6	Nov. 10	Monowai
*Wanganella	Nov. 8	—	Nov. 12	Nov. 15	—	Nov. 19	*Wanganella
Monowai	Nov. 12	Nov. 16	—	—	Nov. 17	Nov. 21	Monowai
*Wanganella	Nov. 22	Nov. 26	—	—	Nov. 29	Dec. 3	*Wanganella
Monowai	Nov. 24	—	Nov. 28	Dec. 1	—	Dec. 5	Monowai
*Wanganella	Dec. 6	Dec. 10	—	—	Dec. 13	Dec. 17	*Wanganella
Monowai	Dec. 10	—	Dec. 14	Dec. 17	—	Dec. 21	Monowai
*Wanganella	Dec. 20	—	Dec. 24	Dec. 28	—	Jan. 1	*Wanganella
Monowai	Dec. 24	Dec. 28	—	—	Jan. 3	Jan. 7	Monowai
*Wanganella	Jan. 3	—	Jan. 7	Jan. 10	—	Jan. 14	*Wanganella
Monowai	Jan. 11	Jan. 15	—	—	Jan. 18	Jan. 22	Monowai
*Wanganella	Jan. 17	Jan. 21	—	—	Jan. 24	Jan. 28	*Wanganella
Monowai	Jan. 24	—	Jan. 28	Feb. 2	—	Feb. 6	Monowai
*Wanganella	Jan. 31	—	Feb. 4	Feb. 7	—	Feb. 11	*Wanganella
Monowai	Feb. 7	Feb. 11	—	—	Feb. 12	Feb. 16	Monowai
*Wanganella	Feb. 14	Feb. 18	—	—	Feb. 21	Feb. 25	*Wanganella
Monowai	Feb. 18	—	Feb. 22	Feb. 23	—	Feb. 27	Monowai
Monowai	Feb. 28	Mar. 4	—	—	Mar. 5	Mar. 9	Monowai
*Wanganella	Feb. 28	—	Mar. 4	Mar. 7	—	Mar. 11	*Wanganella
Monowai	Mar. 11	Mar. 15	—	—	Mar. 16	Mar. 20	Monowai
*Wanganella	Mar. 14	—	Mar. 18	Mar. 21	—	Mar. 25	*Wanganella
Monowai	Mar. 21	—	Mar. 25	Mar. 26	—	Mar. 30	Monowai
*Wanganella	Mar. 28	Apr. 1	—	—	Apr. 4	Apr. 8	*Wanganella
Monowai	Apr. 1	—	Apr. 5	Apr. 6	—	Apr. 10	Monowai
Monowai	Apr. 11	—	Apr. 15	Apr. 16	—	Apr. 20	Monowai
*Wanganella	Apr. 11	Apr. 15	—	—	Apr. 18	Apr. 22	*Wanganella
Monowai	Apr. 23	Apr. 27	—	—	Apr. 29	May 3	Monowai
*Wanganella	Apr. 26	—	Apr. 30	May 2	—	May 6	*Wanganella
Monowai	May 4	May 8	—	—	May 10	May 14	Monowai

* NOTE: Dates shown for "Wanganella" and "Westralia" have been supplied by the vessels' Owners, Messrs. Huddart Parker Ltd.

1956–57 sailing schedule published by the Union Steamship Co.

been stowed for years as ballast. Hundreds of tons of gravel and bags of crushed bluestone were distributed on the wharf from the various holds, having served their purposes in stabilising the vessel for many thousands of miles in her voyages across the Tasman.

Rust was in evidence on all decks and superstructures, but preparations were under way for a complete and thorough overhaul.

Flame cleaning, chipping, new plates where required, and an army of men are transforming 'Wanganella' into a condition which will again give her pride of place as the flagship of the Fleet.

The ballast will be returned to the vessel in the form of concrete blocks and when next it has to be removed for tank top examination we will not again be faced with a costly task as on this occasion. Among many innovations which will prove attractive to the passengers is the painting of the passenger accommodation in pastel shades. Cabins already finished in varying colours are restful to the eye and being of a wide range of shades give an individuality to the rooms.

On A Deck three small single rooms have been sacrificed to provide six de-luxe rooms with toilet and shower. A number of three-berth have been converted to two-berth rooms.

The dining room accommodation has been completely changed, provision now being made for most of the tables to seat only four people. The Master's and Chief Engineer's tables will be circular, thus enabling conversation to be conducted between all those seated at these tables, which hold eight people.

When she resumes running in the Trans-Tasman service, we are confident that 'Wanganella' will maintain the popularity with the travelling public which has been established over the years.

On 23 October *Wanganella* left Cockatoo Dock, and moved to 4 Darling Harbour to be prepared for a return to service. On Thursday, 25 October, *Wanganella* departed Sydney on a voyage to Wellington. *Wanganella* made a second voyage to Wellington, departing on 8 November, then on 22 November departed on a voyage to Auckland.

It was also during 1956 that the future of *Monowai* came under close scrutiny. *Monowai* was a heavy consumer of fuel oil and had also reached the age when a classification survey was due, to allow her to operate another four years. The Union Line thought the high cost of building a new ship would prohibit competitive fare charges, so it was planned that the trans-Tasman passenger service would be abandoned when the *Monowai*'s survey certificate expired in 1960.

(Above) Suite on *Wanganella* after the 1956 refit   (Below) First Class Smoke Room on *Wanganella* (*The Beacon*).

14

Cruising

As 1956 drew to a close the Huddart Parker office in Wellington was kept busy with preparations for a four-night Christmas cruise that had been organised for *Wanganella* from Wellington to the South Island Sounds. Among the extra attractions engaged for this trip was a five-piece orchestra. With Captain Norrie going on leave, Captain C. T. Copping took over command for the round trip from Sydney to Wellington and the cruise, which departed Wellington on Christmas Eve. A report on the cruise, which was unfortunately beset with bad weather, appeared in the March 1957 issue of *The Beacon*:

> Over 300 passengers left Wellington on Christmas Eve for a cruise to Queen Charlotte and Milford Sounds. The Company had spared no efforts in making provision for the entertainment of the cruise passengers, but a depression crossing the Tasman Sea brought with it strong westerly winds and heavy rain. A passage down the West Coast of the South Island was marred by this weather, but the heavy rain failed to dampen the ardour of the passengers who were determined to have an enjoyable time.
>
> On arrival at the entrance to the Sound, low driving rain clouds obscured the entrance and the lower slopes of the mountains, and Captain C. T. Copping dared not risk his ship going too close in. However, through the breaks in the clouds some memorable glimpses of the Southern Alps were afforded the passengers.
>
> Card parties and deck games enlivened the passage and gala dances on both overnight stops at Queen Charlotte Sound were very successful.
>
> The Christmas Day festivities were carried out in traditional fashion and the ship's catering staff excelled itself in providing meals that were as memorable as the views of the Alps.
>
> Arriving back in Wellington on the morning of the 28th of December, *Wanganella* sailed the same day for Sydney.

> The task of the ship's complement in making the ship ready for sea in the short time between the conclusion of the cruise and the sailing hour for Sydney was a mammoth one and was carried out with efficiency and despatch.

In the Wellington notes from the same issue of *The Beacon* it was reported:

> At 7.30 am on 28th December, when *Wanganella* had just berthed, the Chief Steward was noticed rushing away from Queen's Wharf as though a brace of Tax Collectors was at his heels. In response to a hurried query as to where he was going at such express speed, he just had time to answer; 'To the marts – the ...'s have eaten me out of house and home.'

Wanganella and *Monowai* continued to operate their regular services throughout 1957 with almost no interruption. However, *Wanganella* was due to depart Wellington on Friday, 10 May, when a major storm struck the area, with winds gusting up to 105 mph. The storm continued into Saturday, and the weather did not moderate until Sunday, with *Wanganella* finally getting away from Queen's Wharf at noon, arriving back in Sydney two days late, on Thursday, 23 May.

Wanganella made news in Auckland when it arrived on 15 October 1957 carrying the animals for an Australian circus, which were offloaded. In the December 1957 issue of *The Beacon*, the Auckland office of Huddart Parker reported:

> We do not seem to have experienced anything of any great moment to report, beyond the fact that Bullen's Circus arrived on the trip in mid-October and the discharging of the elephants caused some excitement. We have handled Wirth's elephants many times and they were easily catered for, being well-seasoned deck passengers, but in the case of Bullen's outfit, this did

Wanganella in Wellington Harbour after the refit in 1956 (*The Beacon*).

Captain H. F. Norrie and *Wanganella* deck officers in 1956 (L to R) D. Robert (3rd), L. Cole (Chief), Capt. Norrie, P. Cheek (2nd), F. Klima (Extra 3rd) (*The Beacon*)

not apply, and the elephants, apparently having enjoyed the trip so much, were loathe to leave the ship, and protested strongly.

The arrival of the circus animals was reported in the *New Zealand Herald* as follows:

SYNCOPATED ELEPHANTS GO ON STRIKE
Gang-Plank Rebellion

Elephants with syncopation invaded Auckland yesterday. A troupe of nine that arrived in the *Wanganella* from Sydney caused uproar in the Customs shed on Captain Cook Wharf and then strolled stolidly up Queen Street on the way to Western Springs stadium. Motorists gaped and at the top of Queen Street a startled traffic officer directed the plodding pachyderms into side streets.

The nine elephants, plus a menagerie of lions, tigers, leopards, Himalayan bears and other animals, were brought by an Australian circus which will tour New Zealand. Chained on the forward deck of the ship, they had a calm Tasman crossing, but when they berthed at Auckland the fun began.

A gang-plank was lowered, to allow them to leave the ship. But, after testing it with their feet, the elephants decided it was unsafe and refused to use it. They began a sit-down strike. Circus hands tried the ancient donkey trick, dangling carrots in front of them to entice them, but the elephants took the carrots and stood their ground.

For the next three hours there was a pitched battle on the deck between elephants and about 20 circus hands. A mixture of carrots, curses and brute force was successful in getting three of the most compliant off the ship. During the row a pachyderm named Alice got hold of the carrot sack and ate most of the bribes inside. The other elephants refused to be pulled down the plank by ropes attached to the animals ashore.

Then, on the wharf, the elephants successfully landed swayed slowly in a syncopated rhythm to light music being broadcast through the loud-speakers.

On deck it was decided to use slings.

This operation started badly. Alice, the first to be hoisted by crane, began to pull the *Wanganella* up after her. Just in time it was realised that she was anchored to the deck by ankle chains.

The fifth elephant screamed so loudly when her sling rose that those on the wharf took fright and broke away from their keepers. They turned to stampede into the wharf Customs shed. A crowd watching from the shed doorway scattered. Circus hands stopped the elephants with goads before they could present their trunks at the Customs barrier.

More screams came from the sixth elephant as it was swung up over the wharf, but were drowned by roars from lions in the hold, and shouts from about 20 people, all giving conflicting directions to the crane driver.

During 1957 the two main diesel engines on *Wanganella* were converted from air, or blast injection to airless, or solid injection. The work was done over a period of months during each four-day period the vessel was in Sydney between voyages, and involved the fitting of a new combined fuel pump and valve to each of the sixteen cylinders in the two 8-cylinder diesel engines.

Blast injection required a heavy three-stage blast air-compressor to be coupled to the forward end of each engine, which absorbed about 6 per cent of the engine power to generate the air required to ignite the fuel in the cylinders. This air was cold when it entered the cylinder, and from time to time caused the piston heads to crack, as had happened to *Wanganella* on several occasions.

Over the years various refinements had been made to the diesel engine, resulting in the development of airless, or solid injection, so that the blast air-compressor could be removed and the 6 per cent of power it had previously absorbed made available for other uses, such as turning the propeller shafts. This in turn resulted in a reduction in fuel consumption of about 5 per cent, and improved the reliability of the engines.

As 1957 drew to a close, preparations were in full swing for another special Christmas cruise from Wellington, though following a different itinerary to

Alice goes ashore from *Wanganella* (*The Beacon*).

the previous year, visiting the Marlborough Sounds. The cruise was announced in September, and was sold out within a short time. This was obviously very pleasing for the company, and it was noted in *The Beacon* that 'The impression created by a successful cruise of this type can have far-reaching effects as the popularity of the vessel can have marked results on future passenger lists'.

A full schedule of events was organised by the Wellington office, as this report published in the December 1957 issue of *The Beacon* indicates:

> All at Wellington Office are now in the throes of the Marlborough Sounds Cruise turmoil. Despite the fact that it was announced only in September, we have a full passenger list, and we are hoping that it will be successful in every other respect, too. A very great deal will depend upon the weather, but even if it rains we feel that we are well prepared to cope with the entertainment problems. We are keeping our fingers particularly tightly crossed for a fine 'first night'.
>
> On Christmas Eve, *Wanganella* is scheduled to anchor in the Bay of Many Coves (which is just as lovely as its name suggests), at 6.30 p.m. About 8 p.m. a Maori Concert Party is expected out from Picton, and the twelve members will give a concert for the 'Cruisers'. Later in the evening we hope that a very much larger party, some 70 strong, will come out in launches and cruise round the ship, singing Christmas Carols. Given a fine night, this should provide a quite unforgettable experience.
>
> To add to the fun, Selwyn Toogood, New Zealand's leading radio personality, will be going as compere, and during the cruise he will record a programme for his weekly 'It's in the Bag' broadcast. This will be quite something, as all the prizes have to go along with him. If some lucky passenger wins the first prize, they can save a taxi fare home – just drive their new Austin A-35 away as soon as it is landed back on Queen's Wharf!

A report on the cruise from the Wellington office appeared in the March 1959 issue of *The Beacon*:

> Though she was only half lucky with the unseasonable weather, *Wanganella*'s Christmas cruise to the Marlborough Sounds was thoroughly enjoyed by the 400 passengers who filled the ship.
>
> Most of them were from Wellington, but others came from many parts of New Zealand. There were a number of tourists from Australia and a Dutch family from outlandish Hollandia, in West New Guinea.
>
> *Wanganella* is said to be the largest ship ever to make the passage through winding Tory Channel into Queen Charlotte Sound. After a pleasant run from Wellington on Tuesday afternoon, 24th December, she anchored overnight in the Bay of Many Coves.
>
> An excellent concert was given on board by a party of Maoris from Picton. Trained and compered by Mrs. T. Riwaka, the costumed performers were young girls who made good their first appearance in public with self-accompanied duets and action songs. The concert was followed by a dance to music by George Miller and his orchestra.
>
> Starting early on Christmas Day morning, *Wanganella* made a fine weather run round to Pelorus Sound and anchored in Tennyson Inlet shortly before 10 o'clock. Passengers were interested to identify many features of the rugged, broken coastline and the intricate windings of the sound by means of the excellent maps provided by the company.
>
> There was much excitement among the 40 or 50 children when Father Christmas (impersonated by Mr. Selwyn Toogood) arrived on board and summoned each one by name to receive a gift.
>
> A pleasantly hot midsummer day ended with a sumptuous dinner at night, followed by the singing of Christmas carols.
>
> The weather changed for the worse early on Thursday morning and *Wanganella* made the return trip to historic Ship Cove, Queen Charlotte Sound, in a strong northerly wind and thick driving rain which persisted for the rest of the day, but failed to damp the spirits of the passengers.
>
> *Wanganella* went up to Picton in the afternoon and was escorted to her anchorage by a large number of speedboats taking part in the New Zealand water skiing championship events. When the ship returned to Ship Cove, a children's fancy dress parade was held, and after a gala dinner there was a fancy dress ball.
>
> Despite the weather, there was not a dull minute throughout the cruise. Captain H. F. Norrie and his

Maori entertainment group on *Wanganella* (*The Beacon*).

Wanganella anchored off Picton (*The Beacon*).

officers and crew spent long hours and broken periods on duty to ensure its success. They were ably supported by Mr. S. A. Marris, assistant manager at Wellington, and his wife, and Mr. and Mrs. R. H. C. Taylor.

The chief officer (Mr L. Cole), his boatswain (Mr. B. D. Box), and their men, the chief electrician (Mr R Thomson) and his assistants, Mr. J. Carmichael and Mr. J. Crothers, saw to it that there was no hitch in the deck arrangements.

The providoring staff rose to the festive Christmas occasion under the chief steward (Mr. E. Fookes) and his chef (Mr. J. Balkind). Captain D. McLeish, formerly master in the Union Company's inter-island steamers, was coastal pilot for the cruise.

The cruise of *Wanganella* to the Marlborough Sounds ended with a storm of great violence. Following continuous heavy rain on Thursday, the north-west wind increased to strong gale force during the night and in the early hours next morning there was a violent thunderstorm.

Wanganella, which was lying in Ship Cove, began to drag her anchor and Captain Norrie decided to put to sea. In a torrential downpour of rain which reduced visibility to nil, *Wanganella* got under way in the grey light and headed out past Motuara Island for the entrance to Queen Charlotte Sound and so into open water, where she met the full force of the gale.

Once clear of the land, the ship ran out of the rain into clear weather, the crossing of Cook Strait being made in bright sunshine. There was a considerable sea running and passengers *on* deck got quite a thrill when an occasional cloud of spray swept over the foredeck.

A few late risers were seasick, but their trouble was probably caused by good Christmas living rather than the slight motion of the ship.

Wanganella arrived in harbour on time, but went to an anchorage off Kaiwharawhara to wait for a tug to assist her in berthing in the strong wind. She got alongside Queen's Wharf shortly after 10 o'clock.

Despite the inclement weather the cruise was an enormous success, and Wellington office reported that 'a considerable number who made it came straight in and put their names down' for next Christmas in the hope that it may be repeated. With the two short Christmas cruises in 1956 and 1957 having been so successful, it was decided early in 1958 that *Wanganella* would make a similar cruise at the end of the year, and also be sent on a more extensive cruise to the South Pacific islands in the winter, with departure from Wellington scheduled for 12 June. In addition, a decision was made to begin operating cruises from Australian ports to New Zealand in the summer, with two departures, both to be operated by *Westralia*.

In the meantime *Wanganella* continued to operate fortnightly departures from Sydney to either Auckland or Wellington, in conjunction with *Monowai*. Early in 1958 Captain Norrie was stricken with a serious case of pneumonia, and while he was recuperating Captain J. Gilbertson was in command of *Wanganella* for several voyages. There was also the occasional incident that affected the timetable, one of which occurred under very unusual circumstances during a scheduled drydocking.

Wanganella arrived in Sydney from Auckland on Sunday, 6 April 1958, and was booked to enter the Sutherland Dock at Cockatoo Island on Tuesday, 8 April for two days, then resume service with a departure for Wellington on 11 April, and a voyage to Auckland on 24 April. However, on 11 April the following item appeared in the *Sydney Morning Herald*:

> The Huddart Parker liner *Wanganella*, which was to have sailed from Sydney today for Wellington (N.Z.), will not sail until next Thursday.
>
> The *Wanganella*'s bow was damaged when the ship was caught by the wind and hit the Cockatoo Island floating dock [sic] while entering it for a normal overhaul on Tuesday. Repairing or replacing stoved-in plates will take until next week. The manager of Huddart Parker Ltd., Mr. A. Nichol, said yesterday that some passengers had asked the company to arrange alternative travel to New Zealand.

The damage was actually incurred when the bow of *Wanganella* struck the entrance to the Sutherland Dock, not the floating dock. Repairs were completed within the week, though quite a few bow plates had to be removed and replaced, and the ship departed Sydney for Wellington on 17 April.

Wanganella arrived there on the morning of 21 April, but instead of spending several days in port, departed the same evening for Sydney. The departure for Auckland was put back two days from the original schedule, requiring *Wanganella* to again make a quick turnaround in both Sydney and Auckland, but the vessel was then able to resume its voyages as previously scheduled.

On 6 June *Wanganella* departed Sydney on a regular voyage to Wellington, but instead of returning to Sydney, departed Wellington on 12 June 1958 on a 15-day cruise around the Pacific islands, visiting Suva, Apia and Nukualofa. While *Wanganella* was in Wellington a portable swimming pool was lifted on board, and erected on the port side of No. 2 hatch.

To cover the period *Wanganella* would be cruising, *Westralia* was taken off the service between Sydney and Fremantle to make two trips from Sydney to Auckland, the first departing on 13 June, the second on 27 June. On these voyages *Westralia* was under the command of Captain W. H. Uttley, and the accommodation was advertised as being first, intermediate first and third class.

This report from Wellington office appeared in the September 1958 issue of *The Beacon*.

The cruise was an outstanding success, so much so that we already have a registration list for 'next year's' (if there should be one) which will more than half fill the ship. *Wanganella* left Wellington at 10 pm on June 12th, in fine but cold weather, and the following day, running up the East Coast of the North Island, was beautifully fine, and the views of the coastline were most interesting. On the Saturday and Sunday, the weather deteriorated, the latter day being quite unpleasant, but fortunately it had cleared again by Monday, and we saw no more bad weather until we were within six hours of Wellington.

We arrived at Suva early on Tuesday morning and were favoured with excellent weather for our stay there. It was not too hot, and, strangely enough for Suva, it didn't rain. Most of the passengers took advantage of the shore excursions arranged for them, and also spared time for shopping. They descended on the sports goods shops like a cloud of locusts, and we understand that Suva golfers have had to go practically into recess until the next shipment of golf balls arrives from U.K. In case you didn't know it, we have import restrictions in N.Z.

The run from Suva to Apia is nearly two days, and during that time we were inundated with complaints (about the only ones we heard for the whole trip) about having only a day and a half at Suva, with all its wonderful 'shopping', and having to spend two whole days at 'this A-peer place'. We tried to point out that it should be pronounced Ah-pia, and that we thought they would find it well worth the extra time. (It did seem that to spend over £100 to go on a shopping expedition was a little extravagant.) However, by the time we sailed from Apia, the disgruntled types were without exception saying that we should have had longer *there*, and they

Wanganella berthed in Suva on 16 June 1958 with *Mariposa* and *Beaverbank* astern (*The Beacon*).

This postcard of *Wanganella* was sold on board in the 1950s (Dallas Hogan collection).

Wanganella berthed in Auckland (Ron Knight photo).

Wanganella in Marlborough Sound during a cruise in the late 1950s (both photographs by Ron Knight).

Cruising 159

Monowai departing Sydney in the mid-1950s (Dennis Brook photo).

Postcard view of *Monowai* cruising in Milford Sound.

Wanganella departing Sydney in the mid-1950s (Ron Knight photo).

Westralia berthed in Wellington during a cruise (Dennis Brook photo).

wouldn't have cared if we'd left Suva out altogether ... how can you please 'em?

After having a quick look at Vavau, a very lovely harbour, which treated us to a most magnificent double rainbow as we arrived, with the pot of gold hovering right under *Wanganella*'s bow, we arrived at Nukualofa. Only a short stay was made here, and the general opinion amongst the passengers was that it was quite sufficient. The homeward run was made in really remarkably fine weather, only the last six hours producing an 'old man southerly' which rolled us into Wellington Harbour.

At Apia, it was surprising the number of people who made the early morning (6 a.m.) trip up Mount Vaea to Robert Louis Stevenson's tomb. About 100 did the climb, which is quite a stiff one, and the average age of the passengers was not young. We understand that the report that they started to prepare an extra tomb when they saw the chief engineer heaving into sight is quite without foundation.

And now we have another cruise looming up – we're going to give the Marlborough Sounds one more chance to prove that they can turn on their much-publicised beautiful Christmas weather. (It's not safe to ask Captain Norrie what he thought about it last year.) So down goes the nose to the grindstone again ... still, it's all very interesting, this cruise business. We take this opportunity to extend a welcome to *Westralia* in December, and wish Sydney Office all the best in organising her two jaunts to New Zealand.

Wanganella returned to Sydney on 2 July, and two days later departed for Wellington to resume the regular schedule of fortnightly departures alternately to Auckland and Wellington, while *Westralia*, having completed her two voyages to Auckland, returned to the coastal trade between Sydney and Fremantle.

As 1958 drew to a close, it was time for Captain Norrie to retire, after ten years in command of *Wanganella*. His final departure as master of *Wanganella* was from Wellington on 14 November, and as the ship pulled away from Queen's Wharf Captain Norrie cast a lei into the waters of Wellington Harbour, signifying his desire to return to these shores in the future. He was replaced as master by Captain Uttley. Sadly, Captain Norrie did not return to New Zealand, nor did he enjoy his retirement, as only a few weeks after leaving his beloved *Wanganella* he died.

Over the summer months of 1958/59 Huddart Parker Limited had scheduled two 14-day cruises to New Zealand to be operated by *Westralia*, now under the command of Captain R. H. Clay. The first departed Sydney on 24 December 1958, the second on 7 January 1959, and both cruises followed the same itinerary, going first to Milford Sound, then on to Wellington and Auckland. The following report on these trips, written by the second officer aboard *Westralia*, Mr P. Bradley, appeared in the March 1959 issue of *The Beacon*:

Westralia departing Sydney on 7 January 1959 (*The Beacon*).

I think our New Zealand cruises warrant a detailed report. On both of these we were accompanied by New Zealand Government Tourist Representatives in the interest of the passengers and to assist them in their New Zealand land tours. They did make themselves very popular with the staff and imparted much information on New Zealand history and plant life.

On the first voyage we were blessed with excellent weather, during which the portable swimming pool was put to good use, the children, in particular, thoroughly enjoyed themselves splashing in the pool. Photographers were active in great numbers, and, without exaggeration, the total value of cameras of all types amounted to hundreds of pounds.

To anyone who has not seen Milford Sound, it is a very difficult sight to describe, as its magnificence affects different people in different ways, and even the weather has a great influence on what has been described as the 'mood' of the Sound. Try to imagine that it is late afternoon, with the sun low in the west – this is how it was the first time we approached it. There was quite a lot of low cloud about, and some doubt as to whether Captain Clay would risk entering ... under these conditions. However, as by this time the excitement and expectation amongst the passengers was very noticeable, he decided to enter. Whilst we were approaching the narrow entrance (¼ mile), the New Zealand Tourist Rep. gave a running commentary from the Bridge microphone to the passengers adorning the foc'sle head, and you could almost hear the gasps of astonishment as we steamed into the narrows and became surrounded by the sheer snow capped mountains which tower on either side up to a height of 5,500 ft. We found it almost impossible to photograph; even a wide angle lens was unable to take in most of the views.

The Sound itself is about six miles long and has two prominent waterfalls, both over 500 feet in height, which compare favourably with the world's highest waterfalls (Niagara Falls, 167 feet). The Sound has many large gullies seemingly cut into the mountains, which were actually cut away by the glaciers many years ago.

The widest navigable part of the Sound is ¾ mile across. Captain Clay will verify this, because this is where he swung the vessel. The most noticeable thing when you are actually inside Milford Sound is the loss of height scale, and it became very difficult to judge distances from the shore. At this time of the evening a wind springs up from nowhere in the Sound, reaching moderate gale force, and on this occasion we had great difficulty in turning around, but finally succeeded and sailed out in haste. We steamed off the coast all night and arrived back to enter the Sound at breakfast time the following morning. There was less cloud, and consequently more sunlight inside the Sound.

After our second entry into the Sound, we cruised down the coast with the intention of entering Bligh Sound, but unfavourable weather conditions at this stage and the doubtful charts of the area made us decide not to do so.

The good weather prevailed on the trip to Wellington, where passengers went on various tours of the city. A large number of our passengers commenced their three day overland tour, taking in many places of interest in North Island, including the thermal areas and volcanic regions. The New Zealand Government Tourist Bureau obligingly provided a car and driver for the Master, and the Chief Engineer and myself were invited along for a tour of the city environs.

We continued the voyage to Auckland under admirable weather conditions, and, as we neared the East Cape, we closed into the land to give passengers an opportunity of seeing some New Zealand scenery and taking photographs if they wished. At Auckland, passengers disembarked into the many tourist buses waiting to take them to Rotorua. Again the Tourist Bureau provided a car and driver, and Captain Clay, Chief Officer, Chief Engineer and myself embarked on a most interesting day tour, covering over 400 miles.

Passengers from the overland tour rejoined us on the following day, and we departed from New Zealand's shores on the final leg of the cruise to Sydney.

The second cruise was marred by adverse weather in the nature of a blanket of fog which followed us for a week. It did not deter us from entering the Sound twice on this trip, and I think *Westralia* has created a record here. What we did see on this cruise was a different Milford Sound again, and this time we ventured nearer to the head of the Sound, weather conditions enabling us to steam stern first almost to the Bowen Falls, which are situated near the Milford Hotel. From this position we could clearly see the Pembroke Glacier in all its beauty. Even the fog on the second cruise, which was

Captain Clay on the bridge of *Westralia* in Milford Sound (*The Beacon*).

Wanganella berthed in Darling Harbour, with *Westralia* on the other side of the wharf building, the Huddart Parker cargo vessel *Adelong*, and *Lakemba* at far right (*The Beacon*).

considerably trying to the Master and Officers, failed to dampen the enthusiasm of the passengers.

The Wellington and Auckland trips continued as before, and on the homeward trip we passed *Wanganella* in mid Tasman.

Some mention should be made at this stage of the excellent fare provided by the catering staff, the *Westralia* really 'turned it on'.

When *Westralia* returned to Sydney from the second cruise it resumed its place on the service to Fremantle, departing Sydney on 23 January. However, in early January 1959, Huddart Parker had announced that *Westralia* was to be withdrawn from service, and would be offered for sale. Shortly after this announcement was made, a delegation from Hobart approached the Federal Government with regard to their providing a subsidy of £133,000 per year to enable *Westralia* to operate a service between Sydney and Hobart, but this was refused.

Meanwhile, *Wanganella* had operated her Christmas cruise, but it had not been as successful as previous years. A report from Wellington office in *The Beacon* for March 1959 commented:

> Although we didn't manage to fill it as we did the previous year (the Government's increased taxation rates came thundering down in October!), the 300 who went all had a wonderful time, despite a really wretched and unseasonable Christmas Eve. As *Wanganella* moved out from the wharf into the teeth of a southerly, with pouring rain, the prospects for a happy cruise seemed remote. However, the weather man relented, and after the first afternoon, turned on better weather than for the 1957 cruise. The entire ship's company played their parts nobly, and Bob Taylor did a great job as Cruise Director. It wasn't an easy row to hoe, but he successfully overcame all the unexpected setbacks.

Another report in the same issue was supplied by Mr T Harris, the chief officer of *Wanganella*:

> We have had a break from our usual routine with a Christmas Cruise to Queen Charlotte Sound. The weather didn't treat us too kindly on sailing day, but cleared quite well on Christmas Day, and turned on a beautiful day on Boxing Day, when we were down at Picton.
>
> A wide variety of entertainment was laid on for the passengers, with shore excursions at Tennyson Inlet, Ship Cove and Picton; Selwyn Toogood's Giveaway Show; a horse race meeting; community carol singing and an impromptu concert when our Maori Concert Party failed to arrive; dancing to George Miller's Band; Father Christmas with toys for all the children; a film show; a deck sport's meeting for children (and adults); a Gala Christmas Dinner, with all the trimmings; a Fancy Dress Ball and a rocket display, as well as the usual deck games.
>
> We are pleased to report that our efforts were appreciated by the passengers, who thoroughly enjoyed the trip. Their only complaint seemed to be that it ended too soon.

After the cruise ended, *Wanganella* returned to its regular trans-Tasman routine. Meanwhile, on 20 February, *Westralia* departed Sydney on its final voyage to Fremantle, returning to Sydney on 16

Westralia and *Wanganella* together for the last time in Darling Harbour (*The Beacon*).

March to be laid up at anchor in Sydney Harbour, and offered for sale.

Westralia was purchased in April 1959 by a Fijian firm, converted into a livestock carrier, renamed *Delfino*, and left Sydney on 3 July carrying 30 000 sheep to San Diego. After making one further trip, with 25 000 sheep, the former liner was again laid up in Sydney.

The following letter regarding *Westralia* in her new role, written during the second voyage, appeared in the March 1960 issue of *The Beacon*:

An interesting letter from Captain Lucas to Captain Holthe tells of some of the problems that have to be faced in the carriage of sheep across the Pacific. He writes:

'You would not recognise your old ship now if you stepped aboard her and looked around, as there just isn't anything of the inside left. We carry sheep from Promenade Deck right through to C Deck where the Saloon was and then in what we call Lower Fo'cstle Area, upper Fo'cstle, No. 2 Tween deck and Shelter Deck, also No. 4 Tween deck and there are pens in forepart of No. 5 Hold two tiers high.

'The main stairways that were are not any more, and it's sheep pens right through and on the outside of the Promenade Deck. Boat Deck, apart from removing two boats abreast Bridge and right aft is the same, the boats from abreast Mainmast and on Poop have been removed. We have sheep pens put on Deck along the rails abreast No. 4 Hatch and mainmast two high, all pens are in tiers of two high in each deck. We had to pull out the pens immediately abaft the engine room in B and C Deck owing to heat from engine room bulkhead.

'There is a lot more ventilation in the ship and we are fitting even more in this trip on the way home, and at Suva or Sydney, and I am feeling that the next trip will be even better than the one just completed, which was a 100% improvement on last trip. Our losses this trip were under 2½% from time of loading to completion of discharge. We discharged the full 24,509 in nineteen and a quarter hours' working time.

'On the way across to the U.S. on the first trip I was overside with one of the Technical Advisers at sea painting white to try out the effect in the tropics, and after finding it successful, we made her a complete white ship in Suva homeward bound.

'We have 28 x 4,000 gallon round tanks in No. 2 Lower Hold and that gives us an extra 500 odd tons, there is 750 tons of Blue Metal in No. 3 Lower Hold and 500 tons in No. 4 Lower Hold, and in spite of this, Navigation Department issued orders for Peak Tanks and No. 2 Hold Tanks to be ballasted with salt water when the fresh water is used up. I have experimented and found that she does get a little tender with all fresh water just about used up and no ballast in these tanks, but not dangerously so.

'We use about 60 to 65 tons daily fresh water in normal weather and up to 75 and 80 in very hot weather, so we can carry ample F.W. for our longest hop between Suva and Honolulu, but the owners would like to cut out Suva and I insist on all of another 300 tons in that case. It is possible we may get No. 2 Double Bottom taken out and cleaned for F.W. and a couple or three more tanks in No. 2 Hold, then we might make it.

'It's not practical to clean out the pens by washing down as we have to keep areas as dry as possible, as it's not heat, but humidity, that is our biggest enemy, and the scuppers are not big enough to cope with the manure.

'We therefore work a "DEEP LITTER" system, starting off with sawdust and superphosphate to cut down the ammonia, and when it builds up it's quite hard and dry unless we get high humidity in the area. We estimate that at least three hundred and fifty tons to four hundred tons of manure had to be shovelled over the side on the way back to Suva and Sydney, and we can't land it anywhere owing to chance of plant disease.

'We have our saloon in the well that was above the Lounge in the centre of the Officers' accommodation. It's quite handy for us, really, otherwise there hasn't been much change in the accommodation on Boat Deck. Sparks, a Chinese R.O., lives in his Radio Room, and we have made two cabins in the space that was above the Smoke Room in the centre of the Engineers' Accommodation, where we accommodate the Veterinary Officer, etc. The ship's Surgeon is in the 1st room abaft the Engineers' mess and the Chief Steward is in the next room to that. We carry eight Engineers and two Electricians and four Chinese fitters, and next trip will carry another Electrician and an apprentice engineer and, I hope, a 4th Mate to relieve the Mate for day work which will in turn relieve me a bit.

'Our Fijian Crew numbers 79 including the Stewards, Indian-Fijians, and we can only carry 110 as our two lifeboats on each side limit us to that. Port Number one was fitted with a new Diesel Engine and that cut down its capacity somewhat. We kept the accommodation for crew on starboard side of C deck alongside the engine room otherwise all Fijians and Chinese are For'ard or aft in Poop. On top of Poop we have the four Chinese fitters and two rooms for White stockmen.'

Despite Captain Lucas' references to future voyages, *Delfino* remained laid up in Sydney, and at one stage was renamed *Woolambi*, but did not make another voyage until it left Sydney under tow on 19 December 1961 bound for the scrapyard in Japan.

The sale of *Westralia* in April 1959 left *Wanganella* as the last surviving passenger liner owned by Huddart Parker Limited. The joint service across the Tasman with *Monowai* continued as before, and in January 1959 it was announced that *Wanganella* would be making another cruise from Wellington to the South Pacific islands, departing on 22 July. *Monowai* was also taken off the route during the winter months to operate a cruise to the Pacific islands from Auckland, and also made at least one cruise in the summer to the fjords in South Island.

A colour postcard of *Wanganella* departing Sydney, which was sold on board at the time, carried a very interesting caption:

The 3½ day leisure with pleasure. Ten thousand ton Huddart Parker Liner T.S.M.V. "Wanganella". The Line has been serving the travelling public between Australia and New Zealand with gratification since 1893, and looks forward to carrying on the same service in the future.

One of these postcards, purchased by a passenger who travelled on the ship from New Zealand in April 1959, was posted in Sydney on 21 April and carried the following message about the voyage:

Dear Diane,
I thought you would like to see what the ship looked like on a sunny day. We haven't seen much sun, although it hasn't been very rough, just overcast. I am enjoying the voyage, just eating and sleeping and lying on deck reading. There is plenty to do if you want to – quoits, table tennis and other games, with films or some other entertainment every night. The meals are very good

Delfino anchored in Sydney Harbour (Fred Roderick).

"WANGANELLA" DECK OFFICERS

Back row (from left): Mr. G. Semple (3rd Officer), Mr. T. Harris (Chief Officer), Captain W. Uttley, Mr. R. King (Radio Officer), Mr. W. Dalgleish (Extra 3rd Officer), Mr. R. Taylor (Purser). Front row: Mr. R. Gadsby (2nd Officer), Mr. J. Cowan (Assistant Purser).

Mr. E. J. LYONS, CHIEF ENGINEER, AND ENGINEER OFFICERS "WANGANELLA"

too, five course every time you sit down, and of course I have them all.   Ivor.

On 5 May 1959, when *Wanganella* arrived in Sydney from Auckland, the vessel's regular berth was occupied, and the liner was directed to berth at 9 Woolloomooloo, to my knowledge the only time she ever berthed in Woolloomooloo other than during the war years. *Wanganella* remained there until departing for Auckland again on 8 May. This alteration to standard procedure was not appreciated by the passengers, as was indicated in the report from Chief Officer Harris that appeared in the June 1959 edition of *The Beacon*:

Since the previous issue the only slight deviation we have had from our two grooves across the Tasman was last trip when we berthed down the Loo, much to the disgust of our passengers who did not, therefore, have the thrill of wondering whether our masts would safely clear Jack Lang's Coathanger or just snap off – you know, if they ever did it would be frightfully embarrassing, wouldn't it.

I am pleased to report that we have just enjoyed six months of what, for the Tasman, is quite good weather with the exception of two really bad trips. During the first we ran into a cyclone with the barometer down to 972 mbs (28.7 inches) and the wind howling, mainly from the south and east, at up to 60 knots (69 mph to you landlubbers). We were hove to for a while during the worst of it and did not arrive in Auckland until 2226 hours on Tuesday night when we had to anchor until the next morning. But then what else could we expect after sailing on Friday, the 13th of March! The other bad trip was when we sailed for Wellington on 10th April. There was a 40 knot (46 mph) southerly gale blowing when we left Darling Harbour and it just blew steadily from the one direction until Tuesday morning, when we reached the Cook Strait. Such a prolonged wind, of course, caused a very high sea and a very heavy swell and one freak wave stove in the bulwark doors at No. 2 Hatch and also shattered two half inch plate glass windows on the Promenade Deck! That trip we did not berth until 1810 hours on Tuesday and, as you can no doubt guess, were very pleased to do so to get a decent night's sleep.

During the influenza epidemic that has been sweeping the country we have had our fair share of casualties, but I don't think people were really worried until the Bosun was seen checking up on the position of the Red Crosses that go on the funnels.

In conclusion, we would ask – have you ever noticed that all the articles from *The Beacon* are written by Navigating Officers? Which raises the old query – can Engineers write?

A potentially serious situation occurred aboard *Monowai* when it was berthed in Sydney on 27 May 1959. Workers were using oxy-torches on repairs above the boilers when sparks ignited oil floating in the bilges. The flames became so intense the firefloats *Bennelong* and *Burrowaree* were brought alongside to fight the blaze with foam. Once the fire was extinguished an examination showed that the boiler room had been quite badly damaged, but the ship was still able to depart on schedule.

Wanganella continued to operate regular trips across the Tasman until mid-July, when it made a second cruise to the South Pacific islands from Wellington. The following report on the cruise, again provided by Chief Officer Harris, appeared in the September 1959 issue of *The Beacon*:

Wednesday, 22nd July, Wellington   The day opened fine, clear, and calm. For Wellington, that sounds far fetched, but it was true enough. A perfect day for the final preparations. During the morning the swimming pool was lifted on to the deck and assembled on the port side of No. 2 Hatch. On the previous cruise, it had been necessary for passengers to enter the water via the crew's alleyway. This time a special platform and ladder had been provided so that swimmers could use the pool direct from A Deck.

On the stroke of noon the ship blossomed forth into a mass of bunting, dressed from stem to stern.

The electricians had strung the deck-heads of the port Prom. Deck and the verandah cafe with fairy lights, and they looked most attractive. The gangway and the main entrance were decked with strings of white lights. By dusk, the ship was completely stored and watered, a blaze of light, and all hands stood by for the 'invasion'.

At 7 p.m. the passengers and their friends streamed aboard. They completed their formalities and then made their dining-room reservations. With these completed, the ship's band struck up and passengers and friends danced on the Prom. Deck. George Miller's four-piece dance band proved most popular and was a feature of many of the ship's evening shows. Visitors were ushered ashore and the sailing time of 9 p.m. approached. Then a passenger discovered that his baggage was still at the Central Station with no instructions for forwarding. The Master and Mr. Marris, our Cruise Director, decided to hold the ship while enquiries were made and the Stevedore set out in his car. Twenty minutes after our scheduled departure time, the car flew on to the wharf, horn blazing. A cheer went up from the crowd and those cases went on board like greased lightning. We were off … months of thought and preparation were over.

Thursday, 23rd July   Travelling up the East Coast, our pilot, Captain Broughton, brought the ship fairly close in, and the passengers were given a running commentary from the bridge. Rather cold and overcast but calm seas.

Thursday was a fairly quiet day, passengers taking it easy after travelling long distances to join the ship, Housie Housie in the afternoon and a film show after dinner being the entertainments.

East Cape Lighthouse provided our last glimpse of N.Z., and then we were really 'off into the blue'.

Friday, 24th July A rather choppy sea. It was the only day of the whole cruise when the weather couldn't be described as perfect. Deck sports were in full swing and Mr. Marris, assisted by Mr. R. Taylor, had a busy time booking passengers for tours in Suva.

Mr Bob Taylor really excelled himself during the evening when he ran a most successful 'Pick-a-Box' Session, where some very nice prizes were given away.

Saturday, 25th July The weather seemed to warm up overnight and there was no doubt that we were heading in the right direction – due north. The verandah cafe came into its own. The awnings were spread and the tables and chairs set out. Canvas screens were rigged round the railings and produced a very snug and attractive place for passengers to relax. By night, the place was lit by coloured lights and as the cruise progressed the verandah became the most popular meeting place. On Saturday evening, a race meeting was held before a very large and enthusiastic audience. The passengers were particularly pleasant and easy to entertain, which must have helped the Cruise Director a great deal.

Sunday, 26th July A beautiful hot day – perfect swimming weather. All hands were out in summer clothes and officers in whites. The feature of the morning was a Church Service conducted by Captain Uttley before a capacity congregation. In the afternoon the pool was to be officially opened. To this end Mrs. Marris had done a lot of work. She produced cases of perfectly made 'neck-to-knee' bathers and Tarzan outfits. About ten passengers and officers rigged themselves out as bathing beauties. Our massive 4th Officer, Mr. K. Urry, looked particularly chic, radiant in a neck-to-knee and doing a ballet dance. Artistic application of cosmetics by Mrs. Marris and Mrs. Taylor completed the ensemble. Two passengers were very good as Tarzan and Son of Tarzan, being the tallest and shortest gentlemen we could find (they went hand in hand).

Led by the band, the group paraded the decks and ended up at the pool. From the bridge, Bob Taylor gave a witty commentary.

The passengers loved the show and were left with no doubts that the pool was truly open.

That night, Mr. Fookes, Chief Steward, did us proud in producing a gala dinner with all the trimmings. Individual

Mr Urry stepping ashore (The Beacon).

Wanganella arriving in Suva on 27 July 1959 (The Beacon).

menus, leis for the ladies and paper hats for the gents. The wine waiter is reported to have clocked 30 mph between tables. After this gastronomic adventure, the passengers turned out for the Mad Hatters' Parade and surprised us by the number and cleverness of their creations. Dancing to the band wound up the day and it was a happy and suntanned crowd that trooped off to bed. It seemed we hadn't stopped laughing since lunch time.

Monday, 27th July Dawn – and Fiji. Another glorious morning as we steamed in between the reefs that guard Suva Harbour. The ship was dressed over all and looked very smart. On the wharf the Fijian Military Band struck up. A wonderful body of men, immaculate in their scarlet tunics and white lava-lavas with the famous picket-like hem line. The gangway was lowered very smartly and the 4th Officer went down to greet the Chief who was waiting to officially welcome the ship. Mr Urry, immaculate in his whites, was escorted to the Chief by two fearsome warriors, in full battle array and bearing large and most effective-looking clubs. A speech of welcome was given and translated, and our representative was invested with a lei. The welcome over, the passengers swarmed ashore, each one receiving a hibiscus flower from a pair of island beauties. Passengers spent the day seeing Fiji on many of the specially arranged tours and dinner was a hubbub as excited passengers exchanged stories of their trips. During the evening a native concert party came aboard and gave us a sample of their singing and expressive dancing. The pool was used in port, many people taking a cold plunge before going to bed.

Tuesday, 28th July More tours and souvenir shopping. An almost tax-free colony, the shops carried a great range of reasonably priced goods. Transistor radios were a big attraction together with Indian silver work, baskets and mats. Between them, the passengers and crew must have spent a fortune. At five o'clock we regretfully said 'Isa Lei' and with Fiji behind us in a lovely sunset we looked forward to Samoa.

Wednesday, 29th July Our passage to Apia would have been very hot, save for a steady south-easterly trade wind which kept things pleasant. During the evening an enjoyable impromptu concert and a sing-song was organised. The passengers seemed to be great singers, breaking into song at the slightest excuse.

Wednesday, 29th July Crossed the date line and repeated the date. What with advancing clocks and retarding the day some passengers were slightly bamboozled, but as we enjoyed each day as it came, the date was immaterial. A race meeting for gentlemen jockeys was held in the morning, something of a novelty for the ship's officers as it had always been an evening entertainment in the ship. Noon saw us passing through the Apolima Strait between the two largest islands in the Samoan Group. The scenery was most impressive. High jungle mountains, some over 7,000 feet, gave way to palm covered plains along the shores where most of the copra, bananas and cocoa are produced.

Apia Harbour was just a gap in the coral reefs. A pilot came out and took the ship in. It was a tricky bit of ship handling, turning in a very confined space. Eventually it was done and we lay secure, head to sea and held by our anchors forward and by wires to a buoy astern. The surf thundered on the reefs close by and we didn't like thinking about what could happen if any moorings gave way. Boatloads of Samoans came out to meet us. Very handsome and courteous people, decked out in their bright lava-lavas and grass skirts, they came aboard and every passenger received a beautiful hibiscus or frangipani lei. A singing and dancing show followed.

The Missionaries have always been very strong in Apia and the sea front of Apia seems to be one long row of churches of every kind and description. Capt. Uttley and Capt. Broughton received an invitation to cocktails with the High Commissioner and the ship's company felt most honoured. After dinner, a stream of launches ferried the passengers ashore. The crew deserve a pat on the back, the A.B.'s being most helpful assisting passengers at the foot of the gangways. In the perfect still tropical night, the ship looked magnificent. A pyramid of coloured lights reflected in the dark waters. With the sound of singing coming from the shore and the scent of flowers, we felt we were in another world.

Thursday, 30th July Thursday was a busy day for the touring passengers. The native handcrafts were most attractive and were sold by native women who sat under every available shady tree. The quiet dignity of the Samoans was so different from the feverish salesmanship of the Indians in Fiji. That night there was a 'do.' organised at the White Horse Inn, a sort of country club with beautiful garden surroundings. We found the grounds brilliantly floodlit and dancing by the natives was enchanting.

A native feast was then provided, cooked in pits. Sucking pigs, yams – the lot.

The tables set out in the gardens groaned under the piles of fruit and tropical delicacies. It's surprising how much one can eat at one sitting. Dancing to a first class native band completed the evening.

Friday, 31st July The ship was honoured to have the High Commissioner aboard to lunch and he was received in the most correct fashion.

The passengers completed their sightseeing and shopping, especially the purchase of their outfits for the Islands Night Ball.

Our faithful native singers, who had provided an apparently non-stop show at the landing stage during our stay, came out in boats to see us off. Reluctantly, we left during the afternoon, the passengers throwing their leis over the side in the traditional fashion, and without any doubt wishing that they might return to this lovely island before very long.

Sunday, 2nd August Crossed the date line again, so dispensed with Sunday, 1st. Capt. Uttley presided at Church in the morning and just before lunch Capt. Broughton took the ship close alongside Fonualei Island.

This island is the summit of an active volcano. Passengers got a close-up view of smoke and steam issuing out of cracks in the ground and got a good whiff from the yellow, sulphur-covered peak.

During the afternoon the ship cruised through Vavau Harbour, miles of beautiful waterways and idyllic islands.

The northernmost of the Tongan group, Vavau is hilly and most attractive. Quite unlike the rest of the group which are flat and covered with dense palm plantations.

We were out by sunset and on the way to Nuku'Alofa. That night we had the Islands Night Ball. Many passengers came down to dinner in Island costumes and Capt. Uttley granted permission for officers to appear in suitable rigs. This consisted of white number 10 uniform coats and coloured lava-lavas. No shoes. Rather becoming, we thought, and especially with a frangipani lei and the bloom behind the port ear.

The Islands Night Ball got under way with an act put on by the Mates, with the Chief Engineer and a Junior Engineer. Mr. Laird did the choreography and with much patience produced a good copy of an island dance. The troupe were suitably arrayed in lava-lavas and grass skirts. Mr. Laird, who was to play the part of a native chief, sported a top hat. Black grease paint was liberally applied and the lady passengers who were to assist blackened themselves and went to their hiding places.

The rhythmic dance, done to the accompaniment of Mr. Semple on drum, proved most popular with the crowd.

Then our warriors, Messrs. Fisher and Margetts, bearing clubs, called for Capt. Uttley, who up to now had been laughing on the sidelines. A rather apprehensive Master was led to a chair in the centre of the arena. Great Chief Laird then delivered a speech of welcome in local dialect, which was translated by your correspondent. He was then given a lei, all same Suva.

Then followed the kava ceremony. One of our lady assistants came forward with a fire bucket containing fire water of great potency. It was said there was a dash of coconut milk somewhere in it. The kava ritual was carried out in the correct manner and a half coconut shell of the brew offered to the Captain. Like a hero, he had a sip, to the great merriment of the crowd.

The show proved most popular and the evening continued with dancing and much merriment.

Monday, 3rd August Our pilot brought us into Nuku'Alofa bright and early, the ship anchoring off. Passengers departed on several short tours, but after Samoa they were a little disappointed.

Queen Salote's Palace was the main attraction. Some nice examples of basket work were brought aboard.

Departed that evening on the final run home.

Tuesday, 4th/Friday, 7th August Good weather stayed with us almost to the last lap. A Fancy Dress Ball was held, during which many weird and wonderful sights were seen. On Thursday, Capt. Uttley presented the prizes, and Mr. Fookes, Chief Steward, turned on his greatest extravaganza, the dinner adieu. Champagne flowed and we all realised, very sadly, that 'the greatest yet' cruise was almost over.

To the strains of island music, we docked in Wellington on Friday afternoon, late but very happy.

Many very kind things were said by passengers and your correspondent believes quite a number have made enquiries about next year's effort.

After the excitement and welcome change of pace and ports during the cruise, it was back to the routine of trans-Tasman voyages for the crew of *Wanganella* for the remainder of 1959. For three months while Captain Uttley took leave, *Wanganella* was under the command of Captain Clay, Captain Uttley returning in mid-November.

No Christmas Cruise was scheduled for 1959. Instead *Wanganella* continued its regular Tasman routine, departing Wellington on 24 December for Sydney, and leaving there on 31 December for Auckland, as was reported by Chief Officer Harris in the March 1960 issue of *The Beacon*:

Christmas and New Year were celebrated in the traditional manner by the passengers, who seemed to enjoy the novelty of spending these holidays afloat. All hands turned to on decorations, which included a Christmas tree hoisted to the fore-masthead. As usual the Chief Steward and the Catering Staff excelled themselves and put on an extensive and succulent Christmas and New Year's Dinner.

Over the holiday season we have had a full complement of passengers both ways and fortunately the weather has been most kind, smooth seas, blue skies and balmy breezes. Also, as is usual at this time of year, we have carried a full team of yearlings for the past two trips. The total value is believed to be around £70,000, so, as can be imagined, we are pleased to see them safe ashore.

Racehorse being loaded on *Wanganella* at Auckland (*The Beacon*).

15

The Final Years

As the 1950s came to a close the future of the entire trans-Tasman passenger liner service was uncertain. At that time, apart from *Wanganella*, Huddart Parker owned five cargo ships, *Warringa*, *Watamurra*, *Woomera*, *Barwon* and *Adelong*, and two tugs based in Melbourne, *Batman* and *Eagle*. In addition, the company had a half share with the Union Line in Tasmanian Steamers, who operated the ferry *Taroona* and a small cargo ship, *Tatana*, between Melbourne and Tasmania, but that operation was to be terminated during 1959. However, Huddart Parker was also one of several Australian shipping companies to have formed Bulkships Limited, to build new bulk carriers for the Australian coastal trades.

Some shareholders in Huddart Parker Limited had publicly recommended that the company withdraw from shipping altogether. This had first been raised early in 1959, and dominated the Annual General Meeting that year. A message from the Managing Director published in the June 1959 issue of *The Beacon* said, in part:

> Members of the Staff will be aware of the unfortunate and disturbing situation which developed prior to, during, and subsequent to the Company's Annual Meeting.
>
> Certain proposals were made which must have resulted in the ultimate extinction of the Company as a shipping entity. The name of Huddart Parker Limited has long been synonymous in the business community with stability and solidity and this unprecedented action by certain shareholders made it clear that they advocated the abandoning of the enterprises on which the Company's success was founded, together with the reputation and tradition built up by service to the community during a period of more than 80 years.

The situation was only aggravated when Union Steam Ship Company announced early in the year that *Monowai* would be withdrawn from service at the end of May, and not replaced.

During her last year in service, berth utilisation on *Monowai* averaged 85 percent of capacity, and during the summer season there were very few voyages that were not fully booked. This high demand for sea travel generated widespread criticism of the Union company's decision to terminate its New Zealand to Sydney service.

The New Zealand Government was hopeful that a service involving a New Zealand ship could be maintained in the future, and approached the Australian Government with an interesting proposal. The basic idea was that a new ship capable of carrying up to 1000 passengers should be built in an Australian shipyard, but manned by New Zealanders. This proposal, however, did not receive approval from the Australian Government.

On 27 May 1960, *Monowai* departed Sydney on her final voyage across the Tasman, arriving in Auckland on 31 May. This terminated the Union Line participation in the trans-Tasman service, which they had maintained since 1876.

The withdrawal of *Monowai* left *Wanganella* to maintain the Tasman service on her own. As before, a schedule of departures every second week from Sydney was maintained, but without *Monowai* as a partner to provide a weekly service, many potential passengers began turning to air travel when they wished to cross the Tasman.

On 2 June *Monowai* departed Auckland on a seventeen-day Pacific island cruise to Tonga, Samoa and Fiji, arriving back in Auckland on 19 June. Three days later the vessel left Auckland for the last time, arriving in Wellington shortly after noon on 23 June. On the evening of 23 June *Wanganella* left Wellington on her third Pacific island cruise from that port, sixteen days to Suva, Apia, Vavau and Nuku'alofa, so for several hours the Tasman liners were together for the last time.

Monowai anchored in Moreton Bay (Warwick Foote).

On 21 June the Union Line had announced the sale of *Monowai* to Hong Kong shipbreakers, Far East Metal Industry & Shipping Co Ltd, who did not rename the vessel, but registered it in Hong Kong, and painted a narrow yellow band on the funnel under the black top.

At midday on Monday, 15 August, *Monowai* departed Wellington on its final voyage to Hong Kong, but in the Tasman Sea ran short of water, and diverted to Brisbane, where no local shipping agent would take on the vessel. When *Monowai* reached Moreton Bay it had to anchor out until something was worked out, and after water was taken on the voyage continued to Hong Kong, arriving there on 6 September.

Although *Wanganella* had developed a very strong following of loyal passengers over the years, there were also those who found the ship less than enchanting. Media personality Derryn Hinch has less than happy memories of his one voyage on *Wanganella* in the early 1960s, as he wrote:

> I booked on one of the most unstable Trans-Tasman 'passenger liners' you could ever entrust with your life and your luggage – the m.v. *Wanganella*.
> It was an uncomfortable, rocking and rolling rust bucket that would have churned your stomach on a mill pond let alone plying one of the most treacherous stretches of water on this planet. It took about three days and seemed like three vomiting weeks. Remember, I was sharing a tiny iron cabin only just above the waterline with three male strangers who didn't seem to wash much or have a second pair of sox.
> It was hardly a love of the sea that put me and the *Wanganella* together. It was solely because it was much cheaper than flying and my duffel bag crammed with all my worldly belongings – including daggy, dated, New Zealie clothes I threw away as soon as I scored an Australian wage – would have incurred a punitive excess baggage charge which I didn't have the money to cover. It cost twenty quid from Wellington to Sydney on the *Wanganella*. That translates to about forty dollars now but it was a fortune in the early Sixties when wages in New Zealand were the equivalent of twenty bucks a week.

Going into 1961, there seemed little doubt that it would not be long before *Wanganella* was withdrawn from service. In the meantime, the liner continued operating across the Tasman from Sydney to both Auckland and Wellington. On one voyage, Pixie Lane and her husband travelled home from New Zealand, and her memories of that voyage were published in the magazine, *World Wide Cruising*, in August 2007. Pixie Lane wrote:

> The year was 1961, my husband and I had lived and worked in New Zealand for the last year and decided to return home to Australia by sea. The haunting strains of 'Now is the Hour' set the scene as we stood on the deck of the *Wanganella*, waving goodbye to friends before quietly slipping out of Auckland Harbour.
> When we could no longer see our friends we set off excitedly in search of our cabin, being first class it was located on the upper deck and we opened our door expecting to find opulence. We were surprised to find a small room with two wooden bunks bolted to the wall on one side and suspended by two chains on the outer corners, there was a tiny bench under the port hole and

a wardrobe also bolted to the wall. No bathroom or toilet, these were later found on the deck below.

We went exploring what was to be our home for the next four days and before we knew it, dinnertime was upon us and with it another surprise. Within the dining room the tables and chairs were long benches that sat eight, and as in our cabin, here everything was bolted down. The food and service were top class, passengers were getting acquainted and having fun over the roll of the waves, but for us, with the afternoon of adventure behind us, it was time for bed.

We woke the following morning to a knock on the door. There stood a butler, with two cups of tea on a silver tray and a cheery 'good morning'. Oh, how posh we felt! Travelling first class on our first ocean voyage with our very own butler. Who cared if the beds weren't really comfortable or the toilets were downstairs, we had our very own butler!

Being an old ship the *Wanganella* was not fitted with stabilisers, and as the lurching sea picked up we quickly discovered why everything was bolted down. The poor old ship tossed and turned and rocked and rolled, waves washed over the deck and up against the portholes in the dining room. Not too many people came to dinner or took a shower that night. We lay curled up in bed, trying to sleep while hanging onto the mattress. Rumours in the morning told of a chap who had fallen out of bed and broken his arm.

Dawn broke to a wonderfully calm day, we breathed a sigh of relief and spent the day lazing about in deck chairs, shopping in the small duty free shop and topping the day off by going to the movies, where we enjoyed Doris Day while sitting on foldout camp chairs which were packed away after the show.

A night of activities was planned for our last evening on board with the highlight being a mock 'horse' race comprising a small wooden horse and jockey on wheels attached to a string and wound in by the contestants.

Each table entered a jockey, I was chosen to wear the number 4 for our table and to the encouraging cries of 'Come on 4' I wound that string as hard as I could and came in a dignified second, just beaten by a head.

A beautiful blue sky greeted us next day as the *Wanganella* made her stately way up Sydney Harbour. What a beautiful sight! There was no Opera House and the buildings were smaller and fewer. We went under the harbour bridge past Luna Park and docked at Darling Harbour Wharf.

We disembarked midmorning and waited for our luggage to be unloaded. A crane lowered a huge rope sling into the hold, up it came full of luggage, passengers took what was theirs and left and down the sling went again. The afternoon wore on and still we waited, by now we were the only ones left and it was 6 pm, the workers were waiting to close up and go home. And so were we!

The last load arrived and so finally did our luggage.

One of the dockworkers found a trolley, watched us load our baggage and pushed it outside the gate, unloaded it and pushed it back inside, and then he locked the gate and walked away without a word being spoken.

Nearly half a century has passed, and that was our one and only cruise. Recently my daughter and I were invited to lunch on the QE2 when she visited Brisbane and my – what a surprise! The furniture wasn't bolted down, the cabins have ensuites, there are swimming pools, shops, a library and the movie theatre has beautifully upholstered seats. What have I been missing?

During 1960 and into 1961 a major battle went on behind the scenes in Huddart Parker Limited. Shareholders had basically split into two groups, one of which wanted the company to stay in shipping, while the other group wanted to sell the shipping interests. In the end the latter group won, and Huddart Parker was sold as an entity to Boral Limited (Bitumen & Oil Refineries Ltd).

There were several parts of the company that Boral was interested in retaining, but *Wanganella* was not one of them. When it was announced that *Wanganella* was to be withdrawn from service, it seemed most probable that the old liner would follow *Monowai* to the scrapyard.

However, in a surprise development, *Wanganella* and the other former Huddart Parker vessels were purchased in September 1961 by another Australian shipping company, McIlwraith, McEacharn Limited, in a share exchange in which Boral became a large shareholder in the company. McIlwraith McEacharn decided to retain *Wanganella* on her trans-Tasman service and, apart from repainting her yellow funnels in the colours of her new owners, red with black top, the liner was not altered.

In early September Huddart Parker had advertised a schedule for *Wanganella* to operate regular trans-Tasman sailings up to the end of 1961, with departures from Sydney for Wellington on 8 and 22 September, 20 October, 17 November, 1 December and 29 December, while departures for Auckland were scheduled for 6 October, 3 November and 15 December, and this schedule was maintained by McIlwraith McEacharn.

Wanganella continued to be advertised under the Huddart Parker banner until the departure for Auckland on 3 November, from which date the schedule was advertised by McIlwraith McEacharn, though the advertisements stated 'for passenger and cargo bookings apply to Huddart Parker Limited, operating agents'.

Wanganella in McIlwraith, McEacharn funnel colours (WSS Victoria).

From 1 December 1961, the Huddart Parker name disappeared completely from the trans-Tasman advertisements, which were subsequently placed by the Union Steam Ship Company of New Zealand, who were listed as 'Principal Agents for MV *Wanganella*'. Going into 1962 a regular schedule was advertised, with alternate departures from Sydney for Auckland and Wellington every second week.

On 23 March 1962, *Wanganella* left Sydney for Auckland, but two days out a piston rod fractured in one of the engines. The liner was able to limp into Auckland on one engine, and temporary repairs were effected. The liner limped back to Sydney, arriving on the afternoon of 4 April, by which time the next voyage, due to depart for Wellington on 6 April, had been cancelled.

The following report on the incident by Doug Taylor, who was an engineer on the ship at the time, was recorded in the book *Workhorses in Australian Waters*:

> In 1962 *Wanganella* was proceeding at full speed when there was an almighty crash from No. 5 cylinder on the starboard main engine, followed by large sections of cast iron, hot water and lube oil being showered out onto the starting platform.
>
> The engineer in charge of the watch, with great courage, rushed to the controls of No. 5 unit and pulled the control lever back to stop but, acting on Murphy's Law, a pin in the control system took this opportunity to drop out and the mayhem continued until the engineer, lying on his stomach, managed to shut the fuel supply valve under the controls. By the time the engine stopped horrific damage had been done.
>
> Initially the piston rod had broken at the crosshead and thereafter the liner, cylinder jacket, cast iron A frames and section of bed plate were all broken. Cockatoo Island Dockyard carried out this major repair using a combination of Metalock and steel sections married up to remaining cast iron sections with fitted bolts. A new liner jacket, piston and rod were fitted and successful engine trials were carried out. Fortunately the crank shaft was not damaged.

Wanganella was moved to Cockatoo Island Dockyard on 10 April, where repairs took so long that the 19 April voyage from Sydney to Auckland was also cancelled. While *Wanganella* was still being repaired it was announced that she had been sold, for £250,000, to the Hang Fung Shipping & Trading Co. Ltd, of Hong Kong, with delivery in three months.

At that time the liner was being advertised to depart Sydney every fourteen days from 4 May to

29 June, when it would make a South Pacific cruise. From 27 July the liner would resume the schedule of departures from Sydney to New Zealand every fourteen days as far ahead as 3 October.

The engine repairs were completed on 3 May, and on 4 May *Wanganella* resumed the Tasman trade with an evening departure from Sydney for Wellington, followed by a departure on 18 May to Auckland, then 1 June and 15 June to Wellington, the last trip *Wanganella* would make there as an Australian flag liner

On 29 June *Wanganella* left Sydney on her final voyage under Australian ownership, a 27-day cruise, with fares from £169/17/6. The first port of call was Auckland on 3 July, then it was on to Suva, Apia, Vavau and Nuku'alofa, the Bay of Islands, and back to Auckland. On 25 July 1962 *Wanganella* arrived back in Sydney.

The liner's final arrival in Sydney would probably have passed without any reference at all in the local newspapers had it not been for the presence of two stowaways on board. On 26 July, the following story appeared in the *Sydney Morning Herald* under the headline, 'Reserved "Cabin" Picked For Trip':

Two stowaways on the liner *Wanganella* made things easy for the Chief Officer, Mr. R. Komoll. They hid themselves in the ship's lock-up, and when they were discovered all Mr Komoll had to do was turn the key.

Mr. Komoll said yesterday he had to go down to the lock-up on Saturday night to lock up a crewman who had been celebrating the liner's departure from Auckland. 'When I opened the cell door there were two stowaways in there,' he said. 'It was late at night and I didn't want to disturb the captain, so I pushed the drunk in and locked the door.'

The two stowaways, Leonard Morris, 27, labourer, of Glenmore Road, Edgecliff, and Maxwell Deidrickson, 24, car salesman, of The Boulevard, Lewisham, were interviewed next morning. They told the master, Captain W. Uttley, a man ashore had said the lock-up would be open when they went aboard. Captain Uttley radioed the men's relatives in Sydney, who agreed to pay their passages.

The *Wanganella*, on its last crossing on the trans-Tasman run, reached Sydney three and a half hours late and with a five degrees list to starboard. Captain Uttley said the liner had run into headwinds on Tuesday. Just off the Sydney Heads the crew emptied some freshwater tanks to prepare the ship for the new owners, Hang Fung (Aust.) Pty. Ltd. This caused the list.

Wanganella arriving in Sydney on 25 July 1962 (Fred Roderick photo).

16

Under Foreign Owners

Although the Hang Fung Shipping & Trading Co. Ltd. was incorporated in Hong Kong, the company actually had an Australian background, involving a major scrap metal company founded in 1920 by Albert G. Sims, which had developed from small beginnings to become a major player in the scrap metal trade, and in 1948 became a public company, Albert G. Sims Ltd. Twenty years later a number of other scrap metal companies had been taken over, and the company was renamed Simsmetal Ltd in 1968, changed to Sims Consolidated Ltd two years later, by which time they were the largest scrap metal merchants in Australia.

During the 1950s there was a considerable growth in the export of scrap metal from Australia to the Far East, and in 1959 the Sims company established their own shipping company, purchasing four cargo ships. In June 1958 the wholly owned subsidiary Hang Fung Shipping & Trading Co. Ltd. was incorporated in Hong Kong for the purpose of conducting the Sims group shipping activities. It was quite a surprise when Hang Fung was identified as the buyer for *Wanganella*, as the company had no experience at all in the passenger trade, and in fact had incurred a substantial loss on their cargo operation.

In early July, however, while *Wanganella* was still operating for McIlwraith McEacharn, advertisements began appearing in the local press for the first cruise, the advertisement published in the *Sydney Morning Herald* on 8 July 1962 reading:

46 day cruise to
THE EXOTIC EAST

Fares from as low as £299

Sail on the famous M. V. Wanganella
Via the Great Barrier Reef to Manila,
Hong Kong and Kobe (Kyoto).
Wanganella leaves Sydney for Brisbane
and the Far East on August 25,
returning through the same ports to
Sydney on October 10.

Comfortable single, double, 3 and
4-berth cabins are available. Relax for
nearly 7 weeks on this finely appointed
ship with its unexcelled cuisine, spacious
lounges and decks, fine service. All
entertainments are available, including deck
games, cinema, dancing to the ship's Orchestra,
shows by popular artists.
And there's plenty of time for shopping
and exploring.
Book now through
F. H. Stephens Pty Ltd

Hang Fung's purchase of *Wanganella*, and the transfer of the ship from the Australian register to that of Hong Kong, incurred the wrath of the maritime unions, and the matter was mentioned in the press during August 1962. The company was accused of 'making a blatant attempt to fly the flag of convenience in Australian waters' and of 'showing a blatant disregard for decency and for its obligation to Australian workers'. The comment was also made that 'the modern shipowner is reverting today to the blackbirding tactics seen last century in employment methods on the Queensland cane fields'.

Mr. A. G. Sims tried to smooth things over by pointing out that all his ships had Australian officers, though the rest of the crew was Chinese, and the ships were registered in Hong Kong because they could not be profitably operated under the Australian register. The matter was raised in Federal Parliament when, in response to a question posed by Labor Party member Dr. Jim Cairns, the Minister for Shipping & Transport, Mr. Opperman, replied that the Hang Fung ships were not competing with any Australian

Wanganella in McIlwraith, McEacharn colours departing Sydney on 25 August 1962 (John Mathieson photo).

Wanganella berthed in Sydney wearing Hang Fung funnel colours (Dennis Brook photo).

Wanganella departing Sydney on 3 November 1962 (John Bennett photo).

Wanganella arriving in Hobart (Lindsay Rex photo).

These two photographs of *Wanganella* berthed in Fremantle during the Empire Games in November 1962 were taken by Richard McKenna (courtesy Western Australia Maritime Museum).

Wanganella tied up in Deep Cove as a workers' hostel (Tim Ryan collection).

Another view of *Wanganella* tied up in Deep Cove (Nick Tolerton collection).

Wanganella departing Sydney on 23 October 1962—note the two elephants on the fore deck (John Mathieson).

ships. Mr Opperman also said he understood that the future employment of *Wanganella* would be in the Australia-Pacific-Far East passenger and cargo trade, and that the existing Australian crew would take the ship to Hong Kong, from where the majority would be repatriated to Australia.

But instead of *Wanganella* being taken to Hong Kong for delivery, after drydocking for a full survey it was handed over in Sydney on 15 August.

Wanganella would be operated for the new owners by Anglo-Japanese Steam Ship Navigation Ltd, and the Sydney agents would be F. H. Stephens Pty. Ltd., who had offices in Bridge Street. An ambitious schedule was announced, starting off with a cruise from Sydney to Asia. There would also be a number of voyages across the Tasman from both Sydney and Melbourne to Auckland and Wellington.

On Saturday, 25 August, *Wanganella* departed Sydney, still in McIlwraith McEacharn colours, on the long cruise to the Far East. While in Hong Kong the funnel colours were changed to black with two silver bands.

The last port of call was Manila, from where *Wanganella* voyaged directly to Sydney, arriving on the morning of 10 October. The vessel remained in port until 13 October, when it left on a seven-day cruise to Norfolk Island, including a circuit of Lord Howe Island. *Wanganella* anchored off Norfolk Island on 16 October for the day, with passengers going ashore in lifeboats.

Wanganella arrived back in Sydney on 20 October, then departed on 23 October for Auckland, berthing there on 27 October. On returning to Sydney, *Wanganella* departed on 3 November for Melbourne, staying in port while passengers attended the running of the Melbourne Cup. Departing Melbourne on 6 November, *Wanganella* crossed the Tasman Sea to Wellington, arriving on 11 November, then voyaging back to Melbourne.

On 16 November, *Wanganella* departed Melbourne on a special voyage to Fremantle, arriving on 21 November, and remaining in port for the next ten days, serving as a hotel ship during the Empire Games held in Perth over that time. *Wanganella* left Fremantle on 1 December, arriving in Melbourne on 6 December, then going on to Auckland, and back to Sydney. On 17 December *Wanganella* left Sydney on a voyage to Auckland, then made cruises from New Zealand through January 1963.

As 1962 came to a close, advertisements began to appear promoting a varied series of trans-Tasman voyages and cruises to be operated by *Wanganella* throughout 1963. There would be two return trips to Auckland, departing Sydney on February 4 and 14, then on February 26 the vessel would leave Sydney on a cruise to the Bay of Islands, Auckland, Hobart and Melbourne, returning to Sydney on 15 March. This would be followed by another cruise, departing on 19 March for Auckland, Norfolk Island and Hayman Island, returning to Sydney on 4 April. On 7 April *Wanganella* would leave Sydney on a return trip to Wellington, arriving there on 11 April.

On 19 April *Wanganella* was scheduled to depart Sydney on a cruise to Brisbane, Hayman Island, Noumea and Brisbane again, returning to Sydney on 3 May. Three days later the vessel would leave on a voyage to Auckland, arriving on 10 May, then go on to Wellington on 13 May before returning to Sydney, to be followed by a return trip to Auckland, departing on 22 May.

On 4 June *Wanganella* was scheduled to depart on a 25-day cruise around the South Pacific, calling first at Auckland, then visiting Suva, Apia, Vavau, Nuku'alofa, the Bay of Islands and Auckland again, returning to Sydney on 29 June. The minimum fare for the entire trip was £151-5-0, but passengers could also travel on various sectors. This offer was also available on the next cruise, departing Sydney on 3 July for Port Moresby, Rabaul and Honiara, returning to Sydney on 19 July.

Wanganella would then make another return trip to Auckland, departing on 23 July, followed by a short cruise leaving Sydney on 6 August for Noumea and Hayman Island, returning on 16 August. The next trip would leave Sydney on 20 August, going to Auckland and Wellington, followed by a return trip to Auckland, departing on 7 September. Another longer cruise would leave Sydney on 20 September, and follow the same itinerary as the 4 June cruise, finishing in Sydney on 16 October.

A round trip to Auckland was then scheduled, departing Sydney on 20 October, while on 2 November *Wanganella* would leave on another cruise, going to Auckland, Suva, Noumea and Brisbane, arriving back in Sydney on 19 November. That was the last voyage being advertised for the liner as 1963 began.

Wanganella began operating this ambitious series of cruises, though financial returns were not good. By the end of June the liner was again being offered for sale, and in July was purchased for £208,145 by

Wanganella arriving in Sydney (Fred Roderick photo).

the Utah Construction Company, who planned to use it as a floating hostel for workers engaged on the construction of the Manapouri hydro-electric project in the South Island of New Zealand.

The final cruise to be operated by *Wanganella* departed Sydney on 6 August 1963, going to Noumea and Hayman Island, returning to Sydney on 17 August. By then the Hang Fung Shipping & Trading Co. Ltd. was in serious financial trouble, having recorded a loss of £231,291 before tax for the business year ended 30 June 1963, most of this coming from the operation of *Wanganella*.

At 3 pm on 20 August 1963 *Wanganella* left her berth at 3a Darling Harbour on her final departure from Sydney, bound for Auckland. (According to records held by the Auckland Port Authority, between January 1933 and July 1963 *Wanganella* had visited Auckland 253 times.)

The last departure of a ship that had been a familiar sight in Sydney Harbour for just over thirty years went almost unnoticed, as the liner slipped quietly down the harbour and out through Sydney Heads, although the next day the *Sydney Morning Herald* printed a brief item on an inside page, headed 'Last Voyage':

> The trans-Tasman liner *Wanganella* left Sydney for Auckland yesterday for the last time.
>
> The 10,000-ton ship, first launched in 1930, has been bought by the Utah Construction Company to act as a floating hotel for 400 workers on its Manapouri hydro-electric project in New Zealand.

On its final Tasman voyage *Wanganella* was under the command of Captain F. A. Simpson. *Wanganella* arrived in Auckland on 24 August, and the final passengers disembarked. The ship was prepared for handover to the new owners, and most of the crew members were flown back to Sydney, leaving just a skeleton crew for the final voyage to Doubtful Sound.

Although both *Monowai* and *Wanganella* had been withdrawn and not replaced due to lack of operating profit, there were still those who hoped that a regular trans-Tasman passenger ship service could be re-established. Despite their previous proposal having been rejected in 1960, in 1964 the New Zealand Government made new overtures to the Australian Government regarding a joint venture agreement being reached to build a new liner for a service between the two countries. Again the proposal did not have a favourable reception in Canberra, and the idea was quietly dropped.

It was still possible to travel by sea between Australia and New Zealand, as various shipping companies offered Tasman passages on liners engaged in the trade from Britain and Europe; however, these voyages were not on a regular basis, and accommodation was only made available if the ship was not fully booked by passengers making longer journeys.

One of the vessels to offer passages across the Tasman on a reasonably regular basis for several years was the former Australian coastal liner *Kanimbla*, under its new name, *Oriental Queen*. Built in 1936, *Kanimbla* had been sold by McIlwraith, McEacharn Limited in 1961, and spent the next two years primarily carrying Islamic pilgrims from Indonesia to Jeddah. Following the completion of the 1963 pilgrimage season, *Oriental Queen* was made available for charter, and in 1964 was taken on a long-term arrangement by the Japanese firm Toyo Yusen Kaisha. With her funnel repainted in their colours, and looking very smart with a white hull, *Oriental Queen* returned to Australian waters, this time to commence a cruise program from Sydney.

The schedule included a series of short cruises to the South Pacific islands, longer trips to Japan and Hong Kong, and some special trans-Tasman trips in the summer months. Over the next two years, *Oriental Queen* became a familiar sight in Sydney Harbour, and visited numerous other ports around the Australian coastline in the course of her cruises. The longer trips to Japan followed a route similar to those pioneered when she was still *Kanimbla*, and proved just as popular.

However, on 13 January 1967, *Oriental Queen* arrived in Sydney from a New Zealand cruise which was the last she would operate in these waters. The vessel then left for Japan, and began a new career cruising from various Japanese ports to Guam. Later in 1967, Toyo Yusen Kaisha purchased *Oriental Queen* outright, and it was eventually broken up in 1974.

17

Workers' Hostel

Wanganella had been purchased to act as a floating hostel for some of the workers employed building the tailrace tunnel and the Wilmot Pass access road to the Manapouri Power Station in the South Island of New Zealand. The ship departed Auckland on 26 August 1963, and arrived in Doubtful Sound on the morning of Thursday 29 August.

In his biography, *Boats and Blokes*, George Brasell recounted his experiences during this period, when he was put in charge of all the marine activities of the Manapouri Power Scheme construction, which also involved *Wanganella*.

When the liner arrived very little work had been done preparing a berthing site. George Brasell and his team only arrived on 28 August, and he wrote:

> Next day *Wanganella* arrived and there was pandemonium. Our first job was to meet her down the sound with Captain Ruegg, Captain Hazard, a pilot from Bluff and several VIPs. The ring bolts had just been put ashore and it would take days of drilling and cementing to fasten them to cliff faces. We had surveyed the entrance to Deep Cove for a suitable place to anchor *Wanganella* and the shallowest water we could find was on a hard ledge outside Halls Arm with 40 fathoms of water over it. This was the limit she could anchor in and if the anchor went down over the edge in 100 fathoms her winches would not be able to handle the weight of chain.

Wanganella dropped anchor at the temporary waiting area located at the mouth of Halls Arm, and was formally handed over to the Utah-Williamson-Burnett construction consortium at 8.30 am on 31 August.

Wanganella moved under its own power for the last time on Tuesday, 3 September, travelling 1.5 nautical miles from the Halls Arm anchoring point into Deep Cove, where it had to perform a 180-degree turn. When *Wanganella* dropped anchor again the captain rang 'finished with engines' for the last time.

A number of mooring points had been cemented into the cliff face ashore (and some strong trees found!), and *Wanganella* was winched into a secure moored location in what became known as Wanganella Cove. George Brasell wrote:

> *Wanganella* was powered with old-fashioned diesel engines which were stopped and started in the opposite direction for reversing. Starting was by compressed air and there was only sufficient air for about six manoeuvres, after which she would be helpless until more air was compressed in her starting tanks. The captain had been on the *Wanganella* on her passenger run from Australia to Hong Kong [sic] and he knew his vessel thoroughly. A marker buoy had been placed where he was to drop anchor while turning in Deep Cove. He dropped the anchor right on the buoy and sank it.
>
> With very little fuss the captain swung his ship in the narrow confines of the Cove and we ran his lines into the bush. He was horrified later to find that some of the mooring lines were fastened to trees! Afterwards the rope lines were replaced with heavy wire ones.
>
> *Wanganella* was first moored off the cliff face because blasting would have to be done to build a road round to the proposed wharf site … Men were already arriving by seaplane as the only other way in at this time was over the Wilmot Pass trampers' track.
>
> The job of changing the old ship from a seagoing passenger vessel to a construction worker's hostel was now in full swing … The captain's quarters on the upper deck were taken over by the project managers. A new hospital was built aft of amidships and the poop deck aft was the quarters of the supervising engineers. Four-berth cabins were changed to two-berth and two-berth to single-berth. No. 2 hold was turned into a warehouse to be used until one was set up ashore. Everything from a needle to an anchor was in that store.

The 38 crew members who had been retained for the final voyage from Auckland were paid off on 29 August, but were forced to remain on board for several more days until the ship was firmly moored, then all except the ship's carpenter and four engineers were flown out of Deep Cove and returned to Australia. The engineers and carpenter stayed on to maintain the generators, which in fact broke down on 5 September. Once repairs were completed these men were also flown back to Australia.

The problems faced with providing a permanent berth for the ship were described in the Dunedin *Evening Star* on Monday, 2 September 1963:

> The *Wanganella* will eventually be pulled hard up against a rock face to be hewn out of the shores of Deep Cove. Though six weeks was suggested as the time she will lie moored about 100yd off shore, Captain H. Ruegg, of the Marine Department, estimates it as four to five months.
>
> The sloping mountain rising out of the sound will be blasted so that a spacious wharf is created. The ship will tie up against a vertical rock face to be blasted and smoothed.
>
> The water in the cove, even right against the shore, is much too deep to allow a conventional wharf to be built, and a floating wharf is thought to be unsatisfactory.
>
> The ship's policeman, Constable J. Clarke, flew in on Saturday and established his police station in what was the ship's shop and hairdressing salon.
>
> Five Australian engineers on board allege that they have been 'shanghaied'. Their resignations took effect from last Thursday and their contracts expired on that day. They expected when they left Auckland early last week to be off the ship no later than Saturday and heading back to Sydney. But they are still on board working sea watches keeping the engines running in case of trouble. They will be on board at least for another three days. By that time it is hoped the ship will be safely moored against any weather contingency.

Meanwhile the task of constructing an access road past the ship to the proposed new cantilever wharf site went on, and included a permanent berth, with direct alongside access to shore. The work involved a considerable amount of blasting, and one incident was reported in the *Taranaki Herald* on 17 January 1964:

> A tremendous explosion at Deep Cove yesterday showered huge rocks on the hostel ship *Wanganella*, shattered windows and portholes and wrecked the newly completed ship's hospital.
>
> A 10lb rock smashed the glass walls of the hospital, knocked out aluminium sliding windows and doors and damaged a X-ray machine.
>
> No one was injured in the blast in which it was estimated that 400lb. of gelignite were detonated. People on the *Wanganella* were sheltered on the starboard side of the vessel. The port side caught most of the explosion.
>
> An eyewitness said that large rocks, many of which men could not lift, smashed into the *Wanganella*. Port

Wanganella berthed at Deep Cove (R W Brookes collection).

side windows and portholes, many half an inch thick, were smashed in by the force of the blast.

The hospital, which workers have just finished building on the deck, was shattered. The outer glass walls were smashed to pieces by a rock which carried on through the double thickness hardboard walls. It struck the X-ray machine a glancing blow on its path. Luckily, the hospital was not occupied.

Late in July 1964 *Wanganella* took up this permanent shore berth, where it would remain for the next six years. To better suit the vessel for its new role the superstructure was altered and extended aft, while the bridge was removed, and additional space made for offices and accommodation. At least two of the ship's lifeboats were removed and sold.

The Manapouri Power Project was one of New Zealand's greatest ever engineering achievements. It was designed to use the waters of Lake Manapouri to generate electric power, with the actual powerhouse to be constructed 700 feet/213 m underground. A key part of the plan was the construction of a huge concrete-lined tunnel to carry the lake water to the underground generating plant, which involved digging through granite, often having to deal as well with freezing underground streams. Work began in August 1963, and the entire project took over 1800 men working 24 hours a day eight years to complete, in September 1971. Sixteen men were killed during the construction work.

The poor weather frequently experienced in the area where the power station was being built made for very difficult living conditions. The *Wanganella* became the base camp for workers employed at the southern section of the project. A land-based camp was established at the West Arm of Lake Manapouri for workers on the northern end of the project. Both camps were in a very rugged and inaccessible part of the country and travel to the nearest towns, which were some distance away, was fairly infrequent and difficult. As a result social clubs were organised to provide entertainment and recreational facilities for off-duty workers.

Apart from providing living quarters for about 400 single men, *Wanganella* was fitted out with a proper cinema and betting shop. Extra deckhouses were built at the stern to provide more lounges and bars for the workers when they were off duty. A full staff was provided to look after these facilities and the workers, including such positions as warehouse foreman, canteen manager, and a Morse-operator to send and receive messages in the wireless room.

The hospital had a permanent medical staff at all times. For several years Sister Bernadette McCarthy was the Chief Assistant to the Medical Officer, and the sole woman on board the ship. Sister McCarthy described herself as 'rather ordinary and plain', but added that she had 'more or less been put on a pedestal' by the men, and her medical skills were in high demand.

Over the years the *Wanganella* often came under media scrutiny, with regular claims of unsafe working conditions and tensions between local and foreign workers. The vessel also became notorious for the drinking culture that was reported to have developed on board, with so many single men thrown together in a limited area for a long time. About the early days George Brasell wrote:

> Before a bar was set up on the *Wanganella* there were a lot of thirsty men and of course spirits were never allowed aboard. The project manager came to me and complained that the men were obtaining spirits from somewhere. Although they had checked all sources, they could not find where it was coming from and my launch drivers and myself were considered the only way it could be brought in. I knew this to be quite unjustified so I had a yarn to my old cobber Bill Gray. He gave me a queer sort of smile and said, 'I think I might have a clue about that, George. I'll do something about it.'
>
> I heard later that there was a beautiful still working in the dummy funnel. The best of materials had been used from the work site and the recipe was the same as the old one from the infamous Hokonui Hills in Southland. The whole lot was lowered gently over the side with many sighs of regret, just before it was discovered. It was very powerful stuff although slightly woody in flavour, about 183% spirit, and to be safe it had to be very well watered down.

Eventually various kinds of beer were made available in the canteens, both on the *Wanganella* at Deep Cove and at the camp at West Arm. Most of it came as draught beer in kegs. However, it was soon discovered that it was difficult to ship the barrels of draught beer to both *Wanganella* and the other base camp, and to store it, and canned beer was more practical.

Bottled beer was not allowed at Deep Cove, as the contractors feared that a lot of empty bottles floating in the fiord would be a hazard to the floats of the seaplanes being used to ferry people and supplies in and out of the project area. It was also considered that cans made less dangerous weapons in a bar fight, should some bored and inebriated workers get into an argument, as they could not smash a can on a bar and used it as a jagged weapon.

From the start the two camps established a

friendly rivalry and after a while the workers aboard *Wanganella* decided they should have their own brand of beer, to be called Deep Cove Beer. A contest among the amateur artists on board was organised to design a suitable label, the winner being a rough black and white sketch of the mountains, valleys and sea surrounding Deep Cove camp with the *Wanganella* tied up at the wharf.

New Zealand Breweries agreed to use the label on cans made especially for the workers at Deep Cove, and Deep Cove Beer was first produced in August 1967. The cans contained their premium lager, Steinlager, which also happened to have the highest alcohol content. Deep Cove Beer was sent only to the *Wanganella*. In January 1968 New Zealand Breweries began producing West Arm Beer in special cans for the other base camp, for a period of six months.

Supplies of Deep Cove Beer ceased being sent to *Wanganella* in November 1968, and the brewer disposed of remaining stock to overseas ships only, so that cans with the special Deep Cove label never came on the New Zealand domestic market; they are now a much sought after collector's item.

When the hydro-electricity project was completed in December 1969, *Wanganella* was no longer needed. During her period at Deep Cove the liner had been home to more than 4000 construction workers.

In October 1969 the old liner had been sold to the New Zealand Government (Ministry of Works), who immediately offered it for sale by tender, with bids to close on 3 November. A week later it was reported that *Wanganella* had been sold to Australian-Pacific Shipping Co., of Hong Kong, who surprisingly announced plans to return the vessel to active service in Far East waters.

However, the engines were in very poor shape after seven years of idleness, and it was not known if they could even be started, never mind power the vessel to Hong Kong. The new owners decided that the vessel would have to be towed all the way from Doubtful Sound to Hong Kong.

The large Dutch salvage tug *Barentz Zee* was brought in to undertake the tow – and it was claimed by some that major problems were encountered trying to move *Wanganella* away from its berth, due to the reef of beer cans that surrounded the vessel, built up by empties thrown overboard during the years spent tied up in the same spot! In fact the waters of Deep Cove are very deep, and no problem was encountered.

On 17 April 1970 *Wanganella* was towed out of Doubtful Sound by the *Barentz Zee*, and the pair headed off to Hong Kong.

When *Wanganella* arrived in Hong Kong an extensive inspection of the engines indicated they were in very poor condition, and could not be restored to active service. It would also be too expensive to consider installing new machinery. As a result *Wanganella* was sold to shipbreakers in Taiwan, and arrived under tow at Kaohsiung on 5 June 1970 to end a forty-year career.

Wanganella in Deep Cove (Nick Tolerton collection).

Index

Aberfoyle 22
Abosso 80
Accra 80
Achimota 80–5
Adelong 171
Airedale 15
Albion 16, 18
Alhambra 15
Anchises 67
Anglian 34–6, 38, 41, 44, 58, 63
Aorangi 41, 42, 60, 122
Apapa (1) 80
Apapa (2) 80
Appam 80
Aquitania 108
Arawata 18
Awatea 102–6, 108, 116, 123
Barentz Zee 187
Barwon 171
Batman 171
Bennelong 167
Britannia 13
Burrowaree 167
Burrumbeet 23, 62
City of Melbourne 17
City of Sydney 21
Claud Hamilton 17
Cobar 127, 128
Coogee 23
Corangamite 23
Dandenong 17
Delfino 164, 165
Despatch 22
Dingadee 40
Dominion Monarch 108
Durraween 105
Eagle 171
Elingamite 23, 33–5, 43–9
Endeavour 13
Express 22
Fort Stikine 112
Georgic 110
Hero 16
Hinemoa 136–7
HMS Penguin 48
Indarra 68
Jalapadma 112
Juno 14
Kahanui 123
Kaikoura 17
Kanimbla 183
Kapiti 108
Katoomba 118–21
Llangibby Castle 86

Lindus 23
Lord Ashley 15
Lord Worsley 15, 17
Macedonia 63
Maheno 51, 52, 54, 63–5, 101, 103
Maitai 65
Makura 65
Malolo 52, 97
Malwa 63
Manapouri 20, 21, 36
Manuka 51, 63–5, 70, 75, 77, 78
Manunda 121
Marama 54, 56, 65, 98, 100, 101
Mararoa 21, 26, 27, 29, 33, 50–1
Mariposa 97, 103, 104, 106
Maunganui 56, 61, 62, 64, 108
Mauretania 108
Medea 22
Miltiades 67
Miowera 23, 27–30, 32, 42
Moeraki 49, 50–1, 64, 65, 75, 77, 78
Mokoia 54, 65, 67
Moldavia 63
Mongolia 63
Monowai (1) 21, 43, 53–4
Monowai (2) 52, 78, 96–101, 103, 104, 108, 116–17, 123, 137, 143–5, 147, 149, 151, 155, 165, 167, 171–3, 183
Monterey 97, 103, 104, 106
Morea 63
Natone 128
Nemesis 23
Niagara 61, 65, 108, 122, 130
Olivia Davies 22
Omeo 15
Omrah 67
Oranje 113
Orcoma 67
Oriana 104
Oriental Queen 183
Orion 108
Otago 17
Paloona 57, 67
Prince Alfred 15, 17
Queen 15
Queen Emma 22
Queen Mary 108
Rakaia 17
Rangatira 101, 108, 109
Razmak 96
Ringarooma 18
Riverina 52–6, 58, 61, 63–8, 73–8
Rotomahana 19–21, 29, 32
Rotorua 18

St Boniface 130
Scotia 16
South Australian 16, 17
Tahiti 64, 96
Talune 29, 57, 58
Tararua 17, 18
Tarawera 36, 40
Taroona 116-17, 145, 171
Tasmania 31–6, 38–42
Tatana 171
Te Anau 19, 34-5
Terawhiti 123, 128
Toia 123, 128, 130, 131, 134
Triumph 21
Turakina 108
Ulimaroa 55–67, 74, 76–9, 82, 96
Victoria (HP) 44, 48, 49, 51–3, 56, 57, 61–3, 66–9, 74
Victoria (P&O) 49
Wahine 136–7
Waihora 27
Waikare 50-1
Wairarapa 20, 21
Wakatipu 18
Walmer Castle 67
Wanganella (1930s) 79, 80, 83–96, 98, 101, 103–7
   hospital ship 108–15
   aground 122–38
   1950s 143–75
   Hang Fung 176, 181–3
   Deep Cove) 184–7
Warrimoo 23–7, 29, 30, 32, 42, 62, 64
Warringa 171
Watamurra 171
Wendouree 23
Westralia (1) 36–38, 41–4, 49, 50, 61-2, 64-5, 67, 73–5, 78
Westralia (2) 85, 86, 95, 96, 107, 148, 155, 156, 161–4
William Denny 14
Willochra 64
Wimmera 51–7, 62, 64, 65, 67–74
Wolff 73
Wonga Wonga 17
Woolambi 165
Woomera 171
Yarra 79
Yongala 59
Zealandia (1) 42–4, 47, 49, 51, 52, 54, 57, 67
Zealandia (2) 59-64, 67–9, 75–9, 82, 96, 100, 111